P9-CKB-240

Core Concepts
in
Cultural Anthropology

Core Concepts
in
Cultural Anthropology

ROBERT H. LAVENDA

EMILY A. SCHULTZ

SEVENTH EDITION

New York   Oxford

OXFORD UNIVERSITY PRESS

Oxford University Press is a department of the University of Oxford.
It furthers the University's objective of excellence in research, scholarship,
and education by publishing worldwide. Oxford is a registered trade mark of
Oxford University Press in the UK and certain other countries.

Published in the United States of America by Oxford University Press
198 Madison Avenue, New York, NY 10016, United States of America.

© 2020, 2017, 2007, 2000 by Robert H. Lavenda and Emily A. Schultz;
© 2013, 2010, 2003 by The McGraw-Hill Companies, Inc.

For titles covered by Section 112 of the US Higher Education
Opportunity Act, please visit www.oup.com/us/he for the latest
information about pricing and alternate formats.

All rights reserved. No part of this publication may be reproduced, stored in a
retrieval system, or transmitted, in any form or by any means, without the
prior permission in writing of Oxford University Press, or as expressly permitted
by law, by license, or under terms agreed with the appropriate reproduction
rights organization. Inquiries concerning reproduction outside the scope of the
above should be sent to the Rights Department, Oxford University Press,
at the address above.

You must not circulate this work in any other form
and you must impose this same condition on any acquirer.

Library of Congress Cataloging-in-Publication Data
Names: Lavenda, Robert H., author. | Schultz, Emily A. (Emily Ann), 1949-
    author.
Title: Core concepts in cultural anthropology / Robert H. Lavenda, Emily A.
    Schultz.
Description: Seventh edition. | New York : Oxford University Press, [2020] |
    Includes bibliographical references and index.
Identifiers: LCCN 2018060667 (print) | LCCN 2019001018 (ebook) | ISBN
    9780190924768 (e-book) | ISBN 9780190924751 (pbk.)
Subjects: LCSH: Ethnology. | Ethnology--Bibliography.
Classification: LCC GN316 (ebook) | LCC GN316 .L39 2020 (print) |
    DDC 305.8—dc23
LC record available at https://lccn.loc.gov/2018060667

9 8 7 6 5 4 3 2
Printed by Marquis, Canada

To Jan Beatty

CONTENTS

PREFACE

This book is a concise introduction to the fundamental key terms and issues of contemporary cultural anthropology. It is not a condensed version of our textbook, *Cultural Anthropology: A Perspective on the Human Condition*; this is something different. Our goal is to provide students with a rapid sketch of the basic ideas and practices of cultural anthropology in a style analogous to an expanded glossary. A good glossary supports beginners in a discipline by expanding the analytic vocabulary at their command and situating this new terminology in the theoretical and practical history of the field. So, too, we hope, will this volume: we introduce the core concepts and key terms in cultural anthropology and indicate briefly where they come from and how they are related to one another to provide students with a context for understanding anthropological writing, especially ethnographic writing, when they turn to it. Our expectation is that this text will be used in conjunction with ethnographies and/or collections of readings during the term. For that reason, we have omitted extended ethnographic examples and other kinds of details found in our textbook *Cultural Anthropology* (and most introductory texts), and we have concentrated on providing a scaffolding on which students can rely as they begin to read more conventional anthropological texts.

FEATURES

- *Flexibility*. This text can be used in many different ways. It can be used by itself as a concise introduction to cultural anthropology when the course time that can be devoted to covering the discipline is limited. It can also be used very successfully in conjunction with other readings, either anthologies or ethnographies or both. *Core Concepts in Cultural Anthropology* may be assigned at the beginning of the term to go along with introductory lectures and be referred to as needed. Another approach, popular with users of earlier editions of *Core Concepts in Cultural Anthropology*, is to assign specific chapters to be read along with particular ethnographies or course topics. To accommodate various uses, we have made each chapter as self-contained as possible. Each chapter has numbered section headings to make it easier for students to navigate the text and to give instructors additional flexibility should they wish to assign segments of chapters in novel ways best suited for the organization of their courses. We have included cross references to related topics in other chapters wherever possible. *If the order of our chapters does not fit your arrangement of topics in your course, we invite you to rearrange the chapters and sections in any order that works for you.* We think our order makes sense, but there are many different ways to arrange a course, and instructors should feel free to assign (or omit) the chapters and sections in whatever way best suits their approach to teaching anthropology.

- *Brief and affordable.* What you have in your hands is an unadorned framework for teaching cultural anthropology. This book was written to be brief and to be affordable. Quite intentionally, there are no photographs, no lavish graphics, no elaborate text boxes, no extended ethnographic examples. A consequence of writing a concise introduction is that many of the details and nuances of the field are left out. We assume that instructors will provide favorite ethnographic examples both in class and in other readings to illustrate the issues they raise in class. It is our hope that the brevity and affordability of this text will allow the assignment of additional course readings and will engender lectures and class discussions that bring back the nuance and subtlety that are a part of every human endeavor, including anthropology, teaching, and learning.

- *Provides useful study aids.* Each chapter opens with a list of key terms discussed in that chapter. Each chapter ends with a list of suggested readings, which—along with an extensive end-of-book bibliography—directs students to more detailed discussions. The index allows students to quickly find the key terms they need.

- *Includes a chapter on theory.* Because all anthropological writing is theoretically situated, we have included a chapter on theory in cultural anthropology. We think it is important for students to get a sense of how the texts they are reading fit into a broader theoretical context of the discipline. We also think they need some intellectual tools for interpreting what they are reading: ethnographic writing often refers to alternative theoretical positions, and it is useful for students to know the issues those positions have raised in the course of ongoing anthropological discussion and debate.

- *Provides a unique appendix on reading ethnography.* Chapters 1 and 2 provide discussion of ethnographic *methods*. The distinctive appendix in this book provides students with a set of tools for reading ethnographic *writing*. It looks at how ethnographies are put together and how they are written; it also offers students strategies for getting the most from their reading.

WHAT'S NEW IN THE SEVENTH EDITION?

There has been a significant amount of revision in this edition.

Based on reviewers' experience with their students, we have reduced the number of primary key terms, which remain **boldfaced**. As in previous editions of the text, secondary key terms appear in *italics*. We have also revised the "For Further Reading" recommendations.

Chapter 1:

- Definition of culture now includes material culture.
- New material on archaeology of the contemporary world.
- New section on engaged anthropology.
- New discussion of anthropological engagement with the Anthropocene.
- Expanded discussion of reflexivity, linking it to the ontological turn in contemporary anthropology, which is further developed in chapters 4 and 12.
- Consideration of recent anthropological work building on insights from the anthropology of science, technology, and medicine.

Chapter 2

- Based on reviewers' suggestions, we have included new material from James Scott's recent work in which he reads "against the grain" archaeological and historical evidence traditionally interpreted in terms of cultural evolution and incorporates the notions of niche construction and the Anthropocene.
- New material on Peircean semiotics in a section discussing role of symbolism in anthropological analyses of culture.
- Discussion of processual approaches in anthropology based on Ingold and Palsson's *Biosocial Becoming*.

Chapter 3

- New discussion of the status of the Sapir–Whorf hypothesis in contemporary linguistic anthropology.
- New material on speech communities, based on Marcyliena Morgan (2014).
- New section on raciolinguistics, based on Alim et al. (2016).
- Revised introduction on meaning-making and art.
- Brief new discussion of recent work on hip-hop.
- New discussion of media ideologies based on Gershon (2017).

Chapter 4

- Extended discussion of consequences of the ontological turn in contemporary anthropological studies of religion and worldview based on work by Descola (2013, 2014) and de la Cadena (2015).
- New material on Christian conversion in the context of the ontological turn based on the work of Holbraad and Pedersen (2017).

Chapter 5

- Extended discussion of race based on Peter Wade's work on genomics.

Chapter 7

- Extended discussion of robots and kinship in Japan.

Chapter 8

- Extended discussion of state, including reference to the work of James Scott (2017).

Chapter 9

- Revised discussion of history of subsistence practices.
- Revised discussion of formalist position in economic anthropology.
- New material on precarity under capitalist production.
- Revised discussion of peasants.
- Discussion of global institutions.
- New material on environmental anthropology.

Chapter 10

- New section on border studies and migration.
- New material on the built environment.
- New discussion of global organizations such as the UN, including material on ethnographic research within such organizations.

Chapter 11

- Significantly revised section on science studies.

Chapter 12

- New discussion about the Anthropocene and its consequences for anthropological theory.
- New material on science and technology studies and anthropological theory.
- Extended discussion of the ontological turn in anthropological theory and practice.

If you prefer to teach the material of your course in a different order, please don't hesitate to assign the chapters in the order that makes sense to you and your approach to the material. We have tried to write the chapters as self-contained units with plenty of cross references.

ACKNOWLEDGMENTS

We continue to be delighted that *Core Concepts in Cultural Anthropology*, now in its seventh edition, has joined our other textbooks at Oxford University Press. It has been a great pleasure to work with Executive Editor Sherith Pankratz, who enthusiastically supported bringing *Core Concepts* to Oxford. Our thanks, too, to Associate Editor Meredith Keffer for all the work she does in taking a manuscript and turning it into a book. Reviewers are extremely important to authors, even when we disagree, because they enable us to look at what we are doing from a wide variety of perspectives. Oxford found a particularly interesting set of reviewers for this edition; responses were thoughtful, supportive, and thorough. We have taken many of their suggestions. Even where we didn't, they pushed us to think through our decisions. So we would like to thank the following people: David M. Buchman, Hanover College; Paula Bulgier, University of Tennessee Chattanooga; Alfonso Peter Castro, Syracuse University; Ellen Dubas, Nebraska Wesleyan University; Huma Mohibullah, Renton Technical College; Boris Nikolov, Towson University; and three anonymous reviewers.

Finally, we would like to thank Jan Beatty, who suggested a book like this to us in the first place. This continues to be an interesting and valuable project for us as we think about new ways to present anthropology to new generations of students. We hope that you find it to be an effective tool for teaching anthropology.

CHAPTER 1

Anthropology

The key terms and concepts covered in this chapter, in the order in which they appear:

anthropology
holistic
comparative
evolutionary

biological anthropology
medical anthropology
cultural anthropology
culture
fieldwork
informants
participant-observation
ethnography
anthropological linguistics
linguistic anthropology
language

archaeology
applied anthropology
engaged anthropology

objective knowledge
positivism
modernism
postmodernism

reflexive
multisited fieldwork

moral anthropology
material culture
Anthropocene
process

Anthropology is a discipline that exists at the borders of the social sciences, the humanities, and the biological sciences. The term comes from two Greek words: *anthropos*, meaning "human beings," and *logia*, "the study of." The "study of human beings" would seem to be a rather broad topic for any one field, but anthropologists take the name of their discipline seriously, and anything that has to do with human beings probably is of potential interest to anthropologists. Indeed, **anthropology** can be formally defined as the study of human nature, human society, and the human past. This means that some anthropologists study human origins, others try to understand diverse contemporary ways of life, and some excavate the past or try to understand why we speak the ways we do.

1.1 AN ANTHROPOLOGICAL PERSPECTIVE

Given its breadth, what coherence anthropology has as a discipline comes from its perspective. Anthropology is holistic, comparative, field based, and evolutionary. For anthropologists, being **holistic** means trying to fit together all that is known about human beings. That is, anthropologists draw on the findings of many different disciplines that study human beings (e.g., human biology, economics, and religion), as well as data on similar topics that they have collected, and attempt to produce an encompassing picture of human life. In the same way, when an anthropologist studies a specific group of people, the goal is to produce a holistic portrait of that people's way of life by bringing together information about many different facets of their lives—social, religious, economic, political, linguistic, and so forth—to provide a nuanced context for understanding who they are and why they do what they do.

However, to generalize about human nature, human society, and the human past requires information from as wide a range of human groups as possible. Anthropologists realized long ago that the patterns of life common in their own societies were not necessarily followed in other societies. And so, anthropology is a **comparative** discipline: anthropologists must consider similarities and differences in as wide a range of human societies as possible before generalizing about what it means to be human.

Because anthropology is interested in human beings in all places and at all times, anthropologists are curious about how we got to be what we are today. For this reason, anthropology is **evolutionary**. A major branch of anthropology is concerned with the study of the biological evolution of the human species over time, including the study of human origins and genetic variety and inheritance in living human populations. Some cultural anthropologists have also been interested in cultural evolution, looking for patterns of orderly change over time in socially acquired behavior that is not carried in the genes.

1.2 THE SUBFIELDS OF ANTHROPOLOGY

Anthropology in North America historically has been divided into four major subfields: biological anthropology, cultural anthropology, linguistic anthropology, and archaeology.

Biological anthropology is the subfield of anthropology that looks at human beings as biological organisms. Biological anthropologists are interested in many different aspects of human biology, including our similarities to and differences from other living organisms. Those who study the closest living relatives of human beings—the nonhuman primates (e.g., chimpanzees and gorillas)—are called *primatologists*. Those who specialize in the study of the fossilized bones and teeth of our earliest ancestors are called *paleoanthropologists*. Other biological anthropologists examine the genetic variation among and within different human populations or investigate variation in human skeletal biology (e.g., measuring and comparing the shapes and sizes of bones or teeth using skeletal remains from different human populations). Newer specialties focus on human adaptability in different ecological settings, on human growth and development, and on the connections between a population's evolutionary history and its susceptibility to disease. *Forensic anthropologists* use their knowledge of human anatomy to aid law-enforcement and human rights investigators by assisting in the identification of skeletal material found at crime or accident sites or at sites associated with possible human rights violations.

Overlapping biological anthropology and cultural anthropology is the vibrant and relatively new field of **medical anthropology**. Medical anthropologists study the factors that contribute to human disease or illness as well as the ways in which human groups respond to them. Medical anthropological research covers a vast range of topics ranging from alcohol use in various societies; to the dimensions of the AIDS pandemic cross-culturally; to social aspects of medical care; to the effects of stress, violence, and social suffering. (See chapter 11 for a fuller discussion of medical anthropology.)

Cultural anthropology (sometimes called *social anthropology* in Great Britain) is another major subfield of anthropology. Cultural anthropologists investigate how variation in the ways of life of different human groups is shaped by **culture**, sets of learned behaviors and ideas that human beings acquire as members of society, together with the material artifacts and structures that human beings create and use. (For a fuller discussion of the concept of culture, see chapter 2.) Cultural anthropologists specialize in specific domains of human cultural activity. Some study the ways people organize themselves to carry out collective tasks, whether economic, political, or spiritual. Others focus on the forms and meanings of expressive behavior in human societies—language, art, music, ritual, religion, and the like. Still others examine material culture—the things people make and use such as clothing, housing, and tools, and the techniques they employ to get food and produce material goods. They may also study the ways in which technologies and environments shape each other. For some time, cultural anthropologists have been interested in the way non-Western peoples have responded to the political and economic challenges of European colonialism and the capitalist industrial technology that came with it. They investigate contemporary issues of gender and sexuality, transnational labor migration, and the post–Cold War resurgence of ethnicity and nationalism around the world. And some cultural anthropologists have begun to examine the ways in which forms of science and technology that originated in the West—biotechnology, computers, and the Internet, for example—have been incorporated into and continue to modify the cultural practices of peoples throughout the world.

In all of these cases, the comparative nature of anthropology requires that what is taken for granted by members of a specific society—the anthropologist's own, as much as any other—must be examined, or "problematized." As a result, there is a double movement in anthropology: anthropologists study other ways of life not only to understand them in their own terms but also to put the anthropologists' own ways of life in perspective. In fact, in recent years, some anthropologists have concentrated on studying their own society, or aspects of it.

Sometimes, this study of the anthropologist's own society takes the form of *cultural critique*, as the tools of ethnographic research are used to call into question the assumption that anyone's own way of life—including that of the society to which the anthropologist belongs—is natural.

To make their discipline comparative, cultural anthropologists immerse themselves in the lives of other peoples. Traditionally, cultural anthropology is rooted in **fieldwork**: an anthropologist's personal, long-term experience with a specific group of people and their way of life. Where possible, anthropologists try to live for a year or more with the people whose way of life is of concern to them. The result is a fine-grained knowledge of the everyday details of life. Cultural anthropologists get to know people as individuals, not as "data sets." They remember the names and faces of people who, over the course of a year or more, have become familiar to them as complex and complicated men, women, and children. They remember the feel of the noonday sun, the sounds of the morning, the smells of food cooking, the pace and rhythm of life. This approach does, of course, have drawbacks as well as advantages: anthropologists are not usually able to make macrolevel generalizations about an entire nation or society, and their attention is not usually directed toward national or international policy-making or data collection. They are often, however, well aware of the *effects* of national or international decisions on the local level. In fact, in recent years, a number of anthropologists have done illuminating work about nations, refugees and migrations, and international and global processes (see chapter 10).

People who share information about their way of life with anthropologists traditionally have been called **informants**. In recent years, however, a number of anthropologists have become uncomfortable with that term, which to some conjures up images of police informers and to others seems to reduce fully rounded individuals to the information they provide. But anthropologists have not been able to agree on an expression that might replace informant; some prefer "consultant," "respondent," "teacher," or "friend"—or simply refer to "the people with whom I work." Regardless of the term, fieldworkers gain insight into another way of life by taking part as fully as they can in a group's social activities as well as by observing those activities as outsiders. This research method, known as **participant-observation**, is central to cultural anthropology. Cultural anthropologists also use a variety of other research methods, including interviews, censuses, surveys, and even statistical sampling techniques, when appropriate. Cultural anthropologists write about what they have learned in scholarly articles or in books; and sometimes they document the lives of their research subjects on film, and increasingly via social media on the Internet. A written text about a single culture or way of life is often called a *monograph*, a term for any scholarly book that is a study of a single topic, from the Greek *mono* ("single") and *graph* ("write"). An ethnographic monograph is more commonly referred to as an **ethnography**. *Ethnology*—a term that is somewhat outdated in anglophone anthropology—traditionally referred to the comparative study of two or more ways of life. Thus, cultural anthropologists who write ethnographies are sometimes called *ethnographers*, and anthropologists who compare ethnographic information on many different ways of life are sometimes called *ethnologists.* The prefix "ethno-" comes from the Greek *ethnos* ("people") and is used a great deal by anthropologists to mean "of (or about) a people" or "of (or about) an ethnic group." Increasing numbers of cultural anthropologists and their field consultants work closely together not only in the course of field research but also in the writing of ethnography based on that research, a practice called *collaborative ethnography.*

A third major subfield of anthropology, called **anthropological linguistics** or **linguistic anthropology**, is the branch of anthropology concerned with the study of human languages. For many people, the most striking cultural feature of human beings is **language**, the system of arbitrary symbols—spoken, signed, or inscribed—that we use to communicate with one another and to encode our experience of the world and ourselves. Anthropological linguists were some of the first people to transcribe non-Western languages and to produce grammars and dictionaries of those languages. They also have worked to show the ways in which a people's language (or languages) serves as the main carrier of important cultural information. In tracing the relationships between language and culture, these anthropologists have investigated a range of topics (see chapter 3 for details).

In all their research, linguistic anthropologists seek to understand language in relation to the broader cultural, historical, or biological contexts that make it possible. Modern linguistic anthropologists are trained in both formal linguistics and anthropology, and some cultural anthropologists study linguistics as part of their professional preparation.

Archaeology, the fourth traditional subfield of North American anthropology, can be defined as a cultural anthropology of the human past involving the analysis of the material remains of earlier human societies. Through archaeology, anthropologists discover much about human history, particularly *prehistory*, the long stretch of time before the development of writing. Archaeologists look for evidence of past human cultural activity such as postholes, garbage heaps, and settlement patterns. Depending on the locations and ages of the sites they are digging, archaeologists may also have to be experts in stone-tool manufacture, metallurgy, or ancient pottery. Because archaeological excavations frequently uncover remains such as bones or plant pollen, archaeologists often work in teams with other scientists who specialize in the analysis of those remains.

The work that archaeologists do complements the work done by other kinds of anthropologists. For example, paleontologists may find that archaeological information about successive stone-tool traditions in a particular region may correlate with fossil evidence of prehistoric occupation of that region by ancient human populations. Cultural anthropologists may use the work of archaeologists to help them interpret contemporary patterns of land use or forms of subsistence technology.

Although the popular media often portray archaeologists as concerned primarily with exotic ancient "stuff" (the "Indiana Jones syndrome," we might call it), archaeologists are usually more interested in seeking answers to cultural questions that can only be addressed properly by considering the passage of time.

For example, archaeologists can use dating techniques to establish the ages of artifacts, which then allows them to hypothesize about patterns of sociocultural change in ancient societies. That is, tracing the spread of cultural inventions over time from one site to another allows them to hypothesize about the nature and degree of social contact between different peoples. Some archaeologists dig through layers of garbage deposited by people within the past two or three decades, often uncovering surprising information about modern consumption patterns. Such research, sometimes called the archaeology of the contemporary world, draws attention to a variety of material dimensions of contemporary human societies. One example is the "Undocumented Migration Project," organized by North American anthropologist Jason de Léon, in which archaeologists, ethnographers, and biological anthropologists collaborate to document and analyze evidence of "living and dying along the migrant trail" from Mexico to the United States across the Sonoran Desert of Arizona (De Léon 2015). Similarly, archaeologists and ethnographers have collaborated with persons experiencing homelessness in the UK by undertaking projects of "counter-mapping" that reveal and make public the material traces of their unrecognized "homeless heritage" (e.g., Kiddey 2014a, 2014b).

The projects just described point toward a long tradition of **applied anthropology** in which anthropologists draw on methods and findings from the other subfields to address practical challenges people face in today's world. In recent years, the proportions of professional anthropologists doing applied work has increased enormously. This subfield has grown rapidly as an area of involvement and employment for anthropologists. Some applied anthropologists doing *medical anthropology* use a particular group's ideas about illness and health to introduce new public-health practices in a way that makes sense to, and will be accepted by, members of that group (for more about medical anthropology, see chapter 11). Others may apply knowledge of traditional social organization to ease the problems of refugees trying to settle in a new land. Still others may tap their knowledge of traditional and Western methods of cultivation to help farmers increase their crop yields. Taken together, these activities are sometimes called *development anthropology* because their aim is to improve people's capacities to maintain their health, produce their food, and otherwise adapt to the challenges of life in the contemporary world. Applied anthropologists with a background in archaeology may be involved with contract or salvage archaeology; or they may work in *cultural resources management* to ensure that the human past is not destroyed by, say, the construction of new buildings, highways, or dams. Biological anthropologists may become involved in forensic work, such as the determination of social characteristics of crime or accident victims or in nutrition. Linguistic anthropologists, in partnership with local activists and social institutions striving to protect threatened cultural heritages, have worked to preserve indigenous languages on the verge of extinction.

In recent years, work in applied anthropology has changed and differentiated into several recognizable fields. Some applied anthropologists have taken a corporate route, working in advertising, marketing, or international business, for example. Others work for government agencies (in the United States, ranging from the Forest Service, to the Department of State, to the Department of the Interior). Recently, there has been a move for anthropologists to work for what Stuart Kirsch (2018) calls "constructive political change," a focus of research and action that is known variously as engaged anthropology, advocacy anthropology, collaborative anthropology, or militant anthropology (Kirsch 230). We will use the term **engaged anthropology** for this field, which includes, for example, participation in social movements, collaborating with activists and nongovernmental organizations, advising lawyers, writing affidavits, and producing expert reports (Kirsch 2018). Kirsch notes that engaged anthropology is concerned with the politics of participation, as practitioners are increasingly involved as expert witnesses, contributors to social movements, and, in general, taking and acting on a political position. As Suzana Sawyer (2005) puts it, "my research [in lowland Ecuador] dispensed with any pretensions of 'objectivity'; it was unabashedly invested and engaged . . . indígenas [Indigenous Ecuadorians] challenged, subverted, and capitulated to power, and it helped me understand the circumstances that produced, politicized, and compromised indigenous people."

Applied anthropology highlights the kinds of collaborations that many anthropologists have developed with scholars not only from other anthropological subfields but also from other scholarly disciplines. For example, cultural anthropologists with interests in the ways that human cultural practices articulate with the wider physical environment have, over the years, established working relationships with ecologists and economists, historians and political scientists, geographers and soil scientists, and botanists and zoologists. These collaborations have produced specialties ranging from cultural ecology (see chapters 8 and 9) to political ecology (see chapter 8) to *environmental anthropology*, an area of expertise that unites anthropologists with others who are concerned about ecology, the environment, and global environmental issues (see chapters 8, 9, and 10). For instance, few anthropologists would challenge the vast scientific consensus supporting the view that, as a consequence of human activities, we are living in the **Anthropocene**, a term used by scientists of many disciplines to describe the current geological epoch in which major transformations in climate and all life processes on earth are driven by the activities of human beings. When exactly the Anthropocene began is debated, as is whether or not our species may be driven to extinction by the climate change, pollution of air and water, and rising sea levels. However, these changes are matters of concern for all life, and especially threaten the livelihoods of the poorest, most vulnerable populations on earth—human and nonhuman. Recognition of this shared fate has reshaped the way anthropologists conceive of our subject matter and has promoted new kinds of ethnographic research. One example is *multispecies ethnography*, which focuses on the interrelationships linking specific human and nonhuman populations. For instance, a multispecies ethnography might investigate distinctive set of beliefs and practices regarding animal domestication in a particular community; or it might explore the tensions generated when people must deal with monkeys that threaten their crops, as well as with tourists who visit their settlements precisely to interact and photograph those same monkeys. We will address these issues in more detail in chapter 11.

In recent years, the number of new anthropologists with doctorate degrees who take up jobs in applied settings outside universities has grown steadily. As a result, increasing numbers of anthropologists have come to view applied anthropology as a separate field of professional specialization—related to the other four fields but with its own techniques and theoretical questions. More and more universities in the United States have begun to develop courses and programs in applied anthropology. This means that the distinction between academic and applied anthropologists is shrinking, as academic positions are taken by anthropologists with applied experience and anthropologists in academia are more likely to undertake applied work.

Anthropology may have begun in Western Europe and the United States more than a century ago, but over the course of its history, it has become an international discipline. Universities and research institutions in many countries around the world have established anthropology departments, offer courses and degrees, and carry out research, both theoretical and applied. Indeed, the theoretical innovations and applied projects that have developed in different parts of the globe have challenged forms of anthropological theory and practice that originated in Europe or the United States, contributing new points of view and fresh evidence to enrich our understandings of human possibility.

Anthropologists in different countries have established national anthropological associations, and there are also international associations of anthropologists for the dissemination of anthropological research.

1.3 IS ANTHROPOLOGY A SCIENCE? MODERNISM, POSTMODERNISM, AND BEYOND

At the beginning of the twentieth century, most anthropologists viewed their growing discipline as a science. They agreed that the truth about the world was accessible through the five senses; that a properly disciplined rational mind could derive universal, objective truths from material evidence; and that a single scientific method could be applied to any dimension of reality, from the movement of the planets to human sexual behavior. Such investigation was supposed to produce **objective knowledge**: undistorted, and thus universally valid, knowledge about the world. Anthropologists felt free to apply scientific methods in any area of anthropological interest, from stone tools to religion, confident that the combined results of these efforts would produce a genuine "Science of Man" (as it was then called). This set of ideas and practices is known as **positivism.**

Today, many critical observers of the natural and social sciences connect these ideas to a complex Western cultural ideology called **modernism.** Modernism can be (and has been) viewed in terms of liberation from outdated traditions that prevent people from building better lives for themselves and their children. Critics have argued, however, that modern Western science, rather than being a universal path to objective truth, is itself a culture-bound enterprise connected to a specific definition of progress (for additional discussion of science, see chapter 11). Many members of non-Western societies agree with these critics that, in their experience, modernist ideas have been used by powerful Western states to dominate them and to undermine their traditional beliefs and practices. This was the most direct consequence, in their view, of Western imperialism in the nineteenth and twentieth centuries, when European (and North American) states imposed political and economic domination, as well as forced cultural change, on territories that they colonized. The "era of empire" was regarded in the capitals of Europe and America as a mark of universal "progress," spreading civilization to less fortunate peoples of the globe. Most of those on the receiving end of colonial domination, however, associate colonialism with the loss of political autonomy, increasing impoverishment, environmental degradation, and destruction of systems of social relations and values that clashed with the "modern" way of life.

This criticism of modernism, accompanied by an active questioning of all the boundaries and categories that modernists set up as objectively true, has come to be called **postmodernism**. Its plausibility as an intellectual position increased after the end of the Cold War in 1989 when many previously unquestioned cultural and political "truths" about the world seemed to crumble overnight. To be postmodern is to question the universalizing tendencies of modernism, and postmodern critique has given rise to a series of other "posts" that question specific modernist assumptions. For example, *postcolonial studies* and *postcolonial theory* were developed by scholars who called into question the modernist premises that justified projects of European colonization. They also questioned the conclusion of scholarly work based on modernist premises, including many ethnographies written by Western anthropologists (see chapter 12).

Within anthropology, specific theoretical positions aligned with modernism have also been called into question. Coming under especially heavy fire, for example, were long-standing anthropological assumptions that each society (or culture or language) could be regarded as a self-contained, bounded entity with a unique internal structure. *Structural-functionalist* thinking within British social anthropology and the *structural anthropology* associated with French anthropologist Claude Lévi-Strauss were both undermined, leading to the development of *post-structuralist* views as a consequence (see chapter 12).

Questioning the universalizing tendencies of modernism has also meant questioning the modernist understandings associated with positivist science. In particular, the critique of positivist science developed in what might be called "post-positivist" *science studies* provided formidable evidence to show how people occupying powerful social positions could often pass off their own cultural or political assumptions as universal truths while dismissing or ignoring altogether the view of powerless groups. Scholars in science and technology studies have widened the frame of analysis to show how philosophical preoccupation with correct or incorrect scientific theories ignored the crucial contributions made by experimental *instruments* and the *skilled labor* of laboratory workers in producing successful scientific outcomes (see chapter 11).

These kinds of challenges to the previously accepted frameworks for doing anthropology have been controversial; but over the past quarter century, they have influenced and reshaped the way anthropology is practiced by increasing numbers of anthropologists in all of the subfields.

Anthropologists had long considered themselves to be debunkers of distorting Western stereotypes about non-Western peoples. Having frequently defended the integrity of indigenous societies against the onslaughts of modernizing missionaries and "development" experts, they had come to assume that they were on the side of those whose ways of life they studied. From the perspective of some members of those societies, however, as well as from the viewpoint of postmodernists, anthropologists looked just like another group of outside "experts" making their own universal claims about human cultures—behaving no differently from chemists making universal, "expert" claims about molecules.

1.4 REFLEXIVE ANTHROPOLOGY AND THE ONTOLOGICAL TURN

Postmodern criticism prompted anthropologists to engage in ongoing reappraisal of their discipline and, in particular, to rethink what was involved in fieldwork and the writing of ethnography. While cultural anthropologists continue to value careful observational methods and accurate, systematic data gathering, many of them also take seriously certain parts of the postmodern critique. Perhaps the earliest reappraisal involved a consideration of how to understand the relationships between anthropological fieldworkers and the human subjects with whom they worked. Modernist, "positivist" views of this relationship likened the fieldwork situation to a "living laboratory": placing the ethnographer in the role of the curious human investigator behind the microscope, and placing the subjects of research in the role of inert matter under the lens. But this analogy ignored the fact that anthropological fieldwork always involved a social relationship involving at least two curious human individuals; that is, research is always entangled with social relations. This meant that the cultural and personal characteristics of fieldworkers had to be taken into account when attempting to analyze and write about the research experience. Put another way, fieldwork had to become a **reflexive** activity in which anthropologists carefully scrutinized both their own contribution to fieldwork interactions and the responses these interactions elicited from the subjects of their research. That is, rather than assuming that they were, for all intents and purposes, invisible to the people they were studying, anthropologists began to recognize that who they were as individuals and as socially situated actors had an effect on their research.

Most contemporary cultural and linguistic anthropologists have long taken reflexivity for granted as a necessary component of the ethnographic research process; indeed, sociocultural anthropologists Martin Holbraad and Morten Axel Pedersen have argued that the contemporary developments in anthropological theory collectively referred to as "the ontological turn" are best understood as efforts to *intensify* the commitment to reflexivity in anthropology. What do they mean by that? First of all, in Western philosophy, "ontology" is the field of inquiry concerned with determining what does and does not exist in reality; and philosophers have relied on traditional Western forms of reason and logic to make these determinations. Euro-American scientists (and social scientists, including anthropologists) have carried out their research largely without questioning basic Western assumptions about what exists in the real world: for instance, the assumption that *autonomous entities* are more basic (more "real") than the *relations* that they might have among themselves. However, a key feature of ethnographic inquiry involves experiencing what Michael Agar (1996) called "rich points," and what Holbraad and Pedersen call "a-ha! moments" (2017, 1). These are experiences that utterly challenge the ethnographer's taken-for-granted assumptions about the way the world works. To take an example, we discuss in chapter 4 that the indigenous *runakuna* in Peru apparently regard Andean mountain peaks like Ausangate as living beings who monitor and intervene in human affairs and with whom bargains may be struck (de la Cadena 2015). But this view is flatly contradicted by Western ontological views of mountains as "really" nothing more than inert matter. Anthropologists have long recognized that a rich point of this kind *relativizes* Western claims about mountains and also pushes ethnographers into more *reflexive* awareness of ontological commitments about mountains that they have always accepted but must now reconsider anew. One outcome might be that the ethnographer writes that although "we know" that mountains are inert matter, indigenous Andean peoples "believe" that they are living beings involved in human affairs.

So what would it mean to *intensify* the anthropological commitment to reflexivity? According to Holbraad and Pedersen, it means to take anthropology's relativizing rich points and a-ha! moments and "to *run with them*. Instead of encasing them within generalizing theories about culture, society, human nature, and so forth, or trying to explain them away with a good dose of common sense, this way of thinking in anthropology seeks deliberately to take these moments as far as they will go, making fully virtue of their capacity to stop thinking in its tracks, unsettling what we think we know in favour of what we may not even have imagined" (2017, 2). To continue the previous Andean example, taking the ontological turn would mean rethinking, from top to bottom, what mountains are—but this time beginning with the ontological assumptions of *runakuna*. This is what de la Cadena attempts in her ethnography *Earth Beings*, exposing in the process just how tricky translation becomes when the ethnographer is not free to ignore (or to dismiss as mere "beliefs") the foundational ontological principles of the people with whom she is working. One way to think about taking the ontological turn in this instance is that it would mean attempting to provide an anthropological account of mountain peaks like Ausangate that might have been produced if the anthropologists, and their theories, had been developed by *runakuna* rather than Western thinkers. In Holbraad and Pedersen's words, to take the ontological turn is "to keep open the question of what phenomena might comprise an ethnographic field and how anthropological concepts have to be modulated or transformed the better analytically to articulate them" (2017, 10–11; for further discussion of "the ontological turn," see chapter 12).

Cultural and linguistic anthropologists are not the only anthropologists who take reflexivity seriously. Reflexivity awareness has become central to the work of biological anthropologists, paleoanthropologists, and archaeologists who regularly confer with members of contemporary indigenous communities to gain permission to study human remains or material culture that members of these communities claim as belonging to their ancestors. Successful recent research in studies of ancient DNA, for example, has been preceded by negotiations with representatives of descendant communities, and with institutions safeguarding ancient bones, to insure that appropriate permissions are granted and treatment protocols are observed. Reflexive researchers are much more explicit about the limitations of their own knowledge and much more generous in the credit they give to the people with whom they work. Ethnographers now often appear in their texts, alongside their research subjects; and their ethnographies sometimes read more like novels than like scientific texts.

In light of the postmodern critique and the emphasis on reflexivity, it should be clear by now that the traditional image of ethnographic fieldwork being carried out on a remote island or in an isolated village, where local culture is very different from the fieldworkers' own culture, is an outdated stereotype. To be sure, fieldwork still goes on in such settings. But in the twenty-first century, remoteness and isolation have been much reduced, and today field sites may be found anywhere. For one thing, it has become more and more common for anthropologists, even in the Western world, to do fieldwork in their own societies. Also, even when fieldwork is still undertaken in places far from the anthropologist's home culture, participant-observation is no longer bounded by the scope of a local community. It is quite common today for ethnographers to engage in **multisited fieldwork** in which the goal is to follow people, or objects, or cultural processes that are not contained by social, national, ethnic, or religious boundaries (see chapter 2). Working in more than one place, and with persons or institutions that have not traditionally been the focus of ethnographic analysis, can reveal interconnections and influences that in the past would have escaped the fieldworker's attention. The challenge of such a task is great, but many ethnographers believe that such research can yield important insights into human cultural practices that can be secured in no other way. For example, the work of medical anthropologists like João Biehl and Adriana Petryna involves "archival, multisited, and long-term field research" as well as "professional and consultancy work in the fields of development, international health, and human rights" (2013, 12; see chapter 11).

The interweaving of fieldwork and other research strategies to grasp the shape of cultural and political processes that escape local communities has become increasingly necessary in a twenty-first-century world shaped by a global capitalist economy, the Internet, and vast movements of people from one part of the globe to another. At a time when cell phone reception is available in the middle of the Kalahari Desert in southern Africa, anthropologists are well aware that the West and the rest of the world have become thoroughly entangled with one another. One consequence has been a growing anthropological recognition of the ways in which members of non-Western societies selectively incorporate "modern" or "scientific" practices originating in the Western world to help them develop their own alternative modernity, even as Western cultures are transformed by cultural practices imported from elsewhere (see chapter 10). At the same time, a reconsideration of the nature of "science" by anthropologists and others has shown that the positivist understanding of science may in fact offer an incomplete account of scientific successes and failures, not only in the social sciences but also in physical sciences such as physics and biology (see chapter 11).

A new generation of anthropologists, whose work begins by taking these developments for granted as part of anthropological practice, are displaying a range of previously unsuspected ways of doing anthropology in the twenty-first century. For example, consider recent work influenced by the anthropology of science and technology, anthropological reflection on the material properties of objects, and concerns at many levels about the role of pharmaceuticals in the contemporary world. A review of recent research traces pharmaceutical production, marketing, regulation, metabolic effects on human bodies, and "leakage" into the environment (Hardon and Sanabria 2017). At each step in the analysis, they show how pharmaceuticals, differently contextualized, enter into processes that can have beneficial or toxic consequences: not just for human health but for the health of the wider environment. They conclude that "there is no pure (pharmaceutical) object that precedes its socialization and interpretation. We argue that molecules are not 'discovered' but made and remade; they are fluid, ever evolving in relation to their context" (Hardon and Sanabria 2017, 118). Indeed, having followed the molecules of interest to drug makers and users in this way, they argue that their survey "points to a methodological horizon beyond multisited fieldwork" (127) as conventionally understood for the past two decades. The pharmaceutical molecules they follow, from laboratory to ingestion to outflow into the wider environment, constitute a subject of anthropological inquiry that seems very much removed, for example, from the Kula exchange of armshells and necklaces in the Trobriand Islands, described by Bronislaw Malinowski a century ago. Nevertheless, the journey of these molecules illustrates the kinds of interconnections linking living and nonliving, human and nonhuman, entities that become serious matters of concern to anthropologists investigating human life in the Anthropocene.

1.5 MORAL ANTHROPOLOGY

Anthropological sensitivity to these kinds of processes owes much to the reflexive stance that has become ever more central to anthropological methods. As Biehl and Petryna stress, reflexivity encourages awareness of "the omnipresence of social relations and . . . our own situatedness as researchers" as well as acknowledgment of "unknowns, the limitations of expert knowledge-making, and an inexhaustible richness at the core of the people we learn from" (2013, 12).

Perhaps most obviously, reflexive awareness promotes consideration of the ethical relationships between fieldworkers and informants. Attention to ethical issues in anthropology has expanded in recent decades, and some cultural anthropologists have begun to advance a perspective on these issues that they call **moral anthropology**. *Morality* in Western philosophy traditionally focuses on distinguishing good from evil, and *ethics* is the traditional name for the part of Western moral philosophy that examines what constitutes right and wrong actions. Yet the role of moral anthropology is neither to support nor to condemn moral judgments—nor to take a particular side when such judgments conflict. Rather, as French anthropologist Didier Fassin observes, the focus of moral anthropology "takes these moral tensions and debates as its objects of study and considers seriously the moral positions of all sides. A moral anthropology has no moralizing project (2012, 3).

Fassin acknowledges that many ethnographers have sometimes studied the systems of morality or ethics of particular societies, and he is not proposing that such accounts be replaced or discontinued. Rather, the critical moral anthropology defined earlier is intended to address broader ethical issues that reach beyond local communities, such as questions of international health, economic development, or human rights, which are the focus of work by anthropologists like Biehl and Petryna. These matters of concern cannot be fully addressed within the boundaries of any particular society or culture, assuming the boundaries of such entities could even be agreed on. Responding to the threats posed to all life now living in the Anthropocene require us to forge joint responses across differences, however awkward these may be (Tsing 2005).

Fassin points out that throughout the history of anthropology, many anthropologists have viewed their work as having a broader moral or ethical dimension. Some of these moral commitments may appear admirable (such as challenging oppression and defending the rights of dominated peoples), whereas others may not (such as entanglements with colonial or imperial projects, or with military intelligence operations). Both kinds of commitments are controversial for some anthropologists, and the purpose of critical moral anthropology is to reflect seriously on such controversies. Contemporary efforts to expand and sharpen the scope of reflexivity offer anthropologists possibilities for dealing with matters of ethical concern we cannot avoid encountering in a global context characterized by concerns about humanitarianism, human rights, and social justice (see chapters 10 and 12).

FOR FURTHER READING

Biological Anthropology   Marks 2011

Archaeology   Feder 2016

Applied Anthropology   Ervin 2004; Gwynne 2003; Kedia and van Willigen 2006; McDonald 2001; van Willigen 2002

Engaged Anthropology   Kirsch 2018; Sawyer 2004

Medical Anthropology   See "For Further Reading" in chapter 11.

Field Research   Bernard 2017; DeWalt and DeWalt 2010; Rabinow 1977

Political Ecology   Biersack and Greenberg 2006

CHAPTER 2

Culture

Culture has long been the central concept in anthropology. At its most basic, **culture** is understood to refer to learned sets of ideas and behaviors that are acquired by people as members of society, together with the material artifacts and structures that human beings create and use. Anthropologists have used the concept of culture in a variety of ways over the years, however, and contemporary anthropologists continue to disagree about how it should be defined. Major debates about the culture concept can be connected to particular intellectual and social struggles in which anthropologists have been involved historically.

2.1 CULTURE AGAINST RACISM: THE EARLY TWENTIETH CENTURY

Culture gained power as an anthropological concept in the early decades of the discipline, around the turn of the twentieth century, in a social and scholarly context in which the distinctiveness of different social groups of people was widely attributed to **race**. Races were thought to be distinct biological subpopulations, or even subspecies, of humanity. Scholars and physicians usually assigned people to various racial categories on the basis of skin color, hair texture, or other visible physical traits. But these physical traits were thought to be inseparable from a number of other, often less visible traits that were also thought to distinguish one race from another—traits ranging from language and dress and musical ability to morality and intelligence. Many early physical anthropologists hoped that if they could succeed in accurately identifying the "races of Man," they would be able to specify which languages and customs originated with, belonged to, or were otherwise appropriate for which races. Unfortunately, this search for a scientific definition of race took place in a historical context in which light-skinned ruling groups in the societies from which the anthropologists came were already convinced that differences in races were real and consequential and so used race-based distinctions to justify their own domination of darker-skinned peoples around the globe.

In this context, the culture concept was a crucial innovation designed to counteract the racism implicit in nineteenth-century physical anthropology and, more broadly, in nineteenth-century social thought. At the turn of the twentieth century, under the influence of Franz Boas (1858–1942), anthropologists were collecting evidence to show that the diverse beliefs and practices that distinguished different groups of human beings from one another were due to differences in *social learning* and not differences in racial biology. This social learning came to be called **socialization**, the process of learning to live as a member of a group; or **enculturation**, the process by which people come to terms with the ways of thinking and feeling that are considered appropriate in the group. For example, immigrants in the United States were assigned by physical anthropologists to a variety of different "races." Yet Boas and his colleagues were able to show that American-born children of immigrants regularly spoke fluent English: they wore the clothing, ate the food, and otherwise adopted ways of life common in the United States. Boas even showed that the head shapes of the children of immigrants differed from the head shapes of their parents, apparently under the influence of nutritional changes. This was important because head shape had been considered until then to be a rigid feature of difference between "races." Boas and his students went out and actually measured skulls, finding a slight but noticeable difference between generations born abroad and those born in the United States who developed a response to changed environmental factors.

The so-called races of Man were, in actuality, a single *human* race (or as we would say today, populations of a single human species). As a consequence, all were understood to possess the same "panhuman rationality" and considered equally capable of creating new cultural traits or adopting cultural traits from others. Another way to emphasize the equal humanity of all human groups was to demonstrate that each of them possessed the same kinds of institutions, or **cultural universals**, designed to achieve the same overall goals for the group's members. This was the path taken by Polish-British anthropologist Bronislaw Malinowski (1884–1942), who argued that all human beings everywhere face the same problems of survival or, as he put it, experience the same basic human needs. The members of each society use culture to devise ways of meeting these needs—for food or clothing or shelter or education or reproduction.

Different societies meet these needs in different ways, however, and it is the ethnographer's job to catalog the variety.

Boasians chose a different line of attack, arguing that race, language, and culture were independent phenomena. To show this was to show that the concept of biological race corresponded to no coherent material reality and thus explained nothing about systematic variation across human groups. That is, a person's physical attributes—skin color, hair texture, nose shape, stature, or the like—in no way compelled that person to speak or behave in any particular way. Indeed, the rapidity with which people of all "races" could forget old languages and customs and adopt new ones demonstrated the superiority of the culture concept in explaining variation across human groups. Because the capacities to create and learn culture belong to the entire human species, nothing prevents members of any subgroup from learning languages, beliefs, or practices originally developed by members of some other human subgroup.

Work by Boas and his students suggested strongly that the boundaries between various human groups are fuzzy and fluid and that firm distinctions are difficult to identify, let alone enforce. They devoted much effort to documenting an enormous amount of cultural borrowing across social, linguistic, and "racial" boundaries. The culture concept provided an explanation for why different social groups often lived lives that were quite distinct from those of their neighbors, without any need to invoke the notion of race. First, people do, initially at least, learn their native language and the bulk of their cultural practices from those among whom they grow up. Second, social groups often deliberately emphasize unique cultural attributes to set themselves apart from their neighbors. Finally, many of the groups that ethnographers first studied had historically been incorporated into colonial empires (as in Africa) or within the boundaries of a larger nation-state (as in the United States). In such situations, the sorting of peoples into named societies, each associated with its own unique way of life, was strongly encouraged by the ruling elites.

It was not until after World War II, and evidence of the horrors of genocide justified by racial thinking in Nazi biology, that racial thinking in anthropology was condemned. The highest-profile critic of racial thinking in physical anthropology was probably Sherwood Washburn of the University of California at Berkeley. Washburn proposed a "new physical anthropology," or biological anthropology, that was firmly situated within the so-called modern synthesis between Darwinian natural selection and genetics, which emerged among evolutionary biologists in the 1930s and 1940s. Drawing on population biology, a research field within the modern evolutionary synthesis, biological anthropologists argued that all humans were members of a single species; and they explained variations both among and within populations of our species as adaptations to particular natural environments, shaped by natural selection on genes. By the late 1960s, in the context of the civil rights movement in the United States and collapsing colonial empires abroad, this orientation became standard in anthropology.

All this work aimed to demolish the concept of biological race for good; and yet, at the beginning of the twenty-first century, the concept of "race" has not disappeared. The concept of culture explains why this is so: people can invent *cultural* categories based on superficial physical features of human beings, call these categories "races," and then use these categories as building blocks for their social institutions—*even if such categories correspond to no coherent biological reality*. Thus, when a particular social order depends on racial categorizations of the population to function in a particular way, racial categories can persist no matter how powerfully scientists demonstrate that they have no material basis in biology or genetics (see chapter 5). Ironically, racial categories that are condemned for stigmatizing different segments of the human population may be reinforced when, for example, a government asks its citizens to identify themselves by "race" to measure the extent to which compensatory government programs have or have not assisted the members of different "racial" groups to overcome past oppression. An ongoing challenge within anthropology has been how to expose the illegitimacy of race as a biological concept without ignoring the continuing vigor of race as a cultural construction in societies like that of the United States. This effort is complemented by ethnographic research illustrating how the concept of "race" has been defined and situated in varying ways in other societies, across time and space (see, e.g., Wade 2017; Amrute 2016; Shoshan 2016).

2.2 THE EVOLUTION OF CULTURE

Rejecting racial thinking led the Boasians to stress the plasticity of human biology under different environmental circumstances. If human beings could learn any language or culture to which they were exposed, this must mean that they required culture to survive and thrive. Along with many founders of the modern synthesis in evolutionary biology, such as Theodosius Dobzhansky and Ernst Mayr, anthropologists came to argue that in the course of human evolution, natural selection on genes produced species (our own and those of our ancestors) whose members adapt and survive as biological organisms by learning the cultural practices of those among whom they live.

Compared even to our nearest primate relatives, we human beings seem to be born remarkably free of specific "survival instincts" or biological programming that would secure food, shelter, and mates for us automatically. Instead, as Malinowski suggested, every human group apparently can invent (and modify) its own particular sets of learned cultural traditions to solve those problems. Thus, human beings must learn everything necessary to survive and thrive from older, culturally experienced members of their group.

Put another way, the way that a human group adapts to the environmental challenges of a particular habitat does not depend only on the physiology of individual human organisms (or the genes involved in the development of such physiological responses). For example, human beings attempting to survive in cold climates are not obliged to wait until natural selection provides them with thick fur. Instead, they can rely on their cultural capacity to learn to control fire, make warm clothing from skins, invent ways of using cold-adapted plants and animals for food, and so forth. Natural selection on genes still plays a role, but selection would favor those whose genetic endowment allowed them to learn especially easily from those around them and who were curious and creative in devising cultural solutions for new adaptive challenges. Evidence for evolution favoring increased human brain plasticity in response to environmental factors continues to accumulate (see Sherwood and Gómez-Robles 2017). Some anthropologists, known as *cultural inheritance theorists*, have used mathematical models borrowed from population biology to demonstrate how the capacity for human culture could have arisen as a result of natural selection on cultural variation. Others have used similar models to propose how natural selection working on genes and on elements of culture could have jointly given rise to *gene-culture coevolution* in the human evolutionary past. Their work grew out of work by *cultural ecologists* like Julian Steward, active in the mid-twentieth century. Steward connected changes in culture over time in particular societies to the nature of the societies' adaptations to their material environment, adaptations in which their culture and technology played central roles (see chapter 9).

If people's cultural activities reshape the environments in which they live (and to which they must adapt), then people also alter the selection pressures that they face. This process, called *niche construction*, remodels the environment to which any population must adapt, and it is by no means exclusive to the human species: birds building nests and beavers building dams are engaged in the same activity. Niche construction buffers a population from some environmental challenges that they might otherwise face, but it subjects them to new selection pressures shaped by the constructed niche. For example, although good eyesight has long been advantageous to human beings, selection pressures that favor individuals with good eyesight have been relaxed in contemporary affluent constructed niches in the United States, where eyeglasses are widely available to correct people's vision. Similarly, most human beings in the contemporary United States live in constructed niches that buffer them from predation by large carnivores but expose them to a different set of dangers: microbes like HIV (human immunodeficiency virus) or the tuberculosis bacillus. When individuals are exposed to such microbes, natural selection will favor those individuals who are more resistant to microbes over those who are less resistant, especially in niches where drug therapy is inadequate or unavailable.

Overall, research into human prehistory strongly supports a view of human beings as a species of "weedy generalists," equipped by our evolutionary history with adaptive traits, including our dependence on culture, that has made it possible for us to construct habitable niches in virtually any environment that the earth has to offer. Some anthropologists have tried to make sense of the patterns of human cultural adaptations revealed by archaeology, history, and ethnography over time and across space since the time, some 6 to 7 million years ago, that the lines leading to apes and humans diverged. As we saw in chapter 1, modern anthropology began by rejecting simplistic unilineal schemes of cultural evolution. Today, there is disagreement among anthropologists concerning whether it is still makes sense to talk about stages of cultural evolution. In this connection, James Scott (whose research spans the fields of anthropology, political science, and others) has recently argued that evidence traditionally interpreted to support such a sequence may tell a rather different story when read "against the grain" (Scott 2017). Notably, Scott situates his analysis within the framework of niche construction. According to Scott, "long before the more explosive and recent 'thick' Anthropocene," human niche construction initiated a "thin" Anthropocene when our ancestors used fire to remodel the landscape some 400,000 years ago—later intensifying our mark on the landscape about 12,000 years ago, when our ancestors developed ways of life based on the domestication of plants and animals and permanent settlement on the land. A decisive shift took place around 4,000 years after that, when some of our ancestors invented the institution of the state (2017, 3).

Scott emphasizes how activities involved in human niche construction expanded as our ancestors entered into coevolutionary relationships with grains such as wheat and animals such as sheep, goats, and chickens. Understanding "domestication" in coevolutionary terms, Scott echoes recent work of anthropologists studying human–animal relations who regard domestication as a process that evolutionary biologists describe as *mutualism*, which acknowledges the active contributions of both human and nonhuman partners. Scott further points out that the domesticated grains on which states relied were important not only as sources of calories but also were "best suited to concentrated production, tax assessment, appropriation, cadastral surveys, storage and rationing. On suitable soil wheat provides the agro-ecology for dense concentrations of human subjects" (2017, 21). In the context of a state, niche construction takes the form of what Scott calls "state landscaping," which involves the building and maintenance of infrastructure like irrigation canals and new fields (but also leads to deforestation and the degradation of soil and water). State institutions succeed when they are able to manage relations among plants, animals, and the human populations required to perform agroecological labor, but they are vulnerable to social breakdown in the face of epidemic disease, raiding, and warfare (Scott 2017, 23). Over time, these processes generate non-linear trajectories that Scott prefers to call *deep history* rather than prehistory or cultural evolution (for more on these matters, see also chapters 5, 8, and 12).

2.3 CULTURE AND SYMBOLISM

Human beings depend on learned culture to survive, but they are certainly not the only animals in the world that learn. Several decades of research, for example, have shown that chimpanzees have invented simple practices of various kinds that other members of their groups acquire through learning, such as fishing for termites with twigs, making leaf sponges to soak up water to drink, cracking nuts open with rocks, and assuming distinctive postures for grooming one another. If culture is defined as practices that are acquired from and shared with other members of one's social group, that mediate one's adaptation to the environment, and that get passed on from generation to generation by means of social learning, then these ape practices certainly can be called culture. At the same time, missing from these forms of ape culture is a key element that is integral to human culture. Unlike the learned behavior of other primates such as chimpanzees, human culture clearly depends on our use of **symbols**.

A symbol is something that stands for something else: "X symbolizes Y." What makes symbols distinct from other forms of representation is that there is *no necessary link* between the symbol (X) and that which it stands for (Y). Put another way, the relationship between a symbol and that which it stands for is conventional and arbitrary. The object that you are reading right now is called a "book" because generations of English speakers have agreed to call it that. It could just as easily be called "libro" or "gludge." Apes such as chimpanzees and bonobos do seem to have some rudimentary symbolic capacities. Just how much remains controversial, however, because the strongest evidence has been produced in the highly constructed niches that are primate research laboratories. In laboratory settings, however, and especially in the wild, these apes do not depend on symbolism to anything like the degree that human beings do. Thus, although learning is not unique to human beings, and some learning of shared traditional practices can be found in nonhuman animals, only with human beings do we find a species whose survival depends on its reliance on learned, shared traditions that are *symbolically encoded*.

To depend on symbolic culture is to depend on learning for survival, but it is also much more. Symbols stand for objects, events, and processes in the wider world. But because their link to these phenomena is purely by convention, that which the symbol stands for can never be specified once and for all. The "same" phenomena may be symbolized differently in different societies, or phenomena that are distinguished as "different" in one society may be grouped together as instances of the "same" thing in another. This slippage between symbols and what they stand for makes possible complex human cultural systems, and it enables their remodeling or dismantling under novel conditions. Such slippage also means, however, that effort is constantly required to keep symbolic systems *systemic*—that is, orderly and coherent. Furthermore, nothing guarantees that existing cultural systems will not change over time, due either to internally generated developments or to exposure to new phenomena introduced from outside.

Debates about symbolism have a long history in anthropology as well as in disciplines such as philosophy and literary studies. In recent years, perhaps the most influential discussion of symbols in anthropology has been based on the writings of the nineteenth-century pragmatic philosopher Charles Sanders Peirce. Peirce, who distinguished symbols (which are linked to what they refer to by arbitrary conventions) from *icons* (which resemble their referents like the graphic that looks like a printer and takes you to the Print screen in a computer app), and *indexes* (which point toward their referents). The Peircean framework has been especially influential in linguistic anthropology (see the discussion in chapter 3) but has also been important in anthropological studies of art and material culture. As we shall see in chapter 12, some proponents of the so-called ontological turn in anthropology have challenged the taken-for-granted assumption that multiple cultures offer different symbolic representations of a single material world. This assumption, they argue, is rooted in the Enlightenment modernist assumptions about what does (and does not) "really" exist in the world, which needs to be challenged by alternative sets of assumptions about what exists in the world and alternative understandings about what Western anthropologists call "culture."

2.4 ETHNOCENTRISM AND CULTURAL RELATIVISM

Early ethnographers were impressed by the high degree of cultural coherence and predictability that they regularly encountered while doing field research in non-Western societies. This was important because it undermined widespread racist stereotypes about tribal or non-Western peoples: such peoples were regularly portrayed as irrational "savages" or "barbarians" leading lives that were, in the words of seventeenth-century philosopher Thomas Hobbes, "nasty, brutish, and short." Such portrayals of tribal peoples by Western observers were based on the universal human tendency to view one's own way of life as natural and as naturally better than other, different ways of life. Anthropologists call this attitude **ethnocentrism**—that is, using the practices of your own "people" as a yardstick to measure how well the customs of other, different peoples measure up. Inevitably, the ways in which "they" differ from "us" (no matter who "they" and "us" happen to be) are understood, ethnocentrically, in terms of *what they lack*.

Ethnocentric Europeans and North Americans believed that to be "civilized" and "cultured" meant to follow an orderly way of life graced by refinement and harmony. But early anthropologists found that they could use the culture concept to counter these ethnocentric beliefs. They could show that *all* peoples were equally "cultured" because every group's social practices were characterized by order, harmony, and refinement. The particular set of customs one followed depended on the group one was born into, from whose members one learned those customs. Another group's customs might differ from our customs, but each group equally had its own orderly, refined sets of customs. Thus, the child of an aristocratic European family, if brought up among people who hunted and gathered for a living, would learn the language and culture of hunters and gatherers just as easily as one of their children, adopted by the aristocrats, would learn the language and culture proper to aristocratic Europeans. To emphasize that every society (not merely Western European society) had its own integrated culture was a way of emphasizing that each society was human in its own way—indeed, that all human societies were *equally human*.

The term *culture* came to refer to a coherent set of beliefs and customs belonging to a distinct society. Such a view seemed to entail, at the very least, that those who were outsiders to someone else's culture ought to refrain from assuming that difference automatically meant inferiority. A culture could not be fully appreciated, anthropologists argued, until its various beliefs and practices were seen from the point of view of those who lived their lives according to those beliefs and practices. Ethnographic fieldwork introduced anthropologists to peoples about whom they previously lacked firsthand knowledge. By living side by side with people with an unfamiliar set of beliefs and practices for an extended period of time and learning the local language, anthropologists might hope to get a sense of what the world looked like from their hosts' point of view. This perspective on other cultures developed into the position called **cultural relativism** whereby anthropologists were urged to interpret specific beliefs and practices in the context of the culture to which they belonged. More broadly, anthropologists urged others not to make snap judgments about the value of other peoples' customs. Cultural relativism gave anthropologists (and the members of the societies they studied) ideological ammunition to use against missionaries or colonizers who felt no compunction whatsoever about moving into "primitive" societies and destroying indigenous customs that were not to their liking. In this sense, cultural anthropologists in the first half of the twentieth century believed that the ethnographic evidence they collected in societies throughout the world supported their claims of equal capacity and equal dignity for all human beings.

Still, not everyone was persuaded by their views. Indeed, new stereotypes about "primitive peoples" emerged that took account of anthropological evidence. It no longer seemed plausible to claim that "savages" and "barbarians" were wild, unruly, and irrational. But ethnocentric Europeans and North Americans could now argue that "they" were different from "us" because of "their" mindless and uncritical obedience to traditions inherited from their ancestors. People in "modern" Western societies with "scientific" cultures, by contrast, were portrayed as both able and willing to question the validity and rationality of traditional practices and to replace outmoded customs with better-adapted innovations. To view culture as a prison house of custom from which non-Western and tribal peoples were powerless to escape on their own, however, was to take the anthropological concept of culture and apply it in ways that the anthropologists who first developed it had never intended.

2.5 THE BOUNDARIES OF CULTURE?

In the context of the many social, cultural, and political changes that roiled the last third of the twentieth century, the anthropological portrait of a world made up of particular mutually exclusive societies, each with its own, internally consistent culture, increasingly came under scrutiny, both within and outside anthropology. Some anthropologists had always raised questions about just how sharply bounded, just how internally integrated, any particular culture might be. Boas and his students, as noted previously, had documented much cross-cultural borrowing, which suggested that boundaries between cultural traditions might be rather porous. But if society A borrowed a custom from society B, could that custom ever be made into an "authentic" part of the culture of society A? And if it could be integrated, did that mean that the culture of society A was no longer "authentic"? And who would decide? Furthermore, even if a provisional correspondence could be established between a particular society and a particular set of cultural beliefs and practices, was it plausible to claim that every member of that society shared *every* aspect of its culture—the same beliefs, the same values, the same practices, the same points of view? What if members of the society in question disagreed, say, about how to perform a ritual? Could only one of the parties be correct, and must the others necessarily be wrong? And, again, who would decide?

Ethnographers often sought research settings that seemed to approximate the ideal of cultural uniformity—for example, remote villages or culturally distinct urban neighborhoods. Often they had to acknowledge that this setting was only one part of a larger sociocultural system, even if that larger system was not the focus of their research. This was particularly visible and problematic in the case of ethnographic work carried out during the colonial period: the wider imperial setting would be acknowledged briefly, but little or no reference to that setting would be made in the rest of the ethnography.

In recent years, many anthropologists have begun to question the validity of speaking as if a large and complex society could possess a single, uniform "culture." It has also become obvious that even within relatively small homogeneous societies, members may disagree with one another about what "their culture" actually is. Anthropologists have become increasingly sensitive to the political issues involved in drawing boundaries around a society or a culture or in taking the views of one subgroup of a larger society as representative of "the culture" as a whole. This is why contemporary anthropologists always acknowledge that social and cultural boundaries are not eternally fixed; and why they explicitly question, rather than assume they already know, what any particular set of boundaries means.

2.6 THE CONCEPT OF CULTURE IN A GLOBAL WORLD: PROBLEMS AND PRACTICES

How should ethnography be pursued in a world in which local conditions are never isolated from global processes? As we saw in chapter 1, one solution is to undertake *multisited fieldwork*: doing research not only in a particular local setting (a small village, say) but also in a series of other settings (such as political or corporate centers, whether in the same country or abroad). For example, fieldwork might begin in an urban neighborhood in the United States among a group of immigrants. But it might extend into the urban and national bureaucratic settings in which decisions affecting the immigrant group are made, and it might even continue in the communities abroad from which the immigrants originally came. The popularity of multisited fieldwork today testifies to anthropologists' awareness of the often wide-ranging network of complex processes in which any particular local community is enmeshed. Similarly, contemporary ethnographies are often quite explicit about the date when they carried out their research and about which members of a group have provided cultural information about a particular issue. Thus, anthropologists are careful to distinguish the opinions of, say, older men from those of women; or of younger men because they have learned that these subgroups regularly have differential access to social power and different interests to defend and so have different interpretations to offer about the cultural institutions and practices in which they are involved.

With this new awareness has come the realization that a concept of culture that emphasizes uniformity of belief and practice is not always liberating and can also be used as a way of enforcing inequality. This is clearest when one subgroup within a larger society insists on its version of the tradition as the only correct version and tries to force other subgroups to profess allegiance to that version or else risk persecution. Such practices are perhaps most obvious in those societies that were once colonies but have since become independent states. A common experience in such new states was the discovery that very little, apart from joint opposition to the colonizing power, united the peoples who were citizens of these new states. The ruling groups who had inherited the reins of government following the departure of the colonizer all felt very strongly the need to build some kind of national unity based on a shared "national culture." But the elements of such a national culture could be difficult to find when the only historical experience shared by all the new citizens was the tradition of colonial domination. Sometimes appeal could be made to precolonial customs—religious, economic, or political practices, for example—that were distinct from those that had been introduced by the colonial power. If such practices had once been widely shared or at least widely recognized by the bulk of the population, they might become resources on which to build a new national identity. If, however, such practices belonged only to a tiny proportion of the new citizenry—perhaps a powerful tribal group that had come to dominate postcolonial politics, for example—the practices might well be resisted by other groups. Having expelled one colonial power, they would see no advantage in being recolonized by one of their neighbors.

Paradoxically, however, elements of colonial culture often played an important role in the construction of the new national culture. This included not only the bureaucratic apparatus of governmental administration inherited from the colonial past and the new ways of doing business or educating the young introduced during the colonial period but also the language in which all these activities would be carried out. Anthropologists studying the production of national culture have been influenced by the writings of political scientist Benedict Anderson (especially Anderson 1983), who argued that nation-states are "imagined communities," most of whose members never see one another face-to-face but who nonetheless experience a sense of fellow feeling for one another. In Anderson's view, much of that fellow feeling in new nation-states developed out of their members' shared experiences of colonial institutions and practices.

Once again, language is a good example. If the peoples who were administered within a single colony came from dozens or hundreds of different ethnic groups, speaking numerous mutually unintelligible languages, any shared sense of belonging to the same nation would likely be very slight. However, once children from all those different groups began to attend colonial schools and learn the colonizer's language, they did have things in common. Moreover, they could then speak with and learn about one another in a way that would not have been possible had they not all learned to speak, say, French in French colonial schools. Again and again, the new nation-states chose the language of their former colonizer as the new national language of government, business, and education. Not only was this "efficient," in that it allowed an important element of continuity in changing circumstances, but it also meant that the official language of the state did not favor any particular indigenous language group over the others.

The culture concept thus can be reformulated to describe an emerging national culture, and attempts can be made to relate that national culture to the local cultures of different groups incorporated within the nation-state. What anthropologists did not expect, however, and what led to their most serious questioning of the traditional culture concept, were cases in which national regimes in various countries did not recognize the existence within their borders of such differentiated and partially overlapping cultures. Thus, if outsiders objected to the way that a particular regime was treating its own citizens, spokespersons for the regime might respond that such treatment was "part of their culture" and, as such, beyond the critique of outsiders whose cultures were different. Notoriously, under apartheid in South Africa, it was official government policy to endorse the notion that each people had its own unique culture. The apartheid regime assigned indigenous African peoples to "homelands" in rural areas far from mines and farms and factories on the dubious grounds that Africans properly belonged in rural areas, farming the way their ancestors had done, and were not suited to work in, let alone run, modern commercial or industrial institutions in South Africa because these institutions were part of "European culture." In recent years, debates and clashes over supposed threats to cultural integrity have emerged in Western Europe, North America, and elsewhere, in the context of unprecedented population displacements within nation-states as well as flows of immigrants and refugees across national borders. These movements, entangled in complex political and economic disruptions following the end of the Cold War in 1989, will be examined more closely in chapter 10.

2.7 CULTURE: CONTEMPORARY DISCUSSION AND DEBATE

What has been the outcome of all this discussion and debate about the culture concept? Some anthropologists assert that the concept of culture has been forever tainted by the older usage that assigned every society its own unique, internally harmonious set of beliefs and practices. Because this use of the concept reflects an outmoded understanding of how societies and cultures relate to one another, they argue, and has permitted culture to be falsely understood as a prison house of custom from which people could never escape, the term *culture* should be discarded entirely. They believe that it bears too many traces of the colonial circumstances under which it was developed and to which it proved so useful an intellectual tool in dividing and dominating colonized peoples.

But abandoning the one-society, one-culture model does not mean that the concept of culture needs to be discarded. Many of the anthropologists who reject that model prefer to think of culture as the sum total of all the customs and practices that humans have ever produced. They point out that, with the increasing speed and density of communication and travel, nobody anywhere on the face of the earth is isolated from the major flows of information and activity present in our contemporary world. Fast food, hip-hop music, and computers have a worldwide appeal; there are now more Facebook users outside the United States than inside it. (See chapter 3 for a discussion of Facebook.) Because we are a species that needs to learn how to survive and are willing to learn new things from others, people everywhere now seem to be involved in stitching together their own patchwork of beliefs and practices from both local traditions and the wide range of global culture locally available. In situations like this, many contemporary anthropologists argue that what counts as anyone's culture is "up for grabs."

And yet those processes that turn culture into something individuals put together on their own are frequently countered by another process in which groups defend a uniform and closed view of their own culture in the face of potential inundation by global culture. Thus, much like some early anthropologists, contemporary activists in movements of ethnic solidarity defend a monolithic, internally harmonious view of their own culture against "outside" forces claiming to know what is best for them. Such a defense, however, is not without its own paradoxes. For example, to present the image of a united front, ethnic activists must downplay the same kinds of internal divisions and disagreements that anthropologists have been criticized for ignoring in traditional ethnographies that emphasize cultural uniformity. Activists may be fully aware of this paradox but still believe that it is justified for political reasons.

At the same time, some individuals defend their right to pick and choose from global culture the customs that they want to follow and resist attempts by other members of groups to which they belong to police their beliefs and behavior. More than that, they may challenge those who criticize them for incorporating borrowed cultural practices alongside those they have inherited—asserting that theirs is a living cultural tradition, and all living cultural traditions will sometimes change in this way. Put another way, **cultural hybridization**—the mixing and reconfiguring of elements from different cultural traditions—is acknowledged and even celebrated. Those who creatively recombine local cultural features with features from elsewhere regularly insist that the end result need not be "Westernization" or "Americanization" of their own cultures; rather, they speak of the "Africanization" or "Botswanization" or "Ju/'hoansization"—that is, the **indigenization**—of cultural features that may have originated in the West or in America but have been adopted by local people for local purposes. Because these outside cultural elements are chosen by insiders rather than imposed by outsiders, they are seen to enrich rather than to destroy or replace the cultural traditions into which they are being integrated. Prior to the end of the twentieth century, for example, literacy may not have been part of the cultural heritage of southern African foragers like the Ju/'hoansi. But many contemporary Ju/'hoansi who have learned to read and write and transcribe their own language view these as positive changes that strengthen their ongoing, developing, cultural tradition and also allow them to participate more fully in the political and economic life of the country they live in. Picking up on these developments, some anthropologists are paying renewed attention to the kinds of cultural borrowing highlighted by Boas and his students a century ago (see chapter 12) but with a twist. In the contemporary context, anthropologists take for granted that all living cultural traditions are dynamic and open to change. As a result, they draw attention to the deliberation and choice exercised by members of these societies who selectively adopt elements of other cultures, not as a way of rejecting their own tradition for an alien alternative but to reaffirm and strengthen their own evolving cultural identity.

Another recent strategy is to approach culture from the perspective of how it enters into the life processes of human beings over time. In a recent volume, for example, Tim Ingold, Gisli Palsson, and their contributors ask readers to consider what it might mean to think of ourselves as "biosocial becomings" rather than as "human beings" (Ingold and Palsson 2013). This processual approach begins by locating human persons as always already entangled in a dynamic life-world with other organisms, cultural patterns, social institutions, and manifold additional features of the wider world. It draws attention to possibilities and challenges that persons encounter as they grow more experienced in life processes that remain open to contingency. It provides examples that illustrate how human persons may develop in unpredictable and surprising ways precisely because the processes of life are open-ended, and what we may become can never be reduced to our genetic endowment or fully predicted by the socialization or enculturation to which we have been exposed (see chapter 12).

2.8 CULTURE: A CONTEMPORARY CONSENSUS?

In recent years, the concept of culture has been taken up by many other disciplines, partly as a result of anthropology's success in demonstrating its value. But these other disciplines often use the culture concept in ways that contemporary anthropologists do not. If there is a contemporary anthropological consensus about the nature of culture, it would seem to involve at least the four following propositions. First, nobody questions that culture is learned, not genetically programmed. Second, many anthropologists would argue that the kind of culture that is learned (and the way it is learned) is never innocent but is always shaped by power relations of some kind. Third, power relations and cultural forms that are global in scope have penetrated local communities and local cultures; the ultimate consequences for anybody's culture are still to be assessed. But, fourth, it is incorrect to assume that the penetration of local communities by global culture dooms all local cultural traditions to extinction. On the contrary, local societies can and do indigenize cultural elements that arrive from elsewhere, regularly subverting their homogenizing or "Westernizing" potential and putting them to work in sometimes surprising ways, either to preserve and enhance local goals and interests or to explore new possibilities of what an open future might offer.

FOR FURTHER READING

Ideas of Culture   Bohannan 1995; Fox and King 2002; Gamst and Norbeck 1976; Kuper 1999
Contemporary Critiques   Anderson 1983; Clifford 1988; Hannerz 1996; Marcus and Fischer 1986; Ortner 2006
Race   Baker 1998; Harrison 1998; Hartigan 2015, 2013
Ape Culture   Campbell et al. 2011; Savage-Rumbaugh et al. 1986

CHAPTER 3

Meaning-Making and Language

Human beings, alone among all living species, rely on language to communicate with one another. This fact has puzzled and intrigued people in all societies, has played an important role in religious and philosophical reflections on the human condition, and has been a central focus of attention in anthropology from the very beginning. Trying to define language in a clear and unambiguous way, however, has proved surprisingly difficult. Today, most anthropologists would probably agree, minimally, that **language** is a system of arbitrary symbols that human beings use to encode their experience of the world and to communicate with one another. While most language is vocal, language need not be spoken. For example, language can be read, transmitted in Morse code, or expressed in sign language. The scholarly discipline that pursues a scientific study of language is called **linguistics**. The terms **anthropological linguistics** and **linguistic anthropology** have been used by anthropologists to refer to the study of language in cultural context.

3.1 MAKING MEANING

Language is not the only way that human beings communicate with one another. For instance, many anthropologists would insist that humans convey meanings of many kinds via ritual performance or art, even through the clothes they wear and the food they eat and not only through words. *But what is meaning?* Philosophers, linguists, and anthropologists have all struggled to answer this question. After all, dark clouds in the sky "mean" that a thunderstorm is likely. A dictionary will tell you that the word *mouse* "means" a small rodent with pointy ears and a long tail; but it may also tell you that a *mouse* is a small object, held in your hand, connected to your computer by a long cord, that allows you to move the cursor when you push one of its buttons. And what might a friend "mean" if she tells you "The mouse is under your desk?" Meaning is slippery, but this has not discouraged scholars in anthropology or other disciplines from trying to figure out how it works. The general term used for the study of meaning-making is **semiotics**, which derives from the Greek word for "sign." In general, semiotics refers to the study of signs and the roles they play in the communication of meaning.

But what is a sign? Most anthropologists who try to answer this question have turned to philosophers for help, and the most influential philosopher has probably been the nineteenth-century American scholar Charles Sanders Peirce (1839–1914). Linguistic anthropologists and anthropological archaeologists, among others, have been inspired by Peirce's account of signs because of its richness and subtlety. Peirce distinguishes three main kinds of signs, each of which is associated with its own set of operations (or mode of signification). *Icons,* for Peirce, are signs that resemble what they represent (think of the icon on your software toolbar that resembles a pair of scissors that, when clicked on, will allow you to "cut" text from your document). *Indexes,* for Peirce, are signs that point toward something other than themselves (think of smoke pouring under your door as an index of fire, or of a particular manner of pronouncing your vowels that index the part of the country where you grew up). Finally, *symbols,* for Peirce, are signs whose connection to what they represent is arbitrary. For example, the color red used to serve as a symbol of the Communist Party during the Cold War, but after the Cold War ended, it has been used to stand for the Republican Party in the United States—and in other contexts, it may symbolize blood or the emotion of anger. Red can be used to symbolize any and all of these disparate meanings, which means that there is no necessary link between the color red and *any* of these meanings—that is, each particular symbolic link is conventional and, ultimately, arbitrary.

Symbols are the building blocks of culture, as we saw in chapter 2, and they are also central to the operation of human language. Peirce was not the only person to grasp the arbitrary way in which linguistic symbols are connected to their meanings. Independently, the Swiss linguist Ferdinand de Saussure (1857–1913) made the same observation in the early twentieth century, and it was via his work that the concept of "symbol" was first incorporated into studies of language and culture in anthropology. However, Saussure's discussion of symbols has been somewhat displaced in recent years by Peirce's discussion; we will see, for example, how linguistic anthropologist Michael Silverstein and his colleagues have drawn on Peirce to investigate indexical and iconic features of language, which did not concern Saussure. We will consider Peirce's work again in section 3.6.

In fact, as described by Saussure, the arbitrary link between linguistic symbols and their meanings was an operation that occurred entirely *inside* the speaker's head, connecting the meaning of a linguistic expression and its "sound image." Anthropologist Webb Keane (2005) has shown how Peirce's theoretical framework provides a system for understanding how objects like textiles, sculptures, or houses *outside* our heads can also convey meanings in ways that are not fully captured by Saussure's approach (or, indeed, limited to a symbolic mode of signification). We will briefly look at these matters in section 3.8.

3.2 STUDYING LANGUAGE: A HISTORICAL SKETCH

The study of language was central to early anthropology because it was a dimension of culture that was easy to observe and study in detail. Languages also show tremendous variation, both over time and across space. The European study of systematic linguistic change is usually said to have begun with the work of the British scholar Sir William Jones (1746–1794) who studied Sanskrit in India. He pointed out in 1786 that Sanskrit, classical Greek, Latin, and more recent European languages shared numerous similarities, suggesting that they may have all diverged from a common ancestral language, or *protolanguage*, that came to be called *Indo-European*. All languages believed to have descended from a common ancestral language are said to belong to the same *language family*. By 1822, the German scholar Jakob Grimm (of fairy tale fame; 1785–1863) was able to show that regular changes in speech sounds could be traced over succeeding generations of speakers of a single language or among speakers of related languages as they diverged. The long-standing anthropological focus on the relation between language and culture is sometimes referred to as *ethnolinguistics*.

In the twentieth century, scholars turned their attention away from studies of language that were **diachronic** (concerned with change over time) to studies of language that were **synchronic** (concerned with the patterns present in a particular language at a particular point in time). The terms *synchronic* and *diachronic* were invented early in the twentieth century by Ferdinand de Saussure, one of the architects of this transformation. And from Saussure's time onward, scholars involved in synchronic language studies became known as *linguists*—distinct from *philologists*, who retained a focus on reconstructing linguistic divergence, primarily from written texts. Interest in language history did not disappear; but, influenced by the orientation and practices of scholars like Saussure, it became known as *historical linguistics*. Finally, followers of Saussure called themselves *descriptive* linguists because their goal was to describe the rules that governed language as people actually spoke it; they contrasted this goal with that of old-fashioned *prescriptive* grammarians, who saw their job as correcting ordinary speech to make it conform to some ideal literary model of proper grammatical usage. As noted previously, defining language has always been difficult primarily because it has so many dimensions to which attention might be directed. First, people frequently communicate successfully with one another without using language. Second, people can use language to communicate without actually speaking (e.g., they can use gestures or exchange written messages). Linguists traditionally have focused on spoken language, showing how human speech sounds can be grouped into recurring sequences, often called *words*, which are combined into longer utterances according to specific rules. The elements of language and rules for combining words are generally referred to as **grammar**. But much besides grammar is associated with spoken language, such as the various qualities with which we utter our words (volume, pitch, emphasis, speed, etc.), which some linguists call *paralanguage*. Moreover, grammar and paralanguage do not contain all the meaning we convey when we speak; meaning is also carried by such things as our postures, our facial expressions, and our accompanying gestures. These phenomena, which are sometimes called *body language*, have been studied by anthropologists using special systems of notation; the study of body language is called *kinesics*. In addition, we often choose our words carefully, depending on the person whom we are addressing or the setting in which we are speaking, which highlights the important role that context plays in shaping the meaning of our utterances. Finally, as the philologists showed, the language our grandparents (or more distant ancestors) used often differs markedly from the language that we use today. So how much of all this should we take into consideration when we study language?

To answer this question, Saussure made an important distinction between what came out of people's mouths when they spoke (which he called *parole* ["speech"]) and the underlying rules that generated that speech (which he called *langue* ["language"]). In his view, speech varied from speaker to speaker, reflecting each individual's idiosyncratic interests and stylistic preferences; whereas language referred to the stable, universal rules that all speakers observed. Saussure wanted to define language in a way that would permit him to study it scientifically. Therefore, he recommended paying attention only to the most systematic and unvarying elements of language—what other linguists call the linguistic **code** or grammar. Saussure argued that language (the code or grammar shared by all speakers) was a self-contained system and that the significance of any element in the system (such as sounds or words) depended on its relationship with other elements in the system rather than on some feature of the outside world.

Saussure's approach to language had at least two major consequences. First, it gave linguists a clear-cut object of study, whose intricate details they could probe without distraction; the end result was the birth of the independent discipline of linguistics, which continues this investigation today. Second, it drew attention to the *arbitrariness* of the relationship between the sounds (or words) of language and the meanings they stood for. Saussure showed convincingly that the sounds of language, by themselves, carried no inherent meaning: a flat-topped piece of furniture with four legs called "table" in English is called "mesa" in Spanish. Subsequent anthropological linguists, like Charles Hockett, would argue that the arbitrariness of the link between sound and meaning in human language was one of a number of related *design features* of language. Furthermore, they would argue that this arbitrariness was a consequence of the design feature Hockett called **openness**: the possibility of using the linguistic code to create totally new combinations of elements to articulate meanings never before uttered.

Along with Saussure, Franz Boas often is credited with contributing to the birth of modern linguistics and linguistic anthropology. His focus on language developed as he sought a way of studying culture in a detailed and nuanced way. It seemed clear to him, as it did to other ethnographers of his generation, like Bronislaw Malinowski, that a profound understanding of another culture could not be gained unless the ethnographer knew the language used by members of that culture to articulate their understandings of the world and of themselves. Boas's own observations about language, based on his field experiences, also drew attention to the code-like fashion in which languages were organized.

3.3 THE BUILDING BLOCKS OF LANGUAGE

One tradition of linguistic scholarship that can be traced back to the influence of Boas and Saussure focused on linguistic codes themselves. Early linguists were especially interested in the sound patterns peculiar to particular languages, an area of linguistics that came to be called *phonology*. An important early discovery was that every language has a restricted set of sounds that are recognized by all native speakers and that can be combined according to rules to form all the words of the language. These minimal units of sound recognized by speakers of a particular language, called *phonemes*, are contrasted with the much larger range of speech sounds that human beings are theoretically capable of producing and hearing—the scientific study of which is called *phonetics*.

Many early linguists analyzed the sets of phonemes characteristic of particular languages. They were also interested in minimal units of meaning in languages. Although in languages like English, such units often correspond to *words*, comparative work in very different languages, such as those of indigenous Americans, demonstrated that not all languages are put together the way English is. Even in English, not all minimal units occur independently as words. While *walk* is a word and corresponds to one minimal unit of meaning, *walked* is a word with two minimal units, *walk* and *-ed*, the second of which carries the meaning of "past tense." And so linguists adopted a new term, *morpheme*, to refer to the minimal unit of meaning in a language and studied the rules for combining morphemes in a branch of linguistics known as *morphology*.

But phonological and morphological rules alone could not account for the features of all grammatical sentences, a point forcefully made in 1957 by linguist Noam Chomsky. Chomsky argued persuasively that sentences were themselves units of grammatical structure, and he proposed that linguists begin to study *syntax*, the structure of sentences. Chomsky later argued that every grammar ought to contain a component concerned with how that language dealt with meaning. This justified attention to *semantics*, or the study of meaning, a dimension of language that traditionally had been viewed as too vague and variable to serve as an object of linguistic investigation. The fields of formal syntax and semantics have developed in different directions since the 1960s, but all those developments have roots in the initial orientations provided by Chomsky.

Chomsky also observed that people's actual utterances often were full of errors, hesitations, and false starts that might be the result of physical factors such as sleepiness and thus did not truly represent their underlying grammatical knowledge. And so Chomsky further distinguished between *linguistic competence* (the underlying knowledge of grammatical rules encoded in the brains of all fluent speakers of a language) and *linguistic performance* (the actual things people said, which for the reasons mentioned, might not reflect their actual linguistic competence). Much like Saussure, Chomsky thought linguists should ignore linguistic performance and try to develop theories of linguistic competence. Chomsky's influence in linguistics was nothing short of revolutionary, and it accentuated a split between those linguists who focused on the code alone and other students of language who remained concerned with how speakers used the code in different cultural and social settings. The linguistic anthropologist Dell Hymes summarized the objections of this latter group when he compared Chomsky's notion of *linguistic competence* to his own concept of **communicative competence**.

Chomsky's focus on the linguistic code led him to define linguistic competence in terms of a speaker's knowledge of the difference between grammatical and ungrammatical sentences in a language. But Hymes pointed out that successful use of language to communicate with other people requires far more than just grammatical knowledge. It requires speakers to choose vocabulary and topics of speech that are suitable to different audiences in different social settings. For example, fluent speakers of a language might show linguistic competence in their use of casual, grammatically correct linguistic forms in their conversations with friends. But they would betray a colossal lack of communicative competence if they used the same forms when introducing a visiting foreign dignitary in a formal public setting. To identify what constitutes communicative competence, researchers must pay attention to linguistic performance, to the actual words that come out of peoples' mouths: that is, to parole or speech. According to linguistic anthropologists like Dell Hymes or Michael Silverstein, these phenomena are not wholly idiosyncratic but show far more culturally shaped regularity than the followers of Saussure or Chomsky have ever acknowledged.

3.4 LANGUAGE AND CULTURE

In the middle of the twentieth century, the work of Dell Hymes represented the latest development in an approach to language and culture that could be traced back to Boas. Practitioners in this tradition continued to see the study of a particular linguistic code primarily as a means to a more profound understanding of culture rather than as an end in itself. In addition to Boas, the best-known proponents of this approach in the 1920s and 1930s were Edward Sapir and Benjamin Whorf. Both were struck by the ways in which linguistic form and cultural meaning shaped each other, and each in his own way tried to characterize that relationship. Whorf's analyses of the grammatical codes of indigenous North American languages like Hopi attracted attention (and eventual notoriety) both within and outside anthropology. In several controversial articles, he seemed to be claiming that every language had a unique, self-contained grammar that strongly influenced the thought patterns and cultural practices of its speakers, a phenomenon called *linguistic relativity*.

Following World War II, after Sapir and Whorf had died, other anthropologists, linguists, and psychologists decided to test the validity of claims about linguistic relativity by devising experiments that would measure the influence of language on culture and thought. These researchers advanced what they called the **Sapir–Whorf hypothesis**: the claim that the culture and thought patterns of people were strongly influenced by the language they spoke. Immediately, however, the researchers faced a familiar problem: How do you define "language" and "culture" and "thought" with sufficient rigor so that it becomes possible to measure the degree to which one does or does not influence the other(s)? In practice, "language" was equated with "grammatical code," and tests were devised to measure whether speakers whose grammars possessed (or lacked) certain grammatical structures were correspondingly forced to perceive (or prevented from perceiving) those structures when they looked at the world around them. For example, does an absence of grammatical marking on verbs for past, present, and future tense mean that speakers of that language cannot perceive the passage of time? Or, if a language has only three terms for basic colors (for example, *black*, *white*, and *red*), does this mean that speakers of that language cannot tell the difference between the colors an English speaker identifies as *green* and *blue*?

Actual research showed that questions posed in this fashion were far too simplistic, both about grammars and about human perception. Any language is always a part of some culture—that is, it is learned, not innate—and it is intimately interrelated with all cultural practices in which its speakers engage: and thinking cannot easily be distinguished from the linguistic and cultural activity in which it is regularly involved. Thus, it is virtually impossible to tease language, culture, and thought apart, let alone to figure out the direction of the causal arrows that supposedly link them to one another.

In the 1950s and 1960s, a number of anthropologists developed a research program known as *ethnosemantics* or *ethnoscience* that aimed for greater accuracy and sophistication. As the labels suggest, their goal was to discover the systems of linguistic meaning and classification developed by people in their own languages and used in their own cultures. Borrowing the linguistic contrast between phonetic and phonemic studies of the sounds of language, ethnoscientists explicitly contrasted *etic* categories devised by outside researchers and *emic* categories devised by native speaker-informants. Their goal was to describe as faithfully as possible the emic categories used by informants in their own language, and so they developed a rigorous set of research practices intended to protect their emic data from etic contamination. For all their achievements, however, ethnoscientists continued to work with a theoretical model of language and culture in which researchers and informants were understood to belong to mutually exclusive monolingual and monoculture worlds. It was not that anthropologists failed to recognize the inaccuracy of this model. Fieldwork and study had made many of them bilingual or multilingual and bicultural or multicultural, and a history of colonial conquest followed by linguistic and cultural imperialism had often made many of their informants bicultural or multicultural as well as bilingual or multilingual. Indeed, it was obvious that many people throughout the world were bilingual or multilingual, successfully communicating with speakers of languages with sometimes very different grammatical codes (e.g., Hopi and English), and they called into question the supposition that people typically were monolingual—that is, they knew or spoke fluently only one language from birth to death. This state of affairs became impossible to ignore.

By the 1960s, most linguistic anthropologists had concluded that there was no solid evidence that grammatical features of particular languages *determined* thought patterns or cultural practices. But did this mean that the forms of language had no shaping effects whatsoever on how people spoke to one another? In recent years, scholars have recognized that there are several different ways to ask about the relationship between language and thought. Dan Slobin (1987), for example, proposed a "thinking for speaking" hypothesis, suggesting that the influence of grammatical forms on thought may be greatest when people prepare to speak to others on a specific topic in a specific setting. For example, an English speaker who is trying to say "I like fast food" in Spanish will have to use a passive encoding—*me gusta la comida rápida* ("fast food pleases me"). This encoding is not easy for many English speakers to learn, precisely because it is not the standard English way to encode the thought.

Crucially, how one understands linguistic relativity depends on how one defines language. Dedre Gentner and Susan Goldin-Meadow (2003) have observed that some researchers think of language as *a lens* through which people view the world; others think of language primarily as *a toolkit*, which speakers make use of to build more elaborate conceptual structure; and still others think of language as a *category-maker*, influencing how people classify experiences and objects in the world. In their view, the research that produces the most consistent evidence of the influence of language on thought comes from those who view language as a tool kit. Because not all scholars of language agree to define language in this way, Gentner and Goldin-Meadow concluded that we are unlikely ever to agree on universal "yes" or "no" answers to questions about the influence of language on thought and culture. Straightforward answers to such questions will be even less forthcoming to the extent that we acknowledge the vast numbers of people throughout the world who are fluent in more that one variety of more than one language (see Pavlenko 2014).

3.5 LANGUAGE AND SOCIETY

Recognition of the need to take bilingualism and multilingualism/multicultur-alism into theoretical account prompted Hymes to urge his colleagues to move beyond the study of individual languages to the study of speech communities. A **speech community** is any concrete community of individuals who regularly interact verbally with one another.

In his classic discussions of speech communities, Hymes pointed out that if you delimit a speech community and then do an inventory of all the different kinds of language used by members of that community, you will quickly discover not merely one version of one language in use but rather a variety of forms of one language (and sometimes more than one language) in use. Some varieties will be *regional dialects*: versions of a particular language associated with particular geographical settings such as the Appalachian versus Texan versus New England dialects of North American English. Some will be *social dialects*: versions of a particular language associated with particular social groups such as the "Cock-ney" working-class dialect of London as contrasted with the "BBC English" of the educated British upper middle class. Still others will be social *registers*: ver-sions of a particular language associated with particular social settings such as a court of law or an elementary school playground or a house of religious worship. Every member of the speech community may not be able to converse fluently in all the varieties represented in the community, but all members will ordinarily have control of several varieties, each of which will be called for in a different set of circumstances.

This approach developed in linguistic anthropology by Hymes was sup-ported by similar approaches developed in sociolinguistics by sociologists such as John Gumperz. **Sociolinguistics** is usually defined as the study of the relation-ship between language and society. Traditionally, it has been interested in corre-lations between social variation (e.g., class or ethnic stratification) and linguistic variation (e.g., in the form of regional or social dialects), as well as correlations between particular social settings and linguistic registers. Together, Gumperz and Hymes developed analytic concepts that meshed in interesting ways. For ex-ample, if every speech community is characterized by a number of different lan-guage varieties, then every member of that speech community can be described in terms of her or his **verbal repertoire**: the sum total of verbal varieties a par-ticular individual has mastered.

Gumperz and others were able to show that the number and nature of the varieties within an individual's verbal repertoire not only offer a good set of indi-cators as to that individual's social identity and status but are also a good predic-tor of that individual's probable success in interacting verbally with speakers of different identities and statuses. Gumperz described verbal repertoires as sets of weapons that one could deploy in verbal (and social) struggles with others. Like soldiers with a range of weapons, people with more varieties in their repertoires could attain objectives in a range of social situations. They could switch from one variety (or code) to another as the situation demanded, a phenomenon called **code-switching**. Some sociolinguists have described speech communities in which everyone was fluent in two codes (either two dialects of a single language or two different languages) a phenomenon described as *diglossia*. Where diglossia occurs, speakers generally use each code in mutually exclusive settings (e.g., one at home and the other at school), switching back and forth between codes as the situation demands. One insight provided by studies of verbal repertoires is that speakers with fewer codes at their command are both socially and verbally limited in their interactions with others.

Hymes's suggestion that linguistic anthropology should focus on how people develop communicative competence in speech communities characterized by multiple codes stimulated research in a number of related areas. One was the comparative study of childhood acquisition of communicative competence, which involved mastering not only grammatical rules but also rules for appropriate use. Another was the study of classifications of forms of talk in specific cultures and examination of the various contexts in which these forms were used. A third was the study of culture-specific verbal performances like storytelling in which the codes known by the storytellers and their audiences were resources on which the storyteller could draw in exercising individual artistic agency.

Studies of verbal performance emphasized all those features of language that formal linguists ignored—such as figurative language, wordplay, deliberate rule breaking, and code-switching—to achieve certain rhetorical effects. Linguistic anthropologists carrying out cross-cultural research on verbal performance were able to show that however central the rules of grammar remain for effective linguistic communication, in real life, when people struggle to defend their interests using whatever tools are available, rules of grammar and rules of use can be bent or broken to achieve other communicative effects. And if rules can be broken, perhaps they are as much a product of other social and cultural communication as they are shapers of that communication.

More recent discussions of speech communities have built on these observations. Marcyliena Morgan (2014), for example, characterizes speech communities as dynamic groups whose speakers use the linguistic resources at their disposal to forge identities and engage in political struggles within the larger societies to which they belong. Morgan also draws attention to the way contemporary social media have stretched and amplified the reach of members of some speech communities across the globe. Situating linguistic variation in this way highlights the fact that not all varieties in a speech community are accorded equal respect, and that most formal linguists who talk about "the" grammar of language X ordinarily had in mind only one high-prestige variety of language X. If they were, like Chomsky, educated linguists studying their own native language, the grammar in question was likely to be that language's literary standard, such as standard English. And

because native-speaker linguists were told to trust their own intuitions in deciding whether certain usages were "grammatical," it became increasingly clear that
in practice, "linguistic competence" meant competence in the standard variety.
Despite linguists' assertions that their work was descriptive, not prescriptive, non-
standard varieties inevitably appeared ungrammatical with respect to the standard, making those varieties (and, by extension, their speakers) look defective.

3.6 DISCOURSE

Such judgments looked suspiciously like the old-fashioned opinions of prescriptive grammarians. From the point of view of linguistic anthropologists, they
reflected sociocultural evaluations of speakers associated with those linguistic
varieties, evaluations that inevitably reflected the unequal power relations between evaluators and those being evaluated. Linguistic anthropologists began
to focus explicitly on the way linguistic usage and evaluations of linguistic usage
were shaped by power struggles between various subgroups within a society.
They emphasized that rules of "grammaticality" or "cultural acceptability" often
are based on linguistic forms preferred by powerful groups in society. As a result,
disadvantaged groups may choose to express resistance against a given power
structure by refusing to use the linguistic forms endorsed by the powerful. Some
linguistic anthropologists have shown how this takes place in the course of public
and private performances of different culturally recognized forms of **discourse**
(talk) such as storytelling, oratory, popular theater, and traditional forms of
poetic expression (e.g., funeral laments). Such work made very clear that those
who engage in particular forms of discourse are not forced by rules of grammar
or culture to say some things rather than others. It is quite the opposite: they
struggle to use the rules of grammar and culture as *resources* to convey their own,
often subversive, messages to their audiences.

　　The focus of scholars like Hymes and Gumperz on speech communities
whose members each possessed verbal repertoires consisting of multiple language
varieties displayed the complexity and coordination of cultural and linguistic variation within a society. It also highlighted the sophistication with which
people regularly matched appropriate forms of discourse to appropriate audiences or settings. Following the rise of postmodern critique in anthropology in
the 1980s, however, attention began to shift to the prisonlike rules that aimed to
constrain people's behavior and censor their speech and to the struggles in which
people engaged to resist such limitations. In linguistic anthropology, this reori-
entation was assisted by the adoption of the concepts and approach of a group of
Russian literary and linguistic scholars associated with Mikhail Bakhtin, whose
key texts had recently been translated into English. Hymes and Gumperz's image
of speech communities whose members made use of multiple language varieties
was echoed in Bakhtin's concept of *heteroglossia*, or "many-voicedness," among
speakers in a society. The emphasis of Bakhtin's discussion, however, was on how
different groups of speakers, each rooted in their own particular (and unequal)
positions within society, struggle for control of public discourse.

Linguistic anthropologists influenced by Bakhtin were particularly interested in the discourse of low-status groups whose vulnerable social position made it unsafe for them to verbally challenge those who dominated them. Such linguistic anthropologists found Bakhtin's concept of *double-voiced discourse* very useful, for it emphasized the way the "same" words or expressions can mean different things to different speakers who use them in different contexts. Bakhtin demonstrated how speakers could maneuver around verbal censorship by the *ironic* use of language—when speakers and (some) listeners understand that words used in a particular setting mean the opposite of what they ordinarily signify. Bakhtin also drew attention to the *parodic* use of language—when officially acceptable language is exaggerated or mimicked with the intention of poking fun. Double-voiced discourse highlights the agency of speakers who manage to keep their actual words within acceptable grammatical and cultural boundaries, whereas the context in which their words are spoken imparts to them meanings quite different from their formal denotations. Officially, order is upheld; but unofficially, it is held up to ridicule or critique.

To focus on subversive forms of talk like double-voiced discourse is to emphasize the way in which language in cultural contexts of use twists and manipulates the supposedly unvarying and stable elements of formal grammar. The demonstration was so powerful that even formal linguists began to include a **pragmatics** component in their formal grammars, which purported to catalog universal rules of use obeyed by all speakers of all languages who wanted to communicate successfully with others.

Linguistic anthropologists quickly pointed out that the kinds of rules proposed by formal pragmatics, however, were based on the linguists' incorrect assumption that the primary purpose of linguistic communication is to convey faithfully from speaker to hearer factual information about the world. This communication, moreover, is assumed to take place in a conversational setting between disinterested parties of equal social status.

Communication sometimes does involve the transmission of information between equals. Linguistic anthropologists like Michael Silverstein were able to show, however, that such communication is only a small and highly idealized part of what normally goes on when real people with differential linguistic and cultural knowledge, living in real societies characterized by social inequality, try to communicate with one another. But studying such everyday cultural contexts of use meant that attention would have to be paid to parole (or speech), which Saussure had judged of secondary importance to the idealized langue in the heads of fluent speakers. Nevertheless, paying attention to speech provided important insights. As Silverstein argued, contextualizing language usage in this way exposes the idealizations of formal pragmatics as rationalizations for power-laden patterns of usage—that is, as features of a **language ideology**. Thus, struggles over appropriate usage are also ideological struggles; and everyday speech is an important source of information about these struggles, revealed in what people say and how they say it. Put another way, speech emerges as the practical crucible in which important shifts in language might be generated and spread. For example, Silverstein traced the historical developments that eventuated in shift from "thou" to "you" as the second-person singular pronoun in English. Following the Norman conquest, the custom of using "you" to address superiors and "thou" to address inferiors developed, based on a pattern borrowed from French. Later, during the Protestant Reformation, pronouns of address took on new political meanings: radically egalitarian sects like the Quakers insisted on using "thou" not only to address other members of their sect but also to address their superiors, which was scandalous. Because Quakers used "thou" to address individuals, people who did not want to be identified with the Quakers had to stop using it for that purpose. Because Quakers simultaneously avoided using "you" to address individuals, people who did not want to be identified with the Quakers had to use "you" exclusively for this purpose. The outcome was that English speakers ended up using "you" to address individuals of any status, as well as groups of more than one individual (Silverstein 1985, 242–251). Language use, shaped by political struggle, has the potential to alter even the supposedly unchanging core features of grammar.

Because pragmatic features that shape language use may be quite distinctive from one cultural setting or historical period to the next, linguistic anthropologists insist that every analysis of language use in cultural context must include information from ethnopragmatics. *Ethnopragmatics* is the study of the culturally and politically inflected rules of use that shape particular acts of speech communication among particular speakers and audiences in the specific cultural settings in which they regularly occur. Put another way, the "universal" rules of formal pragmatics turn out to be so narrow and culture bound that they are of little help when we try to understand what is going on in most verbal interactions in most cultural settings in most societies.

3.7 LANGUAGE CONTACT AND CHANGE

Considering linguistic interaction within a context of struggle among speakers with unequal access to valued resources in a society has also refreshed our understanding of languages called pidgins and creoles. A **pidgin** language traditionally has been defined as a reduced language with a simplified grammar and vocabulary that develops when speakers of mutually unintelligible languages come into regular contact and so are forced to communicate with one another. Those who speak pidgins are native speakers of other, fully developed languages and use pidgins only in restricted settings with those who do not speak their native language; for this reason, pidgins are said to have no native speakers. However, when pidgins persist over two or more generations, they often begin to change. Specifically, their grammar sometimes becomes more complex, their vocabularies increase, they are used in a wider variety of social settings, and children learn them as first languages. When this happens, according to the traditional view, the pidgin has developed into a **creole** and functions just like any other natural human language.

For a long time, it was thought that the evolution from pidgin to creole was regular and inevitable, but it has become increasingly clear that pidgins and creoles can persist indefinitely along with other language varieties in the speech communities in which they are found. That is, speakers of pidgins also live in speech communities where different linguistic varieties have specialized uses. As Marcyliena Morgan has emphasized, such speech communities are regularly shaped by unequal power relations, which means that different varieties enjoy different levels of prestige and that those with more prestigious linguistic varieties in their verbal repertoires enjoy decided political and social advantages. Linguistic anthropologists and sociolinguists have pointed out that the most recent wave of pidginization followed European colonization throughout the world. They note further that pidgins and creoles developed under colonial (and postcolonial) political regimes in which mastery of the written language of the colonizer (e.g., English, French, or Dutch) has been a prerequisite for economic and social mobility. Thus, groups in the society that have been deprived of the opportunity to become literate in the colonizer's (or nation-state's) official "standard" language variety are also deprived of access to most of the wealth, power, and prestige in society.

Such a situation helps explain the sometimes violent struggles that occur in contemporary nation-states, especially in those that were once European colonies, about which language or languages will be the "official" language of schooling and of government. If people live in a society whose members speak a number of different languages and language varieties, and if access to the most highly valued resources in society depends on fluency or literacy in only one official language, then it is easy to see that speakers of each language group will want their own language to be the official language.

Debates over "official" languages illustrate the operation of language ideology. The study of language ideology by linguistic anthropologists is central in settings with a history of colonization. Yet even when most members of a society are fluent or literate in the official language, they may be vigilant in policing the "purity" of that language, trying to eliminate linguistic borrowing from other languages. For example, when capitalist business practices and technology, originally developed in European languages, are imported into societies whose members do not speak a European language, the temptation is strong simply to borrow the European vocabulary and expressions for these practices and objects rather than inventing new terms in the local language. The temptation is even stronger if printed instructional materials in the European language are also imported because few poor countries on the periphery of the capitalist global economy have the resources to translate these materials into the languages of the local population. However, the influx of imported vocabulary may well be seen as a form of linguistic colonization. And like political colonization in the past, it is often resisted by *linguistic nationalism*: official, sometimes militant, efforts to proscribe the use of foreign terms and to promote the creation of alternatives in the local language.

Linguistic nationalism is hardly limited to former colonies of European powers. Citizens of European countries like France have periodically displayed linguistic nationalism when they protest the growing popularity among French speakers of expressions borrowed from American English. Like the citizens of former colonies, these French people fear that the influx of American English symbolizes a serious blow to the power and prestige of their own language and the nation to which its speakers belong. Ironically, speakers of regional languages in France, such as Breton in Normandy, have made similar arguments about the way in which the imposition of French by the state has threatened the survival of their own minority tongue! The same dynamics may be observed in the periodic effort—so far unsuccessful—by some citizens of the United States to have English declared the official language of the United States.

As it happens, national, regional, and international languages of business and politics have been spreading very rapidly in recent years, often at the expense of minority or local languages with few native speakers. The growth of schooling in languages of global reach, such as English, has drastically reduced the numbers of native speakers fluent in local, indigenous languages in many parts of the world. By creating grammars, dictionaries, and archival and educational materials designed to teach and preserve these languages in the future, linguistic anthropologists have been active in collaborating with remaining speakers of such languages to prevent *language death* and to promote **language revitalization**. Ironically, even as native speakers of endangered languages want to prevent them from disappearing, they are often torn about what language they want their own children to learn. Many speakers of endangered languages belong to groups that are economically marginal in the regions or nation-states where they live, and they want their children to have more economic opportunities than they have had. One means to such a goal is for their children to learn national or international languages of commerce that, they hope, will give their children a chance to make a better life for themselves in a world of globalizing capitalism.

Indeed, globalized settings are increasingly populated by individuals who regularly speak more than one variety of more than one language, and outside observers are increasingly unable to correctly infer the languages people speak based on the speakers' phenotypes—which are also increasingly difficult to sort into stereotypic racial categories. Linguistic anthropologist H. Samy Alim has called this phenomenon *transracialization* (Alim 2016b), and it is illustrated by President Barack Obama, whose father was Black and whose mother was White. President Obama's public displays of skilled code-switching between African American Vernacular English and Standard Euro-American English also seemed to take many White Americans by surprise. Alim and African American linguistic anthropologist Geneva Smitherman carried out a close study of Obama's speech and its reception by different audiences (Alim and Smitherman 2012). What they learned prompted a further question: "What does it mean to speak as a racialized subject in contemporary America?" (Alim 2016a). Alim and his colleagues have sought answers to this question by exploring relations between languages, race, and power in diverse ethnoracial contexts and societies, a project they call **raciolinguistics** (see Alim et al. 2016). Such work constitutes a promising direction for linguistic anthropology in the twenty-first century.

3.8 MEANING-MAKING AND ART

Although meaning-making is linked most closely to human language use, it has been clear to anthropologists and others for a long time that meanings can be made and communicated by means other than spoken, written, or signed speech. To downplay these other media and favor speech can be seen as an ideological move, favoring some modes of signification over others. For these reasons, we have chosen to address some core concepts anthropologists have developed to describe and analyze these other ways in which humans make meaning.

In Western societies, the term **art** includes sculpture, drawing, painting, dance, theater, music, and literature and such similar processes and products such as film, photography, mime, mass media productions, oral narrative, festivals, and national celebrations. When anthropologists talk about art in non-Western societies, they begin by focusing on activities or products that resemble art in the West. Whether non-Western peoples refer to such activities or products as "art," the activities and products themselves are universal. They seem rooted in playful creativity, a birthright of all human beings, but differ from free play because they are circumscribed by rules. Artistic rules direct particular attention to and provide standards for evaluating the *form* of the activities or objects that artists produce. One anthropological definition of art is that it consists of "culturally significant meaning, skillfully encoded in an affecting, sensuous medium" (Anderson 2004, 277). The term *sensuous* refers to the senses, so a sensuous medium is one that can be perceived by one or more of the human senses. The media through which culturally significant meaning can be encoded are vast and include painting on various surfaces; carving wood, bone, antler, and stone; singing and chanting; creating and playing musical instruments; storytelling; dancing; tattooing; and a theoretically infinite range of other media. These media and the kinds of skills required to work with them are culturally recognized and characterized. For example, the Baule of the Ivory Coast make a number of different kinds of sculptures out of wood, some of which are portrait masks that were supposed to resemble their subjects (Vogel 1997). Others are representations of powerful, dangerous spirits that are not understood as portraits at all.

The first kind of Baule mask might be described, in Peircian terms, as relying on iconic signification; the latter as relying on indexical or symbolic signification. However, as anthropologist Webb Keane (2005) has pointed out, observers may be seriously misled if they assume that representational practices in all cultures are built on the same assumptions that Western people take for granted. He has argued that different cultures depend on different conventional understandings about how signification works, which he calls **semiotic ideologies**. The role of semiotic ideology becomes obvious, for example, when people with different cultural backgrounds discover that their ideas of iconicity do not coincide. This can be seen when Western tourists buy printed cloth made on the Indonesian island of Sumba, take it home, and hang it on their wall as "art." On Sumba, Keane points out, these cloths are traditionally used as clothing, and their makers print images on them in a bilateral, "upside-down" pattern that becomes "right side up" when the cloths are draped on a human body. When Western tourists hang this printed cloth on the wall, however, they overlook these features of the cloth, emphasizing instead what the cloth has in common with other forms of art that Westerners hang on their walls. Keane concludes that iconicity is open: "Determining what features count toward resemblance commonly involves larger questions of social value and authority" (2005, 190).

Such judgments often involve an aesthetic element. Many years ago, Alexander Alland offered a definition of **aesthetic** that is useful for anthropologists: "appreciative of, or responsive to, form in art or nature" (Alland 1977, xii). According to Alland, something that is aesthetically successful generates a positive or negative response for the artist and perhaps for anyone else who experiences it ("I like this," "I hate this"). Indifference is the sign of something that is aesthetically unsuccessful. It is probably the case that the aesthetic response is a universal feature in all cultures and, as with play, may be part of the human condition. This does not mean that everyone in all places and at all times responds in the same way to a given work of art—quite the contrary, there is ample evidence that varies from place to place. Keane would ascribe these variations in aesthetic response to differences in the semiotic ideologies that define what counts as aesthetically successful in different sociocultural contexts.

In recent years, it has become increasingly the case that a very wide range of products of human activity are considered to be art by people in Western societies, and it is equally clear that many of those products were not produced to be "art." Western art museums present furniture, religious or devotional objects, jewelry designed for personal adornment, technology, arms and armor, and much more from Western history as art; and they do the same for objects from non-Western societies as well. Anthropologist Shelly Errington (1998) usefully distinguishes between **art by intention** and **art by appropriation**. Art by intention includes objects that were made to be art, such as Impressionist paintings. Art by appropriation, however, consists of all the other objects that "became art" because at a certain moment certain people (they could be local artists, museum curators, art dealers, art collectors, or interior designers) decided that they belonged to the category of art. Because museums, art dealers, and art collectors are found everywhere in the world today, so too it is now the case that potentially any material object crafted by human hands can be appropriated by these institutions as "art." The set of people and institutions concerned with defining and maintaining art in one form or another make up an *art world*. This includes artists, art historians, art critics, curators, gallery owners, art writers, designers, art collectors, art patrons, museums, galleries, art schools, art magazines, art fairs, paint companies, stone quarries, and so forth. All these people and institutions make it possible for the artist to carry out his or her art but also help define it. Indeed, it is the members of the art world who determine whether a work will be circulated as art or not. This has led anthropologists interested in the arts into studying the ways that non-Western art, tourist art, and "ethnic arts" intersect with or become part of the art worlds of Europe and the United States. Robert Welsch (2006) points out that this is not a new process even if the art worlds that he and his colleagues study are more global than in earlier times. It is also the case that people whose products have been appropriated as art can also begin to produce art by intention. Australian Aboriginal peoples began to produce acrylic paintings to be sold in the art market in the 1970s, based on ancient techniques and styles that were originally of profound religious and spiritual significance.

The development of a global art market has been paralleled in popular music where there has been a tremendous amount of cross-fertilization as well as the development of local traditions that meld rock-and-roll styles from several different parts of the world into creative and satisfying musics. The sharing of music files via the Internet has led to an extraordinary globalization of musical taste such that heavy metal bands from Finland find eager listeners in Chile. The study of the musics of the world, particularly the relationship of music to society and cultural ideas and practices, is the field of **ethnomusicology**. Ethnomusicology can include the study of music and social, cultural, or gender identity; the role of music and musicians in a society; the effect of music on social life; and the study of sound as a form of communication. Recent advances in recording technology have made it possible for ethnomusicologists to include CDs or references to web links of the music they have studied in the books they publish, which has enormously expanded the impact of their work. As with music, so too with dance. Anthropologists who have studied dance in different human societies have demonstrated how dance is connected with the expression of gender; how it is connected with the expression of emotion; how it is connected with sculpture, masking, and religious practice; and how it is a form of self-expression. Indeed, work by anthropologists on hip-hop regularly emphasize that it is not just music or language or a style of performance but that it operates on multiple semiotic levels. They also insist that hip-hop be understood as a way of asserting the political and cultural identity of particular local communities (Morgan 2009). This holds not only for the African American settings where it first emerged but also in the many different settings around the globe where it has been indigenized (Spady et al. 2006).

A number of anthropologists have considered how identity becomes connected with art (and vice versa); for example, how indigenous people in Southeast Alaska use commercial and "tourist" art—blankets, pictures, jewelry—to index membership within a cultural group (Bunten 2006). In other cases, anthropologists have traced the influences of Western art markets on the production of figurines or woven goods or have examined how the Aboriginal acrylic paintings have become significant markers of the Australian state. At the same time, an Australian art world has emerged with connections in the remote areas of central Australia, the major cities of Australia, and such art centers as New York City.

3.9 THE ANTHROPOLOGY OF MEDIA AND THE ARTS

In recent years, anthropologists have begun to direct their gaze at the ways that the media—television, radio, photography, film, and soap operas—are received, understood, created, and used by people around the world. The media have extraordinary power and exceptional reach, and anthropologists have realized that the effect the media have on people's lives can be very great. Some of this work connects to processes of globalization (see chapter 10), including the ways that television programming diminishes, if not erases, the boundaries of time and space (somewhere in the world, *Gilligan's Island* is being broadcast). But at the same time, some of the international cable television companies (Sky, e.g.) have begun regional services that "reterritorialize" the medium by providing programming that is culturally and linguistically appropriate for the different parts of India or China. Some of the most interesting work deals with television and the cultural politics of nation-states—for example, India. Purnima Mankekar (1999) connects television, womanhood, and the nation-state in examining how the television serials (soap operas or mythical or historical serials) on the national television service were created and how they were received by viewers. Mankekar suggests that television broadcasting in India both underlies and undermines the creation of a nationalist consciousness on the part of viewers.

Other anthropologists have been studying computer-facilitated media, including the Internet as an anthropological subject, social media and communication, and the ethnography of virtual worlds. Daniel Miller and Don Slater (2000), for example, were able to show that email and especially chat and instant messaging (IM) were instantly adopted by Trinidadians to facilitate communication among family members on Trinidad and those who had left the island to work. They used these mechanisms to "roll back changes that were dissolving some family relations" (Miller and Slater 2000, 82). However, Miller and Slater warn readers not to assume that the consequences would be the same in another society, emphasizing that anthropology's focus on the local continues to be one of its key contributions to the study of the contemporary world.

As you might suspect, social media like Facebook and Twitter have also been attracting attention from anthropologists. In 2008, Ilana Gershon published a study of how US college students used social media to end romantic relationships (2008, 13–15). Most of Gershon's students preferred to use texting rather than email to break up because texting allowed turn-taking, making the exchange of messages seem like a "conversation." This feature gave the person on the receiving end of the break-up the impression that it was possible to ask "Why?" and get an answer that might provide some closure to the relationship. Gershon was surprised to learn, for example, that her students considered a telephone break-up to be nearly as satisfactory as a face-to-face break-up; this had not been the case with Gershon and her friends when they were in college in the late 1990s. This discrepancy led Gershon to insist that anthropologists pay attention to an important subset of semiotic ideologies that she calls *media ideologies*: sets of beliefs held by users of particular media about how a particular medium shapes a message and how messages received in that medium should be interpreted (2017, 19). Gershon describes different media as existing within a *media ecology* that presents potential users with a range of communicative options (speech, text-messaging, radio, video, etc.), each of which is informed by its own semiotic ideology, and all of which may not be consistent with one another (2017, 19).

As Gershon's work illustrates, the expressive possibilities of social media have become an important avenue for anthropological research that explores contemporary forms of cultural meaning-making. For instance, Dhiraj Murthy studied how young Pakistanis living in the United States and elsewhere outside of Pakistan use Facebook sites that specialize in their own popular culture. These young people do not simply listen to and comment about alternative music; they are also attracted by the opportunity of posting on the Facebook walls of their favorite bands to express themselves creatively and freely (Murthy 2010, 191). Steffen Dalsgaard studied the way that politicians in the United States and western Europe use Facebook and Myspace to mobilize financial and political support in ways that also allow supporters to make a public acknowledgment of their political identities (Dalsgaard 2008).

For at least a decade, anthropologists have been paying attention to cultural meaning-making realized in **virtual worlds**, "places of human culture realized by computer programs through the Internet" (Boellstorff 2008, 17). Tom Boellstorff (2008) and Bonnie Nardi (2010) have done online fieldwork in the online worlds of *Second Life* and *World of Warcraft*, respectively, have done online fieldwork, and both consider ethnography to be an excellent research methodology for the study of virtual worlds. Boellstorff examines ways that *Second Life* enables certain experiences for its players that are not possible in real life. For example, people interact in *Second Life* through avatars, which are customized and customizable visual forms that can be shaped to the desire of the individual. In a virtual world, however, nothing prevents a player from creating several different, alternative avatars (known as "alts") to represent different elements of his or her personality or to allow the player to experiment with a completely invented identity. It is possible for a player logged into *Second Life* to log in a second time as one of his or her alts and to allow the main avatar and the alt to interact in ways that would be impossible in real life.

Nardi studied *World of Warcraft* in the United States and in China, finding many similarities, including the aesthetic response of the players to the online world, but with one big difference: Chinese players tended to play in Internet cafés, often with other people who play the game together (known as a guild). Nardi observed simultaneous online and offline interactions in these settings, both among guild players and among others in the café who were playing the game. She concluded that *World of Warcraft* is becoming a hybrid, mixed reality in which virtual and physical worlds combine (Nardi 2010, 181). *World of Warcraft* combines the pleasure of play, competitive performance, and aesthetic enjoyment. Nardi concludes that *World of Warcraft* is, in fact, an art form.

FOR FURTHER READING

Formal Linguistics   Akmajian et al. 2017

Linguistic Anthropology   Agar 1994; Burling 2005; Ottenheimer 2009; Stanlaw, Adachi, and Salzmann 2017

Linguistic Relativity   Slobin 1987; Gentner and Goldin-Meadow 2003

Speech Communities   Morgan 2014

Readings in Anthropological Linguistics and Linguistic Anthropology   Blum 2016; Alim et al. 2016; Duranti 2001, 2006; Brenneis and Macaulay 1996; Blount 1995

Discourse   Hill and Irvine 1992; Schultz 1990

Language Ideology   Morgan 2002; Schieffelin, Woolard, and Kroskrity 1998

Bilingualism/Multilingualism   Pavlenko 2014; Zentella 1997

Art   Alland 1977; Bakke and Peterson 2016; Burt 2013; Errington 1998; Myers 2003; Kaur and Mukherji 2014; Meintjes 2017; Venbrux, Rosi, and Welsch 2006

Media Anthropology   Gershon 2017; Askew and Wilk 2002; Ginsburg, Abu-Lughod, and Larkin 2002; Mankekar 1999

Virtual Worlds   Boellstorff 2008; Nardi 2010

CHAPTER 4

Worldview and Religion

The key terms and concepts covered in this chapter, in the order in which they appear:

worldview	orthopraxy
religion	rite of passage
animism	liminal period
mana	communitas
oracle	
dogma	magic
orthodoxy	witchcraft
myths	shamans
origin myths	priests
ritual	revitalization
religious rituals	new religious movements
prayer	
sacrifice	secularism
congregation	fundamentalism

Human beings in all cultures try to make sense of their experience in ways that link them meaningfully to the wider world. Anthropologists use the term **worldview** to refer to the result of such interpretive efforts: an encompassing picture of reality based on a set of shared assumptions about how the world works. Anthropologists have long been interested in how worldviews are constructed and how people use them to make sense of their experiences. Worldviews establish symbolic frameworks that highlight certain significant domains of social experience while downplaying others. Multiple worldviews may coexist in a single society, or a single worldview may dominate.

4.1 RELIGION

As they began to compare cultures, anthropologists repeatedly encountered worldviews that reminded them of the religions they knew from Euro-American societies. Over the years, they have tried with mixed success to craft definitions of religion that took these diverse beliefs and practices into account. A recent definition that tries to take account of the complexities of the beliefs and practices found around the world proposes a two-stage approach. First, **religion** is "ideas and practices that postulate reality beyond that which is immediately available to the senses" (Bowen 2008, 4). The second stage in Bowen's definition is to ask how the specific people whom the anthropologist is studying actually conceive of that reality. Here, the anthropologist tries, through careful ethnographic research, to understand what people think and do; the anthropologist is not imposing the model of "religion" from his or her own society. In some cases, the anthropologist may find people with religious worldviews who conceive of the universe as populated by powerful forces that may understand human language and take an active interest in human affairs. Others, as Bowen observes, may speak about impersonal forces like the East Asian idea of a life force that permeates the natural and social world. Another group of people might not talk about belief at all, concentrating on the correct performance of ritual. These forces may monitor human behavior and send punishments to those who violate moral rules; but if approached in the proper manner, they may use their power to confer benefits on the people. When those beings are personified, they have been variously called gods, goddesses, spirits, ancestors, ghosts, or souls.

Although some anthropologists continue to use the term *supernatural* to refer to invisible beings or the realm they inhabit, most contemporary anthropological writing on religion avoids this term because it imposes on other societies a distinction between "natural" and "supernatural" worlds that those societies may not recognize. Similar problems affect many other terms that Western observers, anthropologists included, have used to describe and analyze different religions. For this reason, some influential definitions of religion do not mention beings of any kind but focus on symbols and the ways in which people use symbols to bring meaning and coherence to the interpretation of their experiences. This is also why Bowen proposes a two-stage definition of religion; the second stage consists of trying to understand how specific people understand the world, *in their own terms.*

Remaining faithful to peoples' own understandings of the world has been emphasized even more by those anthropologists who have taken "the ontological turn." These anthropologists would argue, for example, that calling indigenous Andean peoples' (known as *runakuna*) claims about the world religious "beliefs" (in contrast to Western scientific "knowledge") is an analytical error based on the presumption that Western claims about what does or does not exist in the world are valid for Andeans as well as for Europeans. From the Western perspective, only one world exists, but different groups of people may believe different things about it. Peruvian anthropologist Marisol de la Cadena objects to this presumption, and draws attention to the way traditional anthropological ways of writing about Andean "religion" have excluded or truncated elements of indigenous ontology that contradict or exceed what Westerners accept as actually existing in the world. A key example concerns alternative answers to the question, What is Ausangate? Western observers and indigenous Andeans alike would be able to identify Ausangate as a mountain peak near Cuzco. Yet most Western observers are likely to consider it to be inert matter, while many indigenous Andeans consider Ausangate (and other peaks) to be alive, aware, and involved in human affairs. Do these Andeans "believe" that Ausangate is a living "earth being"—or is that just the awkward and partly misleading Western translation? Is it the best Westerners can do, given their unquestioned Enlightenment commitment to an ontology in which mountains are *not* alive, *not* aware, and *not* consciously involved in human affairs? As de la Cadena writes, "Practices with earth beings . . . can be identified as religious, but they cannot be reduced to such, for the notion of religion may not contain all they are" (2015: 207–208).

Anthropologists have suggested a variety of reasons why religion seems to be so important in human societies: it is a way for people to deal with uncertainty that they cannot otherwise control; it is a way to provide meaning for people's lives; it explains the otherwise unexplainable (suffering, death, the mysterious in everyday life); and it helps create social solidarity among those who adhere to it.

Confronted with enormous diversity in the religious traditions of the world, anthropologists initially classified them according to type. For example, some religions propose that objects like trees, stones, or rivers may have souls or spirits associated with them who may interact with people for good or for ill. The nineteenth-century English anthropologist E. B. Tylor (1832–1917) used the term **animism** to describe religions based on belief in the existence of such souls or spirit beings (*anima* is the Latin word for "soul"). In the twentieth century, most anthropologists dropped the term, given its disparaging connotation as a euphemism for "primitive" or "indigenous" religions that contrasted with "world religions" like Christianity or Islam. In recent years, however, animism has been revived by some anthropologists as a concept worthy of respect. Central to this revival was French anthropologist Philippe Descola, whom many consider a foundational figure in the so-called ontological turn in contemporary anthropology. In a manner that echoes his teacher, Claude Lévi-Strauss, Descola insists that the specific cultural practices that ethnographers describe are the outcomes of deeper processes, and that anthropologists "should look for the roots of human diversity at a deeper level, where basic inferences are made about the kinds of beings the world is made of and how they relate to each other" (2014, 273).

With other anthropologists who have taken the ontological turn, Descola insists that the Enlightenment ontology, which claims that there is an original division between "nature" and "culture," is not universal. Instead, is an example of what he calls *naturalism,* one of four types of ontology that Descola argues can be logically established between a human person and another entity. In the case of naturalism, "the entity and I possess similar physicality and different interiority"

(2013, 121). Descola defines *animism* as the ontology in which, "I can assume that . . . we have similar interiorities and different physicalities" (2013, 121). Descola's third ontology is *totemism,* another controversial concept from the anthropological past that he attempts to revive and repurpose. In totemism, "[the entity] possesses elements of physicality and interiority identical to my own" (2013, 121). Descola's fourth type of ontology is *analogism* ("both [an entity's] interiority and its physicality are distinct from mine"; 2013, 121). The extent to which either animism or totemism can be successfully repurposed and take on new conceptual power and popularity may depend on the success of the followers of Descola and other proponents of the ontological turn.

In societies where the connections of relatedness do not end with physical death, religion may take the form of what is called an *ancestor religion* (for more about relatedness, see chapter 7). In these systems, the ancestors are believed to maintain a strong interest in the lives of their descendants and are believed to act to maintain social order by sending sickness or other misfortune when the rules by which people are supposed to live are violated. In these societies, it is often the most senior people who gain great power from the ancestor religion because they are closest to becoming ancestors.

Other societies recognize the existence of sentient and personified forces that are less local and more powerful. The entities may be called *gods*, and traditions in which there are many such beings are sometimes called *polytheistic religions*. The gods in polytheistic religions may have many of the personal attributes of human beings, including gender, and they may produce children with one another or with human beings as the gods did in the religion of ancient Greece. But in some societies, as we saw earlier, the cosmic force or forces recognized are barely personalized at all. This is true in the case of **mana**, a Melanesian term introduced into anthropology in the nineteenth century to designate a cosmic force whose only humanlike attribute is the ability to respond to human beings who use the correct symbolic formulas when they want to harness or channel this force for their own purposes. Another minimally personified cosmic force is an **oracle**, an invisible force capable of understanding questions addressed to it in human language and willing to respond truthfully using symbolic means that human beings with the proper cultural knowledge can interpret. Oracles may speak through people, animals or plants, or other objects.

How people understand the makeup of the world and the beings that inhabit it have traditionally been described as their religious worldview. But societies differ in how systematically they have organized this knowledge and in how much leeway they allow their members to offer alternative interpretations. In some societies, religious knowledge of this kind is highly detailed, carefully organized, and formally passed on from generation to generation. When the truths it is believed to contain may not be questioned, such knowledge is sometimes called **dogma** or **orthodoxy** (correct belief). In other societies, however, religious beliefs are not systematized, and no great emphasis is placed on orthodoxy, with the result that different adherents to the tradition may offer varied or conflicting interpretations of it.

4.2 MYTH

Important components of religious traditions are **myths**: stories that recount how various aspects of the world came to be the way they are. The truth of myths seems self-evident to those who accept them because myths do such a good job of integrating personal experiences with a wider set of assumptions about the way that society or the world in general must operate. (As we saw, the "self-evident truth" of these accounts is taken by some anthropologists to indicate distinct ontologies that may be significantly different from the Western Enlightenment ontology that most ethnographers take for granted.) Those myths that explain the creation of the world, particular features of the landscape, or human beings are often called **origin myths**. Other myths may recount the adventures of the gods, the consequences of their interactions with human beings, or what will happen when the world ends. Although enduring religious myths are believed to embody important insights into life's purposes, they are more than morality tales. They are usually a highly developed verbal art form as well, recited for purposes of both entertainment and instruction; and the occasion of their telling offers verbal artists the opportunity to demonstrate their creative, aesthetic skills. Frequently, the "official" myth tellers are the most powerful or respected groups in society, such as the elders, political leaders, or religious specialists. Myths have a social importance because if they are taken literally, they tell people where they have come from and where they are going and therefore how they should live right now.

The study of myth has always been important in anthropology. Over time, two major approaches to the study of myth have had a lasting impact on the field. The first approach comes from Bronislaw Malinowski, who argued that myths are charters for social action; that is, the beings and places who figure in the myths can be referred to by living people to justify present-day social arrangements. For example, an origin myth about a particular kinship group may describe where members of the group first appeared on the land and the places they subsequently visited. This myth can be used by living members of that kinship group to defend their claims to land in the territories that their ancestors visited and to negate claims to the same land made by other members of the society. In short, to understand why myths have the content they do and how that content changes over time, one must understand the social beliefs and practices of the people who tell them.

The second key approach to myth comes from the French anthropologist Claude Lévi-Strauss (1908–2009). While not denying Malinowski's observations about the practical uses to which myths could be put, Lévi-Strauss showed that the very structures of mythic narratives are meaningful and worth studying in their own right. In this sense, myths are cognitive tools for resolving logical contradictions in human social experience that cannot otherwise be overcome in the world that human beings know. In particular, myths are attempts to deal with oppositions of continuing concern to members of a particular society, such as the opposition between men and women, nature and culture, or life and death—or opposing styles of postmarital residence (postmarital residence is discussed in chapter 7). Although these oppositions may be irresolvable in everyday life, myths offer an imaginative realm in which alternative possibilities and their (frequently undesirable) consequences can be explored.

Many scholars, including Malinowski and Lévi-Strauss, have assumed that the people who accept the claims set forth in myths are typically unaware how their myths are structured or how they use myths to defend their interests. Recent anthropological work, however, acknowledges that ordinary members of a society often *are* aware of how their myths structure meaning. And it is precisely this awareness that permits them to manipulate the way myths are told or interpreted to gain support for the version or interpretation that furthers their goals. As noted previously, anthropologists who have opted for "the ontological turn," like Marisol de la Cadena, emphasize that taking mythic narratives seriously may require ethnographers to struggle when attempting to translate them into terms acceptable for Western audiences. If they genuinely aim to respect an alternative ontology that the myth tellers take for granted, ethnographers will need to resist the temptation to reduce these alternative assumptions to "beliefs" whenever they fail to coincide with foundational assumptions of Western Enlightenment ontology.

4.3 RITUAL

Anthropologists use the term **ritual** to identify certain repetitive social practices, many of which have nothing to do with religion. A ritual is composed of a sequence of symbolic activities, set off from the social routines of everyday life, recognizable by members of the society as a ritual, and closely connected to a specific set of ideas that are often encoded in myth. What gives rituals their power is that participants assert that the authorization for the ritual comes from outside themselves—from the state, society, God, the ancestors, or "tradition." For example, in a courtroom, when people rise as the judge enters or refer to the judge as "your honor," they are not doing so because they feel like it or because the individual judge insists on it but because of the authority of the state and the Constitution. Thus, by responding in court, "Not guilty, your honor," one is accepting the authority of not only the judge but also the court, the justice system, and the Constitution. (Indeed, this is the difference between a wedding rehearsal and a wedding.) Even when rituals are invented or transformed, those involved with them attempt to connect the innovations to external sources of authority. For example, at our university's graduation ceremony, the graduates are asked to applaud the parents, relatives, and friends who have helped them achieve that moment. Although this part of the ritual was proposed by a former president, his justification for the innovation was that it took account of something profoundly important in the social world that the institution needed to acknowledge and it was in keeping with the other elements of the graduation ceremony.

Much work in recent years in anthropology has explored the relationship between ritual and power, and much of this work has concentrated on rituals that are not religious. But the role of ritual in religious contexts remains an important area of study. If the universe is indeed populated by powerful personified beings that take an interest in human affairs, then it is to the very great benefit of human beings to devise ways of dealing with them. All religious worldviews assume that communication between personified cosmic forces is possible and potentially beneficial, but it can take place only if carried out in the correct way. Most religious traditions have developed specialized social routines for communication with the gods that, if performed correctly, should ensure successful communication. As a consequence, **religious rituals** are distinctive in that they regularly involve attempts to influence or gain the sympathy of a particular personified cosmic being. One kind of religious ritual involves addressing these personified forces in human speech, often out loud, while holding the body in a conventional posture of respect; this is called **prayer**. Another kind of religious ritual involves offering something of value (goods, services, money, or an appropriately slaughtered animal) to the invisible forces or their agents; this is called **sacrifice**. Prayer and sacrifice frequently are performed when members of a religious tradition come together in processions, meetings, or convocations; this is called **congregation**.

Members of some religious traditions insist that correct ritual behavior is essential at times of prayer or sacrifice and that any deviation will nullify the ritual. Indeed, some religious traditions aim to ritualize virtually every waking act that adherents perform, a style of religious practice called **orthopraxy** (correct practice). Not all religious traditions that value ritual are orthoprax, however: many entertain a range of opinion regarding correct practice, and individual people or independent religious practitioners are free to develop their own rituals or variants of more broadly recognized rituals.

One particular kind of ritual has drawn considerable attention from anthropologists: the **rite of passage**, which occurs when one or more members of a society are ritually transformed from one kind of social person into another. Rites of passage often are initiations into adulthood when girls are made women or boys made men; but they may also mark marriages (when single people become a married couple), the birth of children (when a new life enters the world), or funerals (when living relatives become ancestors). These and other so-called life-cycle transitions frequently are marked by rituals that connect participants to ancestors, gods, or other cosmic forces. Anthropologists point out that rites of passage regularly follow a three-part sequence. First, the ritual passengers (i.e., the persons who are changing their social position) are *separated* from their previous, everyday existence. Next, they pass through a *transitional* state in which they are neither in the old position nor yet in the new one. Finally, with their new status, they are *reaggregated*, or brought back, into the everyday social world. The second, transitional stage of the ritual was particularly significant for anthropologist Victor Turner (1920–1983), who referred to it as the **liminal period** (from the Latin word *limen*, meaning "threshold"). Turner noted that when people are on the threshold, they are "betwixt and between," neither in nor out. In rites of passage, the symbolism associated with the transitional period often expresses that ambiguity: It is described as being in the womb, being invisible, being in the wilderness, or as death. Ritual passengers in the liminal stage tend to develop an intense comradeship with one another; social distinctions that separated them before the ritual and will separate them again afterward become irrelevant. Turner called this liminal social relationship **communitas**, which is best understood as an unstructured or minimally structured community of equal individuals. In rites of passage concerned with initiation, for example, the liminal period is a time in which those being initiated are tutored in knowledge and skills that their elders believe they must master if they are to be successful in the stage of life they are about to enter.

4.4 MAGIC AND WITCHCRAFT

Anthropologists have also paid much attention to another form of ritual called **magic**. The persistence of definitions of magic that include the term *supernatural* is another indication of the difficulty of using one culture's definitions to describe practices in other cultures. Generally, magic refers to ritual practices that do not have technically or scientifically apparent effects but are believed by the actors to have an influence on the outcome of practical matters. People may believe that the correct performance of such rituals can result in healing, the growth of plants, the recovery of lost or stolen objects, getting a hit in baseball, or safely sailing an outrigger canoe in the Pacific Ocean. The classic anthropological explanation of magic comes from the research of Bronislaw Malinowski in the Trobriand Islands early in the twentieth century. Malinowski suggested that all living societies have developed effective knowledge and practical techniques for dealing with the world. At the same time, however, they also realize that their practical control over the world has limits. Where their techniques and knowledge are sufficient for accomplishing their goals, magic is not used. But when the outcome is uncertain, regardless of the skill and insight people may have, they are likely to resort to magical practices. The use of magic in such situations, Malinowski argued, has the practical function of reducing anxiety, thereby allowing people to concentrate on what they can control. He observed, for example, that Trobriand Islanders whom he knew used outrigger canoes to go fishing in both the protected lagoons around the islands and the Pacific Ocean. When they fished in the lagoons, which were safe and secure, they put their canoes into the water and got straight to work. But when they were going past the lagoons into the open ocean, which was unpredictable and dangerous, they recited spells and used other techniques throughout the voyage.

In the late nineteenth century, when unilineal evolutionary schemes were popular in anthropology (see chapter 12 for details), many anthropologists proposed that magic and religion were separate stages in the progressive evolution of human thought that culminated in science. But subsequent ethnographic research, especially work done in the past few decades, has made it clear that magic, religion, and science may coexist in the same society and may even be used by the same people who resort to different ways of coping with the world in different social contexts. In some cases, people in search of a solution to a serious problem, such as infertility, may be unwilling to dismiss any beliefs or practices that offer a solution, alternatively consulting medical doctors, praying in church, and consulting practitioners of alternative therapies that some might argue are based on magic. (The topic is also discussed in chapter 11.)

It is important to stress that interest in identifying and defining the true nature of magic was historically of greatest concern to two categories of Western critics: missionaries eager to demonstrate the superiority of their version of "religion" over what they considered to be the superstitious "magical" practices of "primitive peoples" and defenders of science who wanted to demonstrate its superiority over both magic and religion. The more that science was stressed as the embodiment of rationality, the more necessary it became to stress the "irrational" features of religion and magic. Anthropologists committed to cultural relativism in the early twentieth century were more interested in stressing the sensible side of seemingly exotic beliefs and practices like magic and witchcraft. Malinowski, as we have seen, focused on the positive practical side effects of belief in the efficacy of magic spells. E. E. Evans-Pritchard (1902–1973), in his classic monograph *Witchcraft, Oracles, and Magic Among the Azande* (first published in 1937), demonstrated that the beliefs and practices associated with all three phenomena were perfectly logical if one accepted certain basic assumptions about the world.

Among the Azande, **witchcraft** involves the performance of evil by human beings believed to possess an innate, nonhuman, "witchcraft substance" that can be activated without the individual's awareness. (Other anthropologists, using Azande witchcraft as their prototype, have applied the term to similar beliefs and practices found in other societies*) For the Azande, witchcraft tends to explain misfortune when other possibilities have been discounted. For example, if a good potter carefully prepares his pots and fires them as he always does, but they still break, he will attribute his misfortune to witchcraft, and his neighbors will probably believe him. But if a careless potter is sloppy when firing his pots and they break, he may claim that witchcraft was the cause—but no one who knows him will believe it.

Evans-Pritchard showed that the entire system of Azande beliefs and practices concerning witchcraft, oracles, and magic was perfectly rational if one assumed that unseen forces exist in the world and that nothing happens to people by accident. For example, when someone falls very ill or dies, the Azande assume that the person has been bewitched. But the Azande are not helpless because they know they can consult oracles who will help them pinpoint the witch responsible. Once the oracle has identified the witch, they can send a ritual message to the accused witch, who can offer a ritual reply that will stop the witchcraft if indeed he (it is usually a man) has been the cause of it. If the bewitched person dies,

---

*This technical use of the term should not be confused with everyday uses of the word in contemporary Western societies, still less with the practices of followers of movements like Wicca, which are very different.

however, the next step is to obtain vengeance magic, which can be used to seek out the witch responsible and kill him.

The Azande do not collapse in fear in the presence of witchcraft because they know how to deal with it. Moreover, they make an accusation of witchcraft only after cross-checking the oracle's pronouncements carefully. Because all the steps in the process are carried out in great secrecy, who has accused whom and who has killed whom with vengeance magic is not open to public scrutiny; so contradictions in the system are rarely exposed. This, Evans-Pritchard suggested, is how all complex belief systems operate, even in the so-called scientific West. After all, the "scientific method" at its most stringent is hardly followed regularly by ordinary citizens or even scientists once they are outside the laboratory. Evans-Pritchard's work has inspired many subsequent studies that debunk ethnocentric Western notions about the supposed irrationality of magic and religion.

Beliefs and practices bearing a resemblance to Azande witchcraft are found in many societies, in Africa and elsewhere. Comparative studies of these phenomena revealed interesting variation in the patterns of witchcraft accusations in a given society. According to Mary Douglas (1970), patterns of accusation fall into two basic types: witches are evil outsiders, or witches are internal enemies, either members of a rival faction or dangerous deviants.

These different patterns of accusation have different effects on the structure of the society in which they are made. If the witch is an evil outsider, witchcraft accusations can strengthen in-group ties as the group unites in opposition to the witch. If the witch is an internal enemy, however, accusations of witchcraft can weaken in-group ties, perhaps to the point in which one or more factions in a community might leave and build a new village; then the entire social structure may have to be rebuilt. This, anthropologists argued, was not really a bad thing because what had prompted the accusations of witchcraft in the first place was a community that had grown too large for the prevailing political organization to maintain order. The witchcraft accusations provided a relatively nondestructive way to restore the community to the proper size for a kinship-based political system. If, on the other hand, the witch is a dangerous internal deviant, to accuse that person of witchcraft might be an attempt to control the deviant in defense of the wider values of the community.

4.5 RELIGIOUS PRACTITIONERS

Anthropologists also have devoted attention to the organization of religion as a social and cultural institution. Virtually without exception, anthropologists have stressed that complex sets of religious beliefs and practices are not merely the byproducts of idiosyncratic individual invention. Rather, they are the products of collective cultural construction, performing social and cultural tasks that involve far more than tending to the spiritual needs of supporters.

The contrast between different kinds of religious institutions in different societies can be illustrated with reference to the existence and role of specialized religious practitioners. In many small-scale societies, specialized ritual knowledge or practice may simply belong to elders who perform required rituals for their kin. Other societies, however, do accord a special status to religious specialists, and anthropologists have classified them in two broad categories: shamans and priests. **Shamans** are part-time religious specialists commonly found in small-scale egalitarian societies. The term *shaman* itself comes from Siberia, and Siberian shamans constitute the prototype that anthropologists have used to classify similar religious specialists in many other societies. They are believed to have the power to contact powerful cosmic beings directly on behalf of others, sometimes by traveling to the cosmic realm to communicate with them. They often plead with those beings to help their people—by curing them, for example—and they may also bring back messages for them. In other cases, the shaman enters an altered state of consciousness to seek and remove the cause of an illness that is afflicting a person who has come for healing. In many societies, it is believed that the shaman has no choice in taking on the role—the spirits demand it. The training that a shaman receives is long and demanding and may involve the use of powerful psychotropic substances. The position of shaman may be dangerous. The effects of entering altered states of consciousness can be long lasting. The power to contact cosmic beings or to heal is itself perceived as ambiguous in many societies: The person who can intervene for good can also intervene for ill, and shamans are sometimes feared as well as admired. Once fully recognized as a shaman, a person remains a shaman in service to the society for the rest of his or her life.

Priests, by contrast, are skilled in the practice of religious rituals, which are carried out for the benefit of the group or individuals within the group. Priests frequently are full-time, formally trained specialists. They are found in hierarchical societies in which status differences between rulers and subjects are paralleled in the unequal relationship between priest and laity. Priests do not necessarily have direct contact with cosmic forces; rather, their major role is to mediate that contact successfully for their people by ensuring that the required rituals have been properly performed.

4.6 CHANGE IN RELIGIOUS SYSTEMS

Much ethnographic work has sought to describe and explain the details of particular religious systems, but the way that change affects religious belief and practice has also been of great interest. When the members of a society are faced with drastic changes in their experiences—because of conquest, natural disaster, or radical dislocation (e.g., by migration)—they frequently seek new interpretations that will help them cope with the changes. In some cases, the individuals or groups in question will adopt an entirely new worldview, frequently a religious system, in the process of *conversion*. But in other cases, the result is a creative synthesis of old religious practices and new ones introduced from the outside, often by force, in a process called *syncretism*. Recently, some anthropologists have pointed out that most studies of religious syncretism have not paid sufficient attention to the unequal relationships between the parties that are syncretizing. Many have assumed that the worldview that changes most is the one belonging to the group with the least power. In some cases, syncretistic practices may indeed be introduced from above by powerful outsiders trying to ease tensions by deliberately making room for local beliefs. In other cases, however, syncretism can be seen as a way of resisting new ideas imposed from outside and above, masking old practices under the labels of the new imported ones.

Sometimes social groups struggling with change defend or refashion their own way of life in a process that anthropologists call **revitalization**: a deliberate, organized attempt by some members of a society to create a more satisfying culture. Revitalization movements arise in times of crisis, most often among groups facing oppression and radical transformation, usually at the hands of outsiders (e.g., colonizing powers). Revitalization may take a syncretistic form, but syncretism also may be rejected in favor of *nativism*, a return to the old ways. Some nativistic movements anticipate a messiah or prophet who will bring back a lost golden age of peace, prosperity, and harmony, a process often called *revivalism*, *millenarianism*, or *messianism*.

One of the most important aspects of religious changes in recent years has been the spread of "nonmainstream" religions, called **new religious movements**, into areas of the world that already have established religious systems of their own. These movements are found throughout the world and range widely in their religious positions, political involvements, and tolerance of other religious movements. Much research has been done in Latin America where Protestant denominations and sects have expanded dramatically in recent decades at the expense of the Roman Catholic Church. These denominations frequently offer a more emotional, dramatic theology as well as altered states of consciousness known as *ecstatic religious experiences*. These include trances, speaking in tongues, exorcisms, and possession. In other cases, they offer a more individualistic theology.

Some ethnographers who have taken "the ontological turn" have closely examined the accounts of people who have converted to Christianity in the societies where they work. Ontological concerns seem central here, given that religious conversion is often portrayed as discarding one understanding of the way the world works and replacing it with a totally different understanding—centered on the convert's personal relationship with God. For Martin Holbraad and Morten Axel Pedersen, however, adopting the ontological turn means setting aside preconceptions about what conversion involves and paying extraordinarily serious attention to converts' own descriptions of their conversion experiences. For instance, Undraa, a Mongolian Christian convert Pederson knew, described her conversion as an ongoing process because it took her a long time and much effort to disentangle herself from a web of preexisting social relationships: "for her, the primordial rupture of becoming Christian must be repeated over and over again . . . despite being a regular church-attendant, she always questions her commitment to God" (Holbraad and Pedersen 2017, 257). Yet Pedersen and Holbraad wonder "what happens to all the social and spiritual connections severed in the processes of conversion—where, as it were, do all the cut-off relationships go?" (2017, 256). Close ethnographic attention to Undraa's descriptions of her conversion experience led them to conclude that Undraa did not totally cut herself off from her pre-conversion social relationships as she enlarged a primary inner relationship with God; instead, she recast these social relationships as secondary to that primary inner relationship. In her case, Holbraad and Pedersen conclude, "Christian conversion is a process of relational transformation and not . . . a process of relational reduction" (2017, 260). But they insist that their analysis of Undraa's conversion experience should not be taken as an account valid for all Christian conversion experiences; rather, they urge other ethnographers to stay close to the ethnographic details in the cases of conversion they study, exploring the possibilities it offers to potentially reveal a different transformational process.

In the United States, anthropologists have studied so-called New Age movements: post-1960s forms of spirituality that explore divinity within the individual. New Age movements have attracted people who seek to break free of the dogmas and restrictions of organized Western religious institutions. Followers of such movements believe that adopting alternative, especially non-Western, religious practices will permit them to develop an individual spirituality free of such restrictions. Among the better known practices are channeling, Harmonic Convergence, and Neo-paganism, sometimes known as Wicca.

In recent years, anthropologists have examined not only the power relations involved in syncretism and revitalization but also the way that different world\ views are related to the creation and maintenance of power relations within societies. For example, power differences may be sustained by differential knowledge as when some groups of people within a society have access to important knowledge that is not available to everyone, or when a limited number of individuals exercise control over key symbols and ritual practices. In many cases, those with power in the society seem to have successfully made use of the self-evident truths embodied in their worldview to continue to control others.

4.7 SECULARISM, FUNDAMENTALISM, AND NEW RELIGIOUS MOVEMENTS

In the context of globalization, it is difficult to talk about religion and not also talk about **secularism**, which can be broadly defined as the separation of religion and state. This separation began in Western Europe in the eighteenth century, in response to the brutal religious wars that had characterized Europe since the beginning of the Protestant Reformation in 1517. To maintain the peace, people were allowed to believe what they chose to believe, and the state did not intervene in favor of one religion rather than another (see Asad 2003). Anthropologist John Bowen points out that secularism is used today in three different ways. First, it refers to how modern states define and regulate the place of religious bodies and religious discourse in political processes. That is, in modern states, religious organizations may make their policy positions known;

but final, legally binding policy decisions for citizens of the state are made by a civilian political body. Second, it refers to a process called *secularization*, in the course of which social institutions become increasingly differentiated from one another, each with its own rules distinct from others. For instance, the institution of the state is increasingly distinguished from religious institutions and from the family, and each becomes a separate form of organization with its own rules and regulations. To be sure, many people continue to see marriage and divorce, for example, as religious events; but in secular nation-states, it is state institutions that regulate marriage and divorce: written laws determine, for example, who may and may not be legally married and the procedures that must be followed to obtain a legal divorce. Third, secularization can also refer to the decline of religion, either in the sense that social life is less controlled by religious practices or in the sense that individuals lose their faith in the existence of religious truth or in the existence of religious beings (Bowen 2008, 231). Sometimes secularism is used to refer to a decline in people's allegiance to organized religions. In a contemporary state, the commitment to secularism has the potential to place all religions on an equal footing. The state may protect free exercise of religion to a greater or lesser degree, but it endorses the teachings of no religion in particular.

Despite occasional tensions and frictions, many citizens believe that life in a secular state is a successful approach to religious coexistence, but others do not agree. Sometimes this disagreement leads to political-religious tensions, as adherents of one faith (or one version of a faith) reject the premises of secular society. Religious movements of this kind have often been called "fundamentalist," and not always accurately. The term **fundamentalism** entered common use in the United States in the late nineteenth and early twentieth centuries. It was applied to a movement in some denominations of Protestant Christianity that promoted a return to what they understood to be the "fundamentals" of their faith. Stressing these fundamentals was intended to serve as a guide for people who had fallen away from the church or who disagreed with more liberal forms of Christian doctrine. Over time, "fundamentalism" has increasingly been used to refer to movements stressing what their followers take to be the "fundamentals" of extremist forms of ideology (Nagata 2001, 483). The world of the secularized state is open and uncertain, and some people respond to the anxieties produced by such openness and uncertainty by becoming uncompromising and antirelativist (see chapter 2). Today, Judith Nagata suggests, the assumption that fundamentalism is primarily a religious phenomenon is incorrect: "[I]t may be sighted in domains such as ultranationalism, extreme or genocidal ethnic chauvinisms, certain political ideologies, in obsessive quests for linguistic and cultural purity of authenticity" (2001, 493). Thus, Nagata suggests it is more accurate to speak about "fundamentalisms," all of which have in common "a quest for certainty, exclusiveness, and unambiguous boundaries, where the 'Other' is the enemy demonized" (2001, 481).

Another response to the pressures of globalization and to the challenges of life in a secular society has been the creation of a range of new religious movements around the world, as discussed earlier. While contemporary study of these religious movements resembles the studies of revitalization or millenarian movements by earlier generations of anthropologists, the new studies place greater emphasis on both the global political context of these religious movements and their connections to other religions that form the context in which they exist.

FOR FURTHER READING

General Anthropological Works on Religion   Bowen 2017; Eller 2015; Winzeler 2013

Readings on Religion   Warms, Garver, and McGee 2009; Lambek 2008; Moro and Myers 2012

The Ontological Turn and Religion   Holbraad and Pedersen 2017; De la Cadena 2015; Descola 2013, 2014

Secularism   Asad 2003

CHAPTER 5

The Dimensions of Social Organization

The key terms and concepts covered in this chapter, in the order in which they appear:

society

status
role
ascribed status
achieved status
social structure
institutions
social organization
functionalism

egalitarian societies
stratified societies
rank societies

caste
class
clientage
compadrazgo
state
bureaucracy
authority

race
racism
antiracism

ethnic group

One of the basic claims of anthropology is that human beings are a social species; that is, we have evolved to live with and depend on others of our own species. Biological anthropologists have demonstrated, for example, that human infants are born earlier in the gestational process than are infants of apes and monkeys and that our young are dependent on other members of the group for far longer (15–20 years and more) before they are capable of establishing themselves as mature adults. Human interdependence means that we cannot survive as lone individuals but need to live with others: that is, we must live in **society**. When anthropologists speak of human society, at minimum they mean a group of human beings living together whose interactions with one another are patterned in regular ways. Such organized groups might also be identified by the particular geographical territory they inhabit, by the particular language they speak, or by the particular customs they follow—any or all of these features might distinguish them from other, neighboring societies. Such distinctive features are in turn mostly cultural, which is why anthropologists developed the habit of speaking as if each identifiable society came equipped with its own culture and vice versa. Still, anthropologists recognize that no culture is monolithic, that cultural patterns may be borrowed or shared by people in different societies, and that a single society may contain within it representatives of different cultural traditions.

5.1 WHAT IS SOCIAL ORGANIZATION?

Anthropologists, together with other social scientists, have developed a set of analytic concepts that help describe and explain the orderly interdependence of human life in society. In particular, they have noted that people who interact in society do so not as unique individuals but as incumbents of publicly recognized social positions. Each such social position is called a **status**, and all individuals come to occupy a range of different statuses in the course of their lives as they take part in a variety of social interactions.

People know what to do in such interactions because each status is associated with a corresponding **role**: a bundle of rights and obligations appropriate for occupants of the status in question. Thus, for example, the kinship status of *parent* might include, among other things, the right to discipline one's children and the obligation to feed them and send them to school. Violation of the role requirements associated with a particular social status generally brings about disapproval from other members of society.

Social scientists also distinguish two basic kinds of social statuses found in all societies: ascribed and achieved. An **ascribed status** is a status over which you have little control: you are born into it or grow into it. Anthropologists often use examples from human kinship systems to illustrate ascribed status. When you are born, you are automatically your parent's child, son or daughter; when you have children of your own, you automatically become a parent, mother or father. Such ascribed statuses ordinarily cannot be discarded, and any person who qualifies will be expected to fulfill the role obligations that go with the status. Very different, however, is an **achieved status**, one that you may not assume until or unless you meet certain criteria through your own (or others') efforts. For instance, being a college graduate is an achieved status, and achieving that status ordinarily requires both hard work and financial resources. Each member of a society occupies a mix of ascribed and achieved statuses.

Statuses and their accompanying roles are not isolated but are often linked to one another in complementary pairs or sets. For example, the statuses of parents and children (or mother and daughter, father and son, mother and son, or father and daughter) are reciprocal relationships. Thus, the right of parents to discipline their children matches the obligation of children to obey their parents (in theory, at least). To describe such a cluster of statuses with complementary roles is to begin to identify key enduring social relationships that provide a foundation for regularized, patterned social interaction, or **social structure**. But social structure is not simply a matter of interlinked and complementary statuses and roles attached to individuals. Most societies regularly associate particular sets of statuses with particular social groups defined in such terms as gender, family, lineage, clan, occupation, and political or religious affiliation. The relationships that link members of these various social groups may also be highly structured, often around a common task or cultural focus. The clusters of social statuses and groups that share such a common focus usually are called **institutions**. Thus, we speak of educational institutions that unite individuals; and groups whose social statuses focus on educational issues; or of political institutions that bring together individuals and groups whose statuses focus on the allocation of power in the society. Sometimes social structure refers only to the arrangement of status positions and groups with respect to each other. By contrast, **social organization** refers to the interlocking role relationships that are activated when statuses have incumbents and groups have members, all of whom are going about the daily business of living.

All this terminology is associated with the school of social scientific thought called **functionalism** (for more about functionalism, see chapter 12). Functionalism was at its most influential in the early twentieth century and has since been much criticized. Drawing attention to the existence of social structures that function to organize and stabilize relations of human interdependence has been historically important in Western societies that support ideologies of *individualism*—the view that society is artificial and nothing more than the sum total of actions performed by individual human actors: that is, separate, autonomous, self-directed human beings whose existence preceded society. These conceptions of the individual and society are *ontological* claims—that is, claims about what does and does not exist in reality. Classic Western political philosophers such as Thomas Hobbes (1588–1679) endorsed the ontological claim that in a "state of nature," "society" did not exist. Instead, autonomous, self-interested individuals were the only real entities, engaging in a war of all against all; life was solitary, nasty, brutish, and short, until individual men agreed to surrender their natural freedom to a new artificial institution, the state, which would protect the weak against the strong. Anthropologist Marshall Sahlins long ago argued that "The development from a Hobbesian state of nature is the origin myth of Western capitalism" (1976, 53), and the social contract continues to be taken as an unquestioned foundational assumption by many political philosophers and ordinary people in contemporary capitalist societies. It has also been taken for granted by Western social scientists, including anthropologists, as valid in all times and places.

However, a number of anthropologists argue that this individualist ontology, which posits autonomous individuals as existing prior to society, is not universally valid. As we saw in chapter 4, French anthropologist Philippe Descola argues for the existence of four basic ontologies in human societies, classifying Western ontology as a variety of what he calls "naturalism." Anthropologist Marilyn Strathern has also challenged the university of Western individualist ontology; she argues that in Melanesia, persons are first and foremost understood as bundles of relations—as *dividual* or *partible* persons—even though different relations may be revealed or masked in different contexts. Analyzing social life from a dividualist perspective challenges many social scientific assumptions presupposed by functionalist analysis; indeed, Strathern's theoretical moves have been regarded as offering a surprising and innovative twist on the concept of social relations originally offered by A. R. Radcliffe-Brown, who formulated structural-functionalism in twentieth-century British social anthropology (Holbraad and Pedersen 2017, 112–113; for more on the so-called ontological turn, see chapter 12).

Many anthropologists and sociologists continue to find some functionalist terminology useful for describing basic social relations. Since the postmodern critique of the late twentieth century, however, most contemporary anthropologists would be cautious about defending the larger claims of functionalist social theory (see chapter 12).

5.2 DIMENSIONS OF SOCIAL ORGANIZATION

One issue of great interest in the early years of anthropology and sociology was the contrast between large and powerful European nation-states, with industrial technology and a complex division of labor, and small-scale societies, with little or no social stratification, whose members used simple tools to make a living and who were socially organized almost entirely on the basis of kinship. The contrast was sometimes phrased as an opposition between so-called civilized and so-called primitive societies. Sociologists were supposed to explain how "civilized" societies worked, and anthropologists were supposed to explain how "primitive" societies worked.

One widely influential model was proposed by Émile Durkheim (1858–1917), a French sociologist considered a founder of both modern sociology and modern anthropology. Durkheim was interested in what held a society together, contrasting societies held together by mechanical solidarity with those held together by organic solidarity. *Mechanical solidarity* characterized small-scale, kinship-based societies in which all the tasks necessary for survival were carried out on a family level, and families stayed together because they shared the same language and customs.

However, because kin groups were more or less self-sufficient in terms of meeting their survival needs, they could split off from one another relatively easily. Thus, mechanical solidarity could not bind together large numbers of people over long periods of time. *Organic solidarity*, by contrast, characterized large-scale societies such as nation-states. In such societies, the tasks necessary for survival became specialties of different subgroups in a complex division of labor. For example, because those who specialized in pot making or metalworking might not have had the time or resources to produce their own food or clothing, they became dependent on other specialists—food producers or tailors—for these goods and services. Such interdependence meant that any single occupational grouping could not easily break away from the larger social whole because it was not self-sufficient. Like the organ systems of a living body, specialized subgroups of complex societies clung together and depended on one another to survive, thereby preserving the overall health and strength of the whole. Thus, organic solidarity could hold much larger societies together far more securely than could mechanical solidarity.

Anthropologists incorporated concepts like these into their own analytic toolkit as they attempted to make sense of the variety of forms that different human societies assumed in different times and places. They also introduced new concepts to highlight further distinctions revealed by ethnographic research. One of the most basic is the fourfold classification of societies on the basis of their form of political organization: band, tribe, chiefdom, and state (discussed at greater length in chapter 8). Another is the very similar fourfold classification of societies on the basis of their form of economic organization: foragers, herders, extensive agriculturalists, and intensive agriculturalists (discussed at greater length in chapter 9). The correlations between these different classifications highlight the connections between the ways that people make a living and the ways that they organize themselves politically.

The correlation is not perfect, however, and this is highlighted by another pair of concepts that crosscuts the earlier classifications. That is, anthropologists distinguish between **egalitarian societies**, in which all members (or component groups) enjoy roughly the same degree of wealth, power, and prestige; and **stratified societies**, in which some members (or component groups) have greater (and often permanent) access to some or all of these three valued resources. But the history of the transition from egalitarian societies (bands and tribes, in the current classification) to stratified societies (chiefdoms and states) is not fully understood. Some anthropologists pay particular attention to societies known through ethnography, history, or archaeology in which egalitarian relations have begun to erode but in which permanent, inherited patterns of social stratification have not yet been established. Such societies, like those of the indigenous peoples of the northwest coast of North America or the Trobriand Islanders of Papua New Guinea, depended on foraging or extensive agriculture for subsistence, just as many egalitarian societies do. But they also have social structures that elevate certain individuals and their families above everyone else, allowing them privileged access to a limited number of high-status positions. Anthropologist Morton Fried called these **rank societies**, some of whose members ranked above others in social honor but did not have disproportionate access to wealth or power.

The labels anthropologists developed to classify forms of human society in twentieth-century North American anthropology combined a desire to avoid the excesses of nineteenth-century cultural evolutionary schemes with an effort to seek out correlations between forms of social organization known from ethnography or history and similar social forms identified by archaeologists that could be assigned firm dates and arranged in a temporal sequence. As we noted in chapter 2, however, James Scott relies on more recent work by ethnographers, archaeologists, and other scholars to read these original accounts "against the grain" by locating changing human social organization within broader, heterogeneous processes of niche construction and by revealing the nonlinear dynamics that pitted settled agrarian states against those who resisted incorporation into state hierarchies. Debates about the origins of social complexity remain lively.

Ethnographic evidence supported Durkheim's observation that small-scale societies tend to be organized primarily on the basis of kinship. As we discuss in chapter 8, kinship systems must be fairly elaborate to carry out this task; and anthropology traditionally has sought to understand and compare the many different kinship systems that human beings have devised. However, even egalitarian societies whose social organization centered on kinship often invented additional forms of social organization that crosscut kinship groups and bound their members together at a more inclusive level; anthropologists often refer to such groups as *sodalities*.

Sodalities can take many forms. Among the best known ethnographically are the age-set systems from Eastern Africa and the secret societies from Western Africa. Found in such societies as the Nyakyusa living in present-day Tanzania, an *age set* is made up of a group of young men born within a specific time span, such as five years; thus, a new age set is formed regularly every five years. Age sets typically progress through a sequence of statuses, or *age grades*, as their members grow older. There might be three age grades through which every age set must pass—for example, a junior, senior, and elder grade. Promotion from one age grade to the next typically is marked by rituals. Many societies with age-set systems devote particular attention to the *initiation* ritual that transforms boys into adult men, but societies differ in the degree of ritual elaboration with which they surround the passage of different sets from one grade to the next. Age-set systems have played different roles in different societies as well. Those sets belonging to junior age grades frequently have been characterized as *warriors*, but it is important to recognize that their activities as fighters or raiders often were subject to the control of men in senior age grades. Moreover, members of societies with age sets and age grades frequently use the age-grade structure as a way of thinking about time and attempting to regulate its passage by ritual means.

The Mende, Sherbro, Kpelle, and other neighboring peoples who today live in the Western African nation-states of Sierra Leone, Ivory Coast, Liberia, and Guinea developed *secret societies* as forms of social organization that crosscut kinship groupings. Some secret societies admit only men as members, others admit only women, and at least one admits both men and women. Only adults may belong to secret societies, and children must undergo initiation rituals to achieve that status and gain admittance; some anthropologists have undergone initiation as part of their research. The "secret" part of secret societies refers to the special knowledge revealed only to initiates, which they are not allowed to share with outsiders. Initiates may also progress to higher positions within the society to which they belong, but they must pay fees and receive special instruction to do so. In addition to these internal activities, secret societies also carry out specific tasks in public. Social relations between men and women tend to be highly egalitarian in cultures with secret societies; for example, the male Poro society and female Sande society of a village might jointly be responsible for supervising public behavior and sanctioning those who violate expected rules of conduct.

Forms of social organization, such as kinship groups or sodalities, can still be found in societies that are socially stratified, but their scope and importance are modified by new features of social structure that sustain the inequalities on which social stratification is based. That is, stratified societies are internally divided into a number of groups that are arranged in a hierarchy. The two most important such hierarchical structures studied by anthropologists have been caste and class.

5.3 CASTE AND CLASS

Anthropologists traditionally describe **caste** societies as stratified societies in which membership in a particular ranked subgroup is ascribed at birth and in which *social mobility*, or movement by individuals out of the subgroup in which they were born, is not allowed. Although the original prototype for caste societies comes from India, anthropologists have used the term to describe similar social arrangements in other societies.

In India and elsewhere in South Asia, each caste traditionally is defined not only as the endogamous group within which members must choose mates (see chapter 7 for a definition of *endogamy*) but also in terms of a traditional occupation with which the caste is identified (e.g., salt maker, farmer, warrior, or priest). Each occupation, and the caste associated with it, is ranked on a scale of purity and pollution, with higher-ranked castes subject to various dietary and other taboos required to maintain caste purity. Highest on the purity scale are the *Brahmins*, the vegetarian priestly caste; lowest are the out-castes, or *dalit* (formerly called "untouchables"), who eat meat and whose occupations (leatherworker, street sweeper) regularly bring them into contact with polluting substances such as dead animals and excrement. Recent studies of caste societies have demonstrated that the high ritual status of the Brahmin caste does not mean that Brahmins dominate the caste system; rather, these studies emphasize the centrality of the king and his warrior caste, the *Ksatriya*. Kings could determine the relative rank of local castes, for example; and from the king's perspective, the function of these other castes, including the Brahmins, was to protect him from pollution. By the end of the twentieth century, caste relations had undergone significant modification in urban India: castes close in rank sometimes came together in political alliances, and members of the same caste but from different regions of the country (e.g., Brahmins) came together to build solidarity on a national level. Unfortunately, Indian cities have also been the site of caste violence in recent years when members of more favorably situated castes clash with those struggling to escape from a permanent position at the bottom of the caste hierarchy.

Social **class**, by contrast, is the term anthropologists use to describe ranked subgroups in a stratified society whose members are differentiated from one another primarily in economic terms—either on the basis of income level or, as

Karl Marx (1818–1883) proposed, on the basis of the kind of property owned by members of different classes. In an industrial capitalist society, for example, Marx argued that class divisions had formed between the *bourgeoisie*, or capitalist class, which owned the means of production (tools, knowledge, raw materials); and the *proletariat*, or working class, which owned only their labor power, which they sold to bourgeois factory owners in exchange for cash wages (see chapters 7 and 10 for further discussion of these terms). Either way, members of some social classes are seen to have privileged access to material resources, while the access of members of other classes to these resources is more or less severely restricted. Moreover, ruling classes use their privileged situation to dominate less powerful classes.

Traditionally, anthropologists have distinguished class from caste on the grounds that social classes are not closed, and social mobility from one class into another is not forbidden. An emphasis on class mobility tends to highlight exceptional, successful individuals who have moved from lower to higher classes while overlooking the enduring rigidity of class boundaries for most people in many societies (e.g., Great Britain) as well as cases of downward class mobility. At the same time, emphasizing the inability of individuals in a caste system to move from a lower-ranked to a higher-ranked caste overlooks the ways in which permanent members of different castes sometimes collectively succeed in elevating the relative position of their caste within the overall caste system.

The members of ranked subgroups in stratified societies do not always accept the position they are supposed to occupy in a class or caste hierarchy, and struggles between such groups do occur. Marx, in particular, emphasized the class antagonism between bourgeoisie and proletariat, which he predicted ultimately would produce class warfare in which the workers would overthrow the capitalist order and establish socialism. Anthropologists working in India have challenged the view that people occupying the lowest ranks in the caste system necessarily accept their low status as right and proper. Indeed, the caste violence that has occasionally erupted in Indian cities in recent decades testifies to the unwillingness of those at the bottom of the system to accept such a position. At the same time, interactions between individuals from different levels of a hierarchical social system is not regularly characterized by such violence; and members of different ranked groups find nonviolent ways to establish relationships with one another. If different groups are associated with different occupations, their members may have only impersonal contact with one another when they need one another's services—for example, in the workplace. But many societies have developed institutionalized cross-hierarchy connections that allow individuals belonging to differently ranked groups to create a more personalized relationship. Anthropologists often call such connections **clientage** or *patron–client relationships* because they normally involve a member of a high-ranking group (the patron) and a member of a low-ranking group (the client). A well-documented example of clientage is the Latin American institution of **compadrazgo**, or co-parenthood. Such a relationship may be created when a lower-ranking married couple (the clients) asks a higher-ranking individual (the patron) to serve as their child's *compadre* or *comadre* (godfather or godmother) at the child's baptism. If the patron agrees and participates in the baptism ritual, then that individual and the child's parents will have a new relationship. They will call each other by the kin terms *compadre* or *comadre*, and their relationship will become less formal and more friendly. Because they are now *compadres*, the child's parents will feel freer to approach their patron (*compadre/comadre*) when they are in trouble, and he or she will be morally obliged to help them out. Conversely, if their patron needs supporters (e.g., in politics), they ordinarily will feel obligated to supply that support. Because clientage institutions like *compadrazgo* frequently remake the relationship of unrelated individuals on the model of formal kinship, anthropologists have sometimes described *compadres* as *fictive kin* (see chapter 7 for more on fictive kin).

Stratified societies with large populations and a complex division of labor ordinarily are associated with the political form called the **state** (discussed in more detail in chapter 8). The organic solidarity of state societies is maintained by a new kind of institution neither present nor needed in small-scale, egalitarian societies: bureaucracy. A **bureaucracy** is a hierarchically organized set of formal statuses, each of which is associated with a highly specific role, and all of which are designed to work together to ensure the smooth functioning of complex organizations such as state governments or business corporations. Persons occupying formal statuses in a bureaucracy possess **authority**: the ability to exert specific forms of influence and control by virtue of the fact that they legitimately occupy a formal office. Ideally, bureaucrats defend the avowed purposes of the organizations they serve, and much of their work involves following proper procedures in performing the particular tasks for which they are responsible. Complex organizations could not function without bureaucracies, but the formality and complexity of bureaucratic procedures often frustrates outsiders and may tempt bureaucrats to manipulate their positions for their own personal benefit.

Descriptions in terms of caste or class may be useful in tracing the gross outlines of the structure of complex stratified societies, but they are rarely sufficient to characterize all the significant dimensions of social organization found in such societies. Anthropologists recognize the importance of additional categories used by members of these societies that may be embedded within or may crosscut caste or class structures. With this in mind, they also have long paid attention to the category of race and have grown increasingly interested in distinctions framed in terms of ethnic identity, gender, and sexuality.

5.4 RACE

The concept of **race** was deeply intertwined with the very origin of anthropology as a discipline (see discussion in chapter 2). Although some late nineteenth-century physical anthropologists hoped to demonstrate a causal connection between the physical attributes of a group and their language and customs, early twentieth-century anthropologists worked hard to expose the flaws in such attempts. The modern concept of culture was developed to explain how individuals could learn *any* language or culture, regardless of their biological origins, and to argue against schemes that tried to classify the world's peoples into mutually exclusive races and to rank them hierarchically.

At the same time, the absence of any underlying biological basis for racial categories has never prevented people in some societies from inventing *cultural* categories based on a group's supposed origins or physical appearance and then using such categories as building blocks for their social institutions. Precisely because racial categories are culturally constructed on the basis of superficial appearances, however, different societies may draw the boundaries around racially defined social groups in different ways. These differences become clear when anthropologists compare the way race is defined and understood in different societies.

Until very recently, for example, the key racial divide in the United States was between two major racial categories: black and white. A history of enslavement of Africans by European settlers in the United States, and continued race-based oppression even after slavery was abolished in the nineteenth century, created in the United States what appeared to be a self-evident divide between black and white. This divide was justified by the ideology of **racism**: the idea that all humanity can be sorted into a few, naturally distinct groups, called "races"; and that some races are inherently biologically superior to other races, which justifies the systematic oppression of inferior races by superior races. But attempting to fix firm boundaries between black and white races has always generated paradoxes. Historically, white male slave owners took sexual advantage of black female slaves, who gave birth to offspring with both white and black ancestry. In the United States, the dilemma of determining racial membership for such individuals was resolved by the rule of *hypodescent*: that is, a single drop of African blood qualified a person as "black" rather than "white." The defense of the "one drop rule" allowed whites to protect the considerable advantages associated with being white, shielding them from the corresponding disadvantages that accrue to those considered black. Indeed, anthropologist Faye Harrison has shown that since the nineteenth century, "blackness has come to symbolize the social bottom" (1998, 612).

A key privilege associated with whiteness in the United States is not having to think about whiteness as a racial identity, taking the privileges associated with white skin for granted, and only associating "race" with nonwhite groups. When whites live in segregated neighborhoods and rarely have face-to-face dealings with people who are not white, it is easy for them to take their ways of doing things as standard, unmarked, "US" ways of doing things and to attribute any variation they see as a matter of individual differences. But whiteness is not experienced in this way by all whites in the United States. Anthropologist John Hartigan studied race relations in three Detroit neighborhoods at the end of the twentieth century and found that *the meaning of race varies from place to place, reflecting localized impacts of economic shifts, demographics, and class compositions*" (2015, 108; italics in the original).

Because most whites in the United States do not regularly acknowledge the advantages associated with whiteness, some scholars and activists in the United States developed an **antiracism** movement whose interventions, such as training workshops, are intended to bring white participants to acknowledge, and denounce, the racist ideology that makes them unaware of their own race-based privileges—thereby disrupting the power and reproduction of racism. Anthropologists who study race in the United States support these efforts but point out that people never experience race in the abstract. For instance, John Hartigan is convinced that ethnographic fieldwork on race relations can enrich our understanding of how racism works by exploring its dynamics in particular communities: "'the field' . . . is also a place that we continually need to learn from in order to understand . . . [the] changing and varied ways that race matters" (2015, 42).

In the early twenty-first century, some observers of race wonder whether it is possible to generalize about the black experience in the United States, both because of the clear emergence of a black middle class and also because of scholarship and activism showing that what it means to be black in the United States is shaped not only by class but also by gender (see chapter 6). In addition, anthropologists and other scholars generally agree that racial identities, like gender or class identities, are better understood as something that people *do* rather than something they *are* (see the discussion of *gender performativity* in chapter 6). The racial landscape in the United States has been further complicated in recent decades by immigration. Hartigan (2015, 152–157) proposes that immigrant populations from Latin American or Asian countries, for example, are marked by *foreignness*, a race-like distinction that bars them from white privilege. At the same time, immigrants are distinguished by cultural and linguistic differences, usually associated with *ethnicity* (see section 5.5), which are seen as less threatening.

Outside the United States, it is clear that continued world domination by societies whose ruling groups trace their origins to Europe continues to sustain a global hierarchy in which light skin is valued over dark skin. And yet, in the Caribbean or Latin America, where Africans also suffered under European slavery, race is understood in different ways. For example, in some places, the racial identity one claims, or is accorded by others, may vary from situation to situation, depending on who else is present. That is, in any particular social setting, those with the lightest skin may claim and be accorded the identity of "white"; but when they move into a different setting and interact with others whose skin is lighter than theirs, they may have to accept being assigned to one of a variety of lower-status, nonwhite categories. Some anthropologists (e.g., Lancaster 1992) use the term *colorism* to describe this pattern of racial classification in contrast to the once and for all pattern of racial classification found in the United States.

Moreover, social mobility and the cultural changes that accompany it—learning the dominant language, getting an education, finding gainful employment, adopting new customs in diet and dress—may be interpreted as movement from one racial group into another. Thus, in some parts of Latin America, indigenous people who cut their hair, speak Spanish, wear European clothing, get an education, and find Western-style occupations may be classified by other members of their society as "white" or "mixed" rather than "indigenous"—even though their outward biological features have not altered. Anthropologists sometimes use the term *social race* to describe these cases in which so-called racial labels are used to refer to cultural rather than physical differences between groups.

Following advances in the new science of human genomics, anthropologists from different subfields have collaborated to produce fine-grained studies of localized understandings of race. One example is the multiyear project called "Race, Genomics, and *Mestizaje* [mixture] in Latin America: A Comparative Approach" (Wade 2017, vii). Three teams of researchers worked in Brazil, Colombia, and Mexico, investigating not only how genetics research was carried on by local scientists in local laboratories but also on how nonscientists in these three countries learned about and responded to genetic information. The project was situated within a science studies framework (for more on science studies, see chapter 11). Project director Peter Wade writes that the first volume of articles based on the project (Wade et al. 2014a) "can be boiled down to the question of how much the practice of genomic science reproduces familiar race-like concepts"; whereas the second volume (Wade 2017b) expands to consider "how genetic science has been and is connected to nodes in an assemblage that encompasses ideas and practices around the governance and imagination of human diversity" (2017, ix).

In Wade's view, the cross-country comparison demonstrated that "Claims about the transformative potential of genomics need to be seen in context and taken with a sizeable pinch of salt" (Wade 2017, 259). Genetics research has dissolved nineteenth-century notions of distinct "races of mankind" in several ways: population variation is now regularly described in terms of clinal distributions of gene frequencies, sometimes connecting these to particular continents; ancestral connections are traced using different genetic markers that are not linked to racialized phenotypic traits and that frequently produce contradictory family trees; and genetic data about ancestry are seen as most relevant to individuals, pointing to medical risks they may face. But it is the factor of medical risk that also helps prop up earlier ideas about race: racialized groups may become the focus of medical research, and drugs may be marketed to treat conditions for which members of their group are said to be at particularly high risk. Racialized genetic data can be used not only to monitor how well certain populations' health needs are being met but also to facilitate racial profiling by the police. Many observers conclude that "continental biogeographic ancestries continue to look like familiar racial categories. . . . Purity might appear an anachronistic concept, but insofar as it stands in for 'racial difference,' one can still detect its magnetic field in constant tension with 'mixture'" (Wade 2017, 250).

5.5 ETHNICITY

As the previous discussion indicates, attempting to sort human populations on the basis of biological criteria is often hard to distinguish attempts to sort them on the basis of cultural criteria. This highlights the ways that people can emphasize or downplay any of a wide range of physical and cultural attributes, either to define an identity for themselves or to assign an identity to others. This ambiguity appears when we consider another important social category investigated by anthropologists, that of the **ethnic group**. Ethnic groups usually are distinguished from other kinds of social groups based on attributes defining group membership that are cultural in nature: shared language, shared religion, shared customs, shared history. However, because all this cultural sharing could never have occurred if group members did not regularly interact and even intermarry, ethnic identity is often thought, by both group members and outsiders, to be rooted in some common biological origin. Indeed, some anthropologists think of racial identity as being no different from ethnic identity—except that racial identity supposedly is biological in origin, whereas ethnic identity has a cultural origin. And in practice, the concepts of both race and ethnic group often overlap with the concept of nation (discussed in more detail in chapter 8).

All such cultural identities—whether understood in terms of kinship or race or ethnic identity—develop in opposition to other, similar identities in a complex social setting. Thus, the boundaries that eventually come to be recognized between races or ethnic groups are a product of both internal self-definition and external definition by others. Of course, a sense of group belonging and the ability to distinguish one's own group from neighboring groups stretch far back into the human past. What makes the study of racial, ethnic, or national identity so important today, however, is the new role such groups take on within the boundaries of contemporary nation-states.

As discussed in chapter 8, nation-states are relatively new forms of political organization, first developing in late eighteenth-century and nineteenth-century Europe and the Americas and later spreading throughout the globe following the dissolution of Western colonial empires. Before the French Revolution, European states were ruled by kings and emperors whose access to the throne was officially believed to have been ordained by God. After the French Revolution, which thoroughly discredited the divine right of kings and proclaimed the "Rights of Man," a new basis for legitimate state authority had to be found. Over the course of the nineteenth century, the notion developed that rulers were legitimate only if they ruled over other members of the nation to which they themselves belonged.

When legitimacy began to depend on the perfect overlap of nation and state, on a recognized bond of cultural, linguistic, or religious—that is, national—identity between ruler and ruled, the persistence of groups with different forms of identity within the boundaries of the nation-state became problematic. If such groups successfully resisted assimilation into the nation that the state was supposed to represent, their existence called into question the legitimacy of the state and its rulers. Indeed, if their numbers were sufficient, they might well claim that they were a separate nation, entitled to a state of their own! This situation describes much contemporary political life at the turn of the twenty-first century when ruling regimes in more and more nation-states, fearful of losing stability and legitimacy in the eyes of the world, engaged in violence against all citizens who challenged their right to rule.

Ethnocide (the destruction of a culture) and *genocide* (the physical extermination of an entire people) have often been the result, generating movements of refugee and immigrant populations whose social and political status is often anomalous and ambiguous in a world of nation-states.

In recent years, anthropologists have paid particular attention to the ways that oppressed racial and ethnic groups, whether resident or immigrant, have struggled to mobilize their members to resist oppression. This has occurred in countries all over the world, including those of Europe and North America. As forces of globalization have weakened nation-states and promoted the flow of large numbers of people of various backgrounds into societies different from their own, new ethnic contacts and ethnic frictions have developed. By the end of the second decade of the twentieth century, debates about immigration had become the focus of polarizing political struggles in both Europe and the United States—as well as an important focus of ethnographic research (e.g., De Genova 2017, De León 2015).

FOR FURTHER READING

Social Organization   Fried 1967; Graburn 1971
Ethnicity   Eriksen 2010; Wade 2010; Williams 1989
Colonialism   Pels and Salemink 1999; Pels 1997; Stoler 2002
Race   Hartigan 2013, 2015; Koenig et al. 2008; Reardon 2005; Lancaster 1992; Smedley 1999
Genocide and Ethnocide   Hinton 2002; Messer 1993; Nagengast 1994

CHAPTER 6

Sex, Gender, and Sexuality

The key terms covered in this chapter in the order in which they appear:

feminism	affect
patriarchy	cyborg
sexism	intersex
sex	disorder of sexual development
gender	
gender binary	sexuality
	heterosexuality
intersectionality	heteronormativity
	heterosexism
gender performativity	homosexuality
men's studies	gay
masculinities	lesbian
women's studies	bisexuality
gender studies	transgender
	queer

Cultural anthropologists have been interested in sex, gender, and sexuality since the beginning of anthropology as a discipline, but their preferred approaches to these topics have changed over time, along with broader theoretical developments in the discipline and wider historical shifts in the world. This chapter focuses primarily on perspectives and concepts that have developed since the 1960s and 1970s in Euro-American sociocultural anthropology. However, scholarship and activism on issues surrounding sex, gender, and sexuality remain intensive and ongoing, extending far beyond the discipline of anthropology. Anthropologists and other social scientists share perspectives and borrow concepts from one another. The result, for sociocultural anthropologists, has been the production of a vast and expanding body of ethnographic research exploring sex, gender, and sexuality both in Euro-American societies and in societies outside the Western world.

6.1 SEX, GENDER, AND FEMINISM IN THE TWENTIETH CENTURY

Some anthropologists would argue that feminism was responsible for one of the most profound transformations of social science scholarship in the twentieth century. **Feminism** argues that women and men are equally human and therefore that women are entitled to enjoy the same rights and privileges as men. As a social movement in North America, the first wave of feminism emerged in the nineteenth century, sparked by the movement to abolish racial slavery. After women in the United States successfully obtained the right to vote in the early twentieth century, the struggle for women's rights lost momentum. But by the 1960s and 1970s, in the wake of the civil rights movement, a second-wave feminist movement rose up, challenging many remaining forms of inequality between men and women. Second-wave feminists pointed out that even though Western societies were supposed to be democratic, and women now had the right to vote, many domains of social life continued to be organized in terms of **patriarchy**, that is, by male domination over women. Feminists coined the term **sexism** (based on an analogy with racism) to describe the systematic sociocultural structures and practices of inequality, derived from patriarchal institutions, that continue to shape relations between women and men. As with racism, sexism was seen to involve more than prejudiced individual beliefs alone; as a result, achieving full equality between women and men was understood to require not only changing beliefs but also dismantling patriarchal institutions and practices.

A rallying cry for many second-wave feminists was that "the personal is political." These feminists confronted the *public/private divide,* a barrier that law and custom had erected between domestic life in the family, conceived as "women's place," and public life, outside the family, conceived as the domain of men. Feminists pointed out that women were oppressed by domestic forms of patriarchy that were considered "private" and thus understood to be matters beyond the "public" reach of the law. Ostensibly, women's husbands or fathers both looked after women's interests within private, male-headed households and protected women from the harsh effects of the public, male domain. However, women who sought education or employment outside the home, or who lacked husbands or private homes altogether, found themselves at the mercy of hostile public institutions that regularly discriminated against them. At the same time, women who stayed at home were not guaranteed protection because the public/private divide allowed men to evade legal accountability for physically abusing the women living in their private households. Indeed, feminist activism around the issue of spousal abuse spurred second-wave feminists to create a battered-women's movement, which has now become global (Merry 2009).

Feminist struggles in their own societies prompted some anthropologists to rethink many long-held assumptions about the contributions of women to human culture. Feminist anthropologists noted that most ethnographies, including those written by women, were based primarily on the views of male informants, even concerning matters pertaining to women. Thus, most discussions of "the culture" of a group in fact portrayed culture from the viewpoint of men (often high-status men). When women were discussed at all, it was usually in the context of marriage and the family, and the assumption seemed to be that women's cultural roles as wives and mothers followed "naturally" from the biological facts of pregnancy and lactation. However, Margaret Mead's demonstration in the 1930s of the lack of correlation between biological sex and culturally expected behaviors of males and females in society was a well-known exception to this pattern.

By the early 1970s, feminist anthropologists were forcing a serious re-examination of traditional assumptions about the roles of women and men in human society. Building on Mead's work, it became commonplace for cultural anthropologists to use the term **sex** to refer to the physical characteristics that distinguish males from females (e.g., body shape, distribution of body hair, reproductive organs, sex chromosomes). By contrast, they used the term **gender** to refer to the culturally constructed roles assigned to males or females, which varied considerably from society to society. The distinction between sex and gender was an important theoretical breakthrough, and it became widely adopted by anthropologists and other social scientists. At the same time, the sex/gender distinction left unquestioned the assumption that people in all societies classified humans into two categories, universally distinguishing women from men. Such a dual categorization has been called a **gender binary**. Many anthropologists and others assumed that even if there seemed to be a demonstrable lack of correlation between physical sex and the content of gender roles, the gender binary itself might be universal. Some feminist anthropologists were also concerned that not only the gender binary, but male domination of females, might also be universal. For example, many human societies trace descent through women (see chapter 7), but no persuasive evidence has ever been found to suggest that there have ever been societies organized as *matriarchies*—that is, societies where women as a group dominated men as a group.

Feminist anthropologist Sherry Ortner wrote a classic 1974 article whose title asked the question, "Is Female to Male as Nature Is to Culture?" The wide-ranging evidence she presented suggested to her that the answer was "yes"—it appeared that regardless of the activities performed by men and women in a society, all human cultures valued culture over nature and associated males with culture and females with nature. At best, women might be seen as mediating between culture and nature, but they were always seen as closer to nature than men, perhaps because of their bodies' ongoing involvement in the "natural" processes of pregnancy, childbirth, and lactation. Ortner's conclusions were challenged by other feminist anthropologists who adopted Marxian perspectives, looking beyond symbolic systems of culture to consider male domination in the context of wider social, political, and economic processes. Gayle Rubin (1975) argued that such processes shaped each society's particular "sex/gender system"; and Eleanor Leacock (1981) argued that cases of male dominance in contemporary societies were less likely to reflect the original human condition than they were to show forms of institutionalized gender inequality influenced by the spread of capitalism. Considering these issues two decades later, after much commentary and additional research, Ortner concluded that "recognizing egalitarianism is not as easy as it looks, that it is a matter of interpretation" (Ortner in Moore and Sanders 2014, 358). Ortner observed in her 1974 paper that she had regarded all indicators of male privilege as equally significant, and equally entrenched, within "cultures," conceived as systematic, self-contained symbolic systems. By 1996, however, she had come to realize that not all gendered distinctions in a particular society were equally significant and that such inequalities might or might not be embedded in larger social, economic, and political orders. Her understanding of culture had also changed: by the end of the twentieth century, she noted, anthropologists had begun to think differently about "cultures," regarding them "as more disjunctive, contradictory and inconsistent than I had been trained to think" (358.) (see chapter 2).

6.2 SEX, GENDER, RACE, AND CLASS

As feminist anthropologists struggled to debunk supposedly universal "truths" about women, they came to realize that "women" itself is a problematic category. This became clear as comparative research revealed ways that other forms of identity, such as race and class, were deeply entangled with the ways women (and men) came to understand the meaning of gender. For instance, second-wave feminism had been energized by many white, middle-class women whose experiences of women's oppression—being denied professional careers in the public sphere, being confined to roles as wives and mothers—were shaped by race and class privilege. But nonwhite feminists pointed out that nonwhite working-class women experienced oppression very differently—frequently as single mothers forced to work outside the home in dead-end jobs. These differences were not simply the consequence of male domination but also of structures of racial and class oppression, a phenomenon now called **intersectionality**. To recognize the reality of intersectionality is to recognize that every woman has multiple identities that intersect and complicate each other; taken together, they locate each woman differently (and sometimes, surprisingly) with respect to other women (or men). Thus, in some settings, a middle-class African American woman might enjoy class-based privileges denied to a working-class white woman; whereas in other settings, the working-class white woman's race would allow her privileges that would override the class status of the middle-class African American women.

At the same time, it was also becoming increasingly clear that *the content* of a woman's gender identity was often shaped by cultural features used to define different ethnic, religious, or national groups and to distinguish them from one another. For instance, a woman might feel that submitting to her husband was part of what it meant to be a proper woman in the religious community to which they both belonged, and that to challenge male domination by leaving a husband who physically "chastised " her could call into question both her proper gender identity and her religious identity.

6.3 GENDER PERFORMATIVITY

As we saw earlier, anthropologists (and others) who distinguish sex from gender long ago rejected the idea that a person's gendered beliefs or behavior were somehow directly caused by that person's biological sex. However, viewing gendered cultural behavior as the unproblematic consequence of conformity to cultural expectations could not explain how people coped with the complications created by intersectionality. Yet women—and men—regularly manage the contradictions that race, class, gender, and other identities create in the course of everyday life. This success suggested to many observers that it was misleading to think of culturally expected gender "roles" simply as obligations to which individuals learned to *conform*. Instead, these roles looked more like scripts that individuals learned to *perform*; and part of each performance involved deciding which features of which identities to highlight or downplay in any given social interaction. Understanding cultural identity as something people perform compels anthropologists to think of individuals as *agents* who have mastered, and are capable of executing, a range of skills appropriate to the public display of particular identities before particular audiences (Butler 2006). Thus, displays of gender identity are examples of **gender performativity**; that is, gender is reconceived as something we "perform" or "enact," something we "do," not something we "are." To put it otherwise, no single identity fully captures the inner life of any individual. From the perspective of performativity, culture can also be reconceived less as a set of imposed beliefs and behaviors and more as a set of *resources*—artifacts, actions, and interpretations— that can be deployed by individuals to enact before others the identities to which they lay claim. The notion of performativity has been widely applied by anthropologists and others to describe the way humans perform not only gender but also other forms of social identity, such as race or ethnicity (see chapter 5).

6.4 THEORETICAL DIVERSITY IN STUDIES OF SEX AND GENDER

Over the past several decades, scholars and activists concerned with women's issues have aligned themselves with different theoretical perspectives. One point of view, sometimes called *cultural feminism,* does not challenge the traditional Western, patriarchal, male–female binary. Cultural feminists accept the view that men and women are fundamentally different from each other; for instance, that men are aggressive, powerful, and rational while women are gentle, nurturing, and emotional. Indeed, cultural feminists insist that men and women have different *essences*—that is, fixed and unchanging natures. However, they also assert that male values and practices threaten women, children, and all life, whereas female values have the opposite effect. Their goal is therefore to promote the cultural values associated with females, to help these values regain an influential position in public policy debates, especially those associated with environmental issues. Such views are regularly encountered among those who call themselves *ecofeminists.*

A second point of view is that of *liberal feminism*, associated with those feminists who base their claims to equality on liberal political principles that were developed in the aftermath of the European Enlightenment in the eighteenth century, principles that are foundational to liberal democratic practice in Euro-American societies. The key liberal concept for these feminists is that of the autonomous individual who is self-directed in pursuit of his (or her) own preferences, and who is capable of reflecting and deliberating rationally on matters of political concern. Liberal feminists clearly reject the cultural feminist notion that women are moved primarily by emotion. On the contrary, they insist that woman are as endowed with rational intelligence as men and therefore should be accorded the same rights and privileges as men. Many liberal feminist activists have worked to change laws and practices that exclude women from various opportunities open to men, such as rights to education and employment.

A third point of view, associated with *socialist feminism*, begins with the idea that contemporary gender inequalities, particularly in Euro-American societies, cannot be understood unless they are situated within the wider Euro-American capitalist political economy. They reject cultural feminist claims about male and female essences because they connect gender divisions, along with race and class divisions, to the broader relations of production that characterize capitalism. They point out that Marx emphasized productive labor of (male) workers but ignored the unpaid reproductive labor of women whose efforts maintained male workers and produced new generations of workers. They also question liberal feminist commitment to the rational autonomous individual, arguing that this notion is an ideological construct that masks the deeper class divisions generated by a capitalist political economy. Finally, they argue that class, race, and gender oppression will not disappear until the capitalist economy itself is transformed. In the second decade of the twenty-first century, several decades after the end of the Cold War and the collapse of socialist economies, the position of socialist feminism may seem to reflect the concerns of a world that no longer exists. However, this tradition of feminist thinking continues to contribute to ongoing critique of systematic forms of gender inequality that persist—or have been exacerbated—by the spread of neoliberal capitalism throughout the post–Cold War world.

The diversification of perspectives within women's studies was accompanied by the recognition by some women's studies scholars that women's gender roles could not be studied apart from the gender roles of men. Again, if one thinks of gender identities as parts of a larger "sex/gender system," studying women or men in isolation becomes immediately problematic. In fact, scholarship by anthropologists and other social scientists contributed to the growth of **men's studies** alongside women's studies; and just as women's studies scholars had found that there were many ways of being a women, so too men's studies scholars identified a range of different ways of being a man, in different places and times: these were called different **masculinities**.

As noted earlier, the study of women's issues sparked by second-wave feminism has drawn attention from scholars in many different disciplines, including anthropologists trained in all the four traditional subfields of North American anthropology. Cross-disciplinary collaboration (and debate) continues today, and it remains theoretically and substantively diverse. One practical consequence, however, has been ongoing discussion about what, in fact, the "field" should be called. Although terms like *feminist anthropology* are still used by some (e.g., Lewin 2006), other scholars prefer to locate their work within the field of **women's studies**. In part, this reflects objections raised in connection with the association of "feminism" with the white, middle-class perspectives of many second-wave feminists; some women of color have preferred to describe their analyses as *womanist* rather than "feminist," to emphasize the distinctiveness of the challenges faced by women who do not enjoy white, middle-class privileges. Many anthropologists and other social scientists have supported the move to combine the study of women, men, sex, gender, and sexuality in an inclusive field called **gender studies**. At the same time, not all women's studies scholars—anthropologists among them—have been convinced that folding women's studies into gender studies was a good move to make. They are concerned that sinking women's studies into gender studies cannot but dilute the attention paid to serious issues that women continue to face. This disagreement remains unresolved, its consequences visible in the many different names given to departments and programs in different universities that specialize in the study of women, men, sex, gender, and sexuality.

6.5 SEX, GENDER, AND THE BODY

An important trend in sociocultural anthropology in recent decades has been attention to "the body," an object of study that is of obvious relevance to discussions of sex, gender, and sexuality. To understand the growth of interest in the body, it is important to remember that for most of the twentieth century, sociocultural anthropology consistently downplayed human individuals (and their individual bodies) and highlighted structures and patterns that characterized the social groups to which individual humans belonged. Such a strategy could be justified because Euro-American audiences, deeply committed to the cultural value of individualism (especially the United States), tended to disregard the powerful ways that broader, shared social structures and cultural patterns shaped the life chances of individuals in society (see the discussion of the social contract in chapter 5).

As ethnographic evidence demonstrating the complexity of women's and men's roles in a variety of cultural settings began to accumulate, anthropologists like Marilyn Strathern (1941–) began to argue that the concept of gender needed to be understood broadly because members of many societies regularly drew on sexual imagery as a resource for categorizing other kinds of people, things, and events. For example, the idea that men are active and powerful and women are passive and weak may be mobilized by members of powerful groups in a society who imagine themselves as "real men" and who treat members of less powerful, dominated groups (perhaps especially men in such groups) as if they were weak and passive, thereby "emasculating" or "feminizing" them. Complex, gen-dered social relations of this kind were characteristic of Western colonial set-tings where a culturally constructed "racial" divide between "white" colonizer and "nonwhite" colonized groups was supplemented by violent opposition to any hint of sexual involvement between indigenous males and "white" women, even as "white" men's sexual relationships with colonized women went unpunished. Colonizers viewed those whom they had colonized (colonized men, in particu-lar) as nonwhite, feminized inferiors incapable of protecting their territories or "their" women from more powerful "masculine," white outsiders (Stoler 2002).

But individual bodies were not entirely ignored. Anthropologist Mary Douglas famously argued that "The social body constrains the way the physi-cal body is perceived" (1970, 93); and she drew on ethnographic and historical data to show how ritual preoccupations with bodily orifices (e.g., food taboos or menstrual taboos, or restrictions governing sexual intercourse) regularly mir-rored preoccupations with the social vulnerabilities faced by a society in rela-tion to its enemies. In recent years, anthropologists have turned to the work of Michel Foucault, whose writings highlight the way social power, particularly in modern Western societies, acts on individual bodies. Social institutions like schools and armies regulate the actions of individual bodies to render them more efficient in the performance of particular skills or practices. At the same time, modern states depend on statistical information about their populations to devise ways of regulating those populations, engaging in what Foucault calls *biopolitics* (see chapter 8). For example, campaigns to improve the well-being of citizens via medical interventions such as inoculations have allowed state insti-tutions to increase the numbers of healthy individuals ready for the labor force or the numbers of healthy recruits eligible to be drafted into the armed forces. Finally, Foucault argues, societies have devised ways of persuading individuals to bring their own bodily activities into conformity with social expectations on their own, a phenomenon he calls "the care of the self." Foucault's theoretical framework has informed work in many areas of anthropological research, but it has had particular resonance for those scholars—such as Foucault himself—who were concerned with documenting the ways these practices of social intervention and regulation were mobilized to classify and produce particular forms of sexual embodiment over time (Foucault 1980, 1990, 1988).

For example, anthropologists have traditionally understood that human beings are plastic organisms who are open to the molding processes of social-ization and enculturation. This resonates with Foucault's understanding of the human body as a *docile* body; that is, a body that is easily taught, or, in Foucault's terms, a body "that may be subjected, used, transformed, and improved" through "disciplinary methods" that apply "an uninterrupted, constant coercion" of bodily activities, making possible "the meticulous control of the operations of the body" (1995, 136, 137). As we observed earlier, however, conceiving of human bodies as nothing more than passive, inert matter that can unresistingly be shaped by sociocultural conditioning raises difficulties. Equally challenging have been liberal Enlightenment views that associated human agency with the exercise of rational deliberation and choice alone. Twenty-five years ago, feminist philosopher Elizabeth Grosz (1994) challenged such views by drawing attention to the experience and forms of consciousness that derived from material processes unique to female bodies, from menstruation through menopause, exploring the implications of these experiences for understanding the connections between sex and embodiment. More recently, theorists in anthropology and elsewhere have drawn attention to the ways in which **affect** (visceral arousal, emotion, or feeling) is not opposed to rational thought but is, in fact, entwined with thought in processes of human meaning-making. Some of this research has focused on how individuals experience visceral feelings of desire that are at odds with cultural ideologies of gender and sexuality. One suggestion is that these forms of affect have the potential to disrupt ideologies concerning sexuality, making room for the development of alternative corporeal relations between individuals. Theoretical approaches of this kind offer ways of bringing material bodies back into discussions of sex, gender, sexuality, and human agency without reducing bodily feelings to genetic or hormonal mechanisms.

Other feminists have explored the connection between the body and technology. Particularly influential in this connection was Donna Haraway's "Cyborg Manifesto" (1991). A **cyborg** is a cybernetic organism, part machine and part living organism. While cyborgs have long been portrayed as monsters in science fiction, Haraway argued persuasively that all humans—women and men alike—were being increasingly drawn into alliances with machines in the contemporary world, for good and for ill. Haraway recognized the negative side of human-machine connections in cybernetically managed forms of economic production, but she refused to condemn technology as contrary to all the needs and goals of feminists, as cultural feminists have done. On the contrary, she argued that thinking in terms of cyborgs could be productive for progressive feminist purposes, particularly as a way of dealing with the conflicts generated by the politics of identity among differently located groups of women. She contrasted the isolating relations promoted by politics based on *identity* (i.e., promoting political solidarity among those who shared the "same" identity) with what she saw as a potentially more promising politics based on *affinity* (i.e., promoting political alliances among those who might claim different identities but who nonetheless shared some partial connections regarding some issues that might allow them to bridge their differences). Relations of affinity were a variety of cyborg relations because they joined unlike entities together but promised political potency that promoted hope. Her model of feminist alliances based on affinity was the set of alliances that produced the hybrid category of *women of color*: although they might be divided by ethnicity or class, all women of color have experienced the consequences of being nonwhite and have been politically effective by coming together on that basis.

One product of Haraway's cyborg thinking has been the development of *cyborg anthropology,* an area of specialization in which anthropologists focus attention on the proliferating cybernetic connections between humans and machines in contemporary societies. Such connections can be found everywhere today, from computerized management of large informational databases in government and private industry, to online computer gaming, to your personal relationship with your smartphone. One area with cyborg properties of interest to many anthropologists who study sex, gender, and sexuality has been the expanding field of *assisted reproduction*. In the past, medicine and technology were not viewed as having any intrinsic connection to the "natural" process of human reproduction, and the failure of this natural process to produce living offspring was understood as equally "natural." Today, however, infertile couples (and, increasingly, same-sex couples) who want children of their own but who are unable or unwilling to adopt, may now call on a variety of complex medical technologies and institutions, from sperm banks and egg banks to fertility clinics that perform procedures like in vitro fertilization for themselves—or for a female surrogate who has agreed, for a fee, to gestate "their" embryo for them. In addition, forms of prenatal testing such as amniocentesis are now standard technological interventions in pregnancies that may be otherwise uncomplicated. Overall, human reproduction has become a cyborg phenomenon, entangling human organisms and technologies in complex ways.

Cyborg thinking asks us to consider connections between "natural" organisms and "cultural" technologies, and doing so inevitably blurs the boundaries between nature and culture. It turns out, however, that a close inspection of that which is considered "natural" can also lead to the blurring of boundaries that once seemed clear-cut. For instance, as we saw earlier, anthropologists have long agreed that "sex," while distinct from culturally shaped "gender," is a "natural" physical attribute that is clearly visible on the body, to be determined by inspection at birth (i.e., males have penises and females have vaginas) or at puberty (i.e., males grow beards and females grow breasts and start to menstruate). However, this way of classifying bodies, based on the presumption of a "natural" gender binary, turns out to be problematic. For one thing, the determination of the sex of newborns by visual inspection is by no means as straightforward as it may seem. Developmental biologist Anne Fausto-Sterling reports that "about one in a hundred infants is born without a consistent body sex" (2014, 313). That is, infants' patterns of sex chromosomes (XX for females, XY for males) may not correspond to the expected outward appearance of their genitals (an XX baby may have enlarged clitoris and fused labia, an XY baby may have a tiny penis), or with their internal gonads (i.e., two ovaries for females, two testes for males).

Individuals who possess ambiguous genitalia have been called **intersex**, although many prefer to describe their condition as the result of a **disorder of sexual development**. Medical scientists are able to identify a number of developmental processes that can produce atypical genitalia in infants, some of which are associated with ongoing risks to the individual's health; however, many newborns with ambiguous genitalia face no such health risks. Still, infants with ambiguous genitalia may cause great anxiety for their parents, which has led to the elaboration of standard medical interventions in the United States soon after the birth of such infants. Decisions are made about the newborn's sex assignment (and the gender in which the child will be reared), and then surgery is performed to bring the external appearance of the infant's genitalia into line with this assignment; sometimes surgery is followed by additional hormonal treatments at puberty. However, many adults who underwent these interventions in childhood have publicly declared that their own personal biographies have been far from "normal." Some have become activists who urge physicians and parents to delay or avoid such surgeries on infants altogether to spare these children the surgical disfigurement and loss of sexual feeling they experienced (Karkazis 2008). The issues are complex, but one thing is clear: the statistical frequency with which infants with ambiguous genitalia are born means that assigning newborns a sex is far from self-evident or unproblematic, and it is powerfully shaped by the cultural expectations and social practices of parents and physicians. This evidence reinforces Judith Butler's well-known insistence that sex is as much a construction of culture as is gender (Butler 2006).

6.6 SEX, GENDER, AND SEXUALITY

Minimally, **sexuality** refers to the ways in which people experience and value physical desire and pleasure in the context of sexual intercourse. But contemporary anthropologists are more likely to refer to sexualities, in the plural, to acknowledge the many ways in which sexual desires and pleasures have always been shaped historically by cultural, social, and political structures of the larger societies in which people live. Until recently, as we saw earlier, many Americans took for granted that biological sex directly determined gendered behavior. These assumptions underlie the view, long popular in the United States, that "normal" sexuality takes only one form—**heterosexuality**—which involves "natural" sexual attraction, leading to "natural" sexual intercourse, between males and females (i.e., individuals of different sexes). To emphasize heterosexuality as the only correct form of human sexual expression is to subscribe to an ideology that anthropologists and others call **heteronormativity**; that is, the view that heterosexual intercourse is (and *should be*) the "normal" form that human sexual expression always takes. For example, heteronormative sexuality has been viewed in Euro-American societies as the appropriate form of sexuality within the nuclear family, formed around a heterosexual married couple who are expected to engage in exclusive sexual relations with one another to produce offspring. Claims that the nuclear family is the building block of US society reflect what Foucault would call the biopolitical concern of the state to manage its population of citizens and regulate their reproduction. However, heteronormative thinking about sexuality has been successfully undermined in recent decades, not only by scholarly work on varieties of human sexual expression but even more by activism by lesbians, gay men, bisexual, and transgender individuals whose preferred ways of doing gender and enacting sexual expression challenge heteronormative standards. From the perspective of these critics, people who continue to support heteronormativity are perceived to subscribe instead to **heterosexism**, a form of bias (like sexist bias) against all those who are not heterosexual.

Historians of sexuality have demonstrated the recency of heteronormative thinking, and heteronormative sexual classifications, in Euro-American societies. Consider, for example, the concept of heterosexuality and its routine opposite, **homosexuality**—sexual relations involving two men or two women, or same-sex sexuality. Many people assume that these terms identify stable forms of sexuality going back deep into the past, but this is not the case. David Halperin observes that the first appearance in print of the word "homosexuality" was in 1869, in German, in a pamphlet urging the German government not to criminalize "homosexual" relations between men; paradoxically, therefore, "'homosexuality' began life as a progay, politically activist coinage" (2014, 481). Before long, however, the term was appropriated by medical specialists called "sexologists" who turned it into a clinical term designating a particular variety of sexual deviance. By the end of the nineteenth century, however, individuals classified as homosexual by the medical authorities began to use the term **gay** to refer to themselves, an affirmative and empowering self-designation that became widespread over the course of the twentieth century. Although the term *gay* may be applied to any person who is sexually attracted to someone of the same sex, it is more commonly used in reference to gay men and the cultures and practices associated with them.

The term **lesbian** did actually emerge in antiquity, but it originally referred to a resident of the Greek island of Lesbos, the home of the female poet Sappho, who was reputed to love women rather than men. Standard use of "lesbian" as to describe female same-sex sexuality, however, only began around the turn of the twentieth century. In fact, the terms "homosexuality," "heterosexuality," and **bisexuality** (i.e., sexual attraction to both males and females) were all invented by Euro-American medical researchers in the late nineteenth and early twentieth centuries; and "heterosexuality" did not assume its current meaning as the opposite of "homosexuality" until the 1930s (see Halperin 2014, 458–461). The term **transgender** is even more recent, proposed in the 1960s in an attempt by medical researchers to clarify differences among individuals who, in one way or another, seemed dissatisfied with the sex and gender assignments they had received at birth. Physicians now recognize *gender identity disorder* or *gender dysphoria* as a formal medical diagnosis; but many persons who claim a transgender identity deny the validity of this diagnosis, arguing that it is based on heteronormative bias. Like individuals diagnosed as "homosexual" in earlier decades, many individuals diagnosed with gender dysphoria insist that their sexuality is not a medical condition to be treated but a valid form of gender variation that requires recognition and support. Some critics have objected to the *homonormativity* professed by those who appear convinced that the only valid alternative to heterosexual identities and sexualities are gay or lesbian identities and sexualities, resisting the legitimacy of transgender gender identities and sexualities.

In the 1990s, some persons whose gender identities or sexual practices fell outside the range defined by "the heterosexual-homosexual continuum" began to refer to themselves as **queer**, taking back as a badge of pride a term once used to insult nonheterosexuals. The status of this term remains controversial, however: some view it as a convenient umbrella term for all those who reject heteronormativity, whereas others use it to signify rejection of *all* categories of gender and sexual classification—including distinctions between lesbian, gay, bisexual, and transgender persons.

In the wake of sociopolitical breakthroughs such as the growing legal recognition of same-sex marriage, debates about how to distinguish and label proliferating varieties of sexuality are ongoing. For example, on June 9, 2015, following the highly publicized transition of former male Olympic athlete Bruce Jenner into a woman called Caitlyn, *The New York Times* published an article describing the difficulty of determining statistically the proportion of the US population that might be classified as "transgender" (Miller 2015). Being able to quantify more accurately the proportion of transgender individuals in the US population would have wide-ranging biopolitical effects, for good or for ill. As Miller notes, "knowing more about this population is important for policy-making in health, education, criminal justice, social services, sports, the military and more" (2015, A3). However, the US Census Bureau does not ask about gender identity, and many transgender persons hide their gender identity to avoid discrimination. At the same time, the article also noted that "gender identity can be hard to define in a multiple-choice list. There are now more than 50 gender options on Facebook, for instance" (Miller 2015, A3); by 2016, there were 71 gender options (see the discussion at https://www.quora.com/Why-does-Facebook-have-71-gender-options; accessed July 20, 2018). Similarly, the "Transgender" page on Wikipedia provides alternative definitions of "transgender" and describes multiple and contradictory ways that people who call themselves transgender might define what that label means (http://en.wikipedia.org/wiki/Transgender; accessed July 29, 2018). In part, the struggle over terminology reflects the desire of some transgender persons to gain public recognition of an identity label of their own choice, as a claim to dignity; at the same time, the proliferation of labels reveals deep disagreements about what that identity might be.

The conclusion seems inescapable that in Euro-American societies today, forms of sexual expression cannot be easily sorted into a handful of unambiguous categories in which sex, gender, and sexuality line up in predictable ways. On the contrary, the phenomena we call sex, gender, and sexuality would appear to be fluid and changing, not only over historical time but also in the biographies of many human individuals, even in the United States. Some scholars speak in terms of a *male-to-female continuum*, along which individuals may plot the development of their own identifications in terms of sex, gender, and sexuality. Others may agree with David Halperin, whose history of the classification of sex, gender, and sexuality in Euro-American societies concludes that "Perhaps the final irony in all this is that the very word sex . . . has had the fine edge of its precise meaning so thoroughly blunted by historical shifts, conceptual muddles, and rearrangements in the forms of sexual life that it now represents that which is most resistant to clear classification, discrimination, and division" (2014, 484).

6.7 SEX, GENDER, AND SEXUALITY
IN ETHNOGRAPHIC CONTEXT

Some Euro-American anthropologists may have been surprised by the variability of sex, gender, and sexuality to be found in their own societies, but at least since the days of Margaret Mead, anthropologists have expected to encounter variation in classifications and practices associated with sex, gender, and sexuality outside the Western world. The classic contributions of anthropology to discussions of these issues—as with other issues—are ethnographic examples from societies other than our own that challenge ethnocentric Western assumptions about sex, gender, or sexuality. Second-wave feminism spurred a reconsideration of older ethnographic and historical accounts of non-Western understandings of sex, gender, and sexuality. One consequence was renewed attention to older writings about the cultural and sexual practices of the so-called *berdache*. Until the last decades of the twentieth century, the term *berdache* was used by anthropologists as a technical term to refer to indigenous (especially Native American) social roles in which men (and sometimes women) were allowed to take on the activities and sometimes the dress of members of the opposite sex. Sometimes *berdache* is defined as "male transvestite," but this definition is inadequate because it ignores the fact that a man who took on other aspects of a woman's role might also, as women did, establish sexual relationships with men. Indeed, the term meant "male prostitute" to the early French explorers in the Americas who first used it to describe the men they observed engaging in such behavior. Today, many anthropologists refuse to use the term, as do many contemporary members of indigenous societies who view themselves as modern embodiments of these alternative-gender roles. Some have proposed using terms like *third gender* or *two spirit* instead, although no consensus has yet been achieved. Given our previous discussion, this lack of consensus is hardly surprising.

In the wake of second-wave feminism and the rise of activism by lesbian, gay, bisexual, and transgender persons, anthropologists have in recent decades produced fresh ethnographic evidence concerning variations in beliefs and practices about sex, gender, and sexuality in the many communities where they carried out fieldwork, both within and outside the Western world. In many cases, the peoples and practices they write about have long histories that predate contact with Euro-American societies, which often came in the form of Western colonialism. As noted earlier, explorers and settlers often wrote about such practices, which scandalized them and which were officially forbidden by Christian missionaries. Today, in the context of globalization, Euro-American ideas about sex, gender, and sexuality sometimes mix uneasily with local understandings, even when those local understandings themselves challenge traditional, Western, heteronormative assumptions. We will briefly describe ethnographic research undertaken in Nicaragua that illustrates some of these issues in a less abstract manner.

Anthropologist Roger Lancaster (1992) began studying gender and sexuality among working-class Nicaraguans in the 1980s when he carried out fieldwork intended to assess the effects of the Sandinista Revolution. While he was living in

Managua, the capital city, he learned about *cochones*. *Cochón* could be translated into English as "homosexual," but that would be highly misleading. To understand what the term meant in its local setting meant that Lancaster needed to find out how working-class Nicaraguans interpreted sexual relations between men, and how these fit into a broader set of Nicaraguan ideas about masculinity. First, working-class Nicaraguans contrast a *cochón* with a "real man" (or *macho*), who is admired as active, violent, and dominant. Macho dominance includes conceiving of the penis as a weapon that can be used to dominate one's sexual partner, who is thereby rendered passive, abused, and subordinate. Second, in working-class Nicaragua, such macho sexual behavior involves the domination of women by men, but it also involves the domination of some men by other men. Indeed, a "manly man" is someone who is the active, dominant, penetrating partner in sexual encounters with women *and* men. A "passive" male who allows a "manly man" to penetrate him anally is called a *cochón*.

A North American gay man himself, Lancaster found that Nicaraguan views about *cochones* and manly men differed considerably from the North American ideas about male homosexuality with which he was familiar. First, only the passive *cochón* is stigmatized, whereas males who always take the active, penetrating sexual role in intercourse with females and other males are seen as "normal." Second, the Nicaraguans he knew found hate crimes such as gay bashing to be inconceivable: *Cochones* were made fun of but were also admired performers during the festival of Carnival. In the United States, by contrast, anal intercourse is not the only form that gay male sexual expression may take; both partners have been considered equally stigmatized by same-sex encounters; and gay bashing has been a sometimes deadly reality. Lancaster found that Nicaraguan ideas about male gender and sexuality created an unanticipated roadblock for Sandinistas who wanted to improve the lives of Nicaraguan women and children. The Sandinista government passed a series of laws designed to encourage men to support their families and to discourage irresponsible sex. However, Lancaster found that working-class men, including committed Sandinistas, resisted these laws; they believed that any man who obeyed these laws—that is, who allowed these laws to govern his conduct—would lose his manly identity, effectively turning him into a *cochón*.

The Sandinistas were replaced in 1992 by an administration supported by the US government; and when anthropologist Cymene Howe visited Nicaragua after this change in regime, the country had been politically transformed. Howe carried out ethnographic fieldwork in the late 1990s and early 2000s on women, sexuality, and social change (2013). The Nicaraguans she knew were familiar not only with the traditional category of *cochón* but also with the category of *cochona*, a "manly woman," although women's same-sex sexuality was less publicly visible than that of men. Howe learned that the partners and girlfriends of *cochonas* were described as *feminina* or *muy mujer* (very womanly). Not unlike the situation of manly men, feminine women could become involved in sexual relationships with *cochonas*, without losing their status as "normal" women.

At the time of Howe's fieldwork, newer labels for same-sex sexuality such as gay, homosexual, and lesbian had entered the vocabularies of many Nicaraguans she knew, especially activists working to transform public understandings of same-sex sexuality in the country, who were the focus of her research. But she was carrying out this research during a period (1992–2007) in which Nicaragua had on the books Latin America's strictest anti-sodomy law. Under these conditions, the activists Howe studied (and Howe herself) had to be very careful, for there were influential groups, like evangelical Christians, who backed the law and were hostile to their work. Howe learned that many women who had been active in the Sandinista revolution had since transformed themselves into "sexual rights activists," working to protect women who engaged in stigmatized sexual practices from the state. In post–Cold War, neoliberal economic conditions, these activists discovered that obtaining funding for their work required meeting the expectations of donors from North America and Europe. Yet they also knew that many of the tactics being urged on them by their donor allies would not be successful in Nicaragua. The fact that they chose to describe their work vaguely, as an attempt to establish "sexual rights," reflects these differences. The activists' work "highlights sexuality as a political object and joins it to rights as a political method, without delineating a particular identity category" (Howe 2013, 13).

One of the activists' most successful efforts was to spread their message using public media like radio and magazines, which protected the identities both of the activists themselves and of those interested in their messages. Perhaps not surprisingly, they ran into difficulties when they attempted to persuade both *cochonas* and *femininas* to adopt a lesbian identity. Many *cochonas*, especially from rural parts of Nicaragua, subscribed to the same distinction between active and passive sexuality as the manly men whom Lancaster knew, and they stoutly refused to recognize any commonality between them and their passive *feminina* partners. In urban areas, however, where nontraditional understandings of women's same-sex sexuality are gaining ground, Howe concluded that *femininas* and *cochonas* were indeed being incorporated into a new, more expansive sexual category (2013, 18).

FOR FURTHER READING

Sex, Gender, and Feminism in the Twentieth Century   Di Leonardo 1991; Lewin 2006; Merry 2009; Miller 1993; Ortner 1974

Sex, Gender, Race, and Class   Andersen and Collins 2012; Collins 2008; Hartigan 2013; Lykke 2012

Gender Performativity   Butler 2006

Theoretical Diversity in Studies of Sex and Gender   Stimpson and Herdt 2014

Sex, Gender, and the Body   Herdt 1994; Karkazis 2008

Sex, Gender, and Sexuality   Blackwood and Wieringa 1999; Gutmann 1997; Howe 2013; Lancaster 1992; Stone 2014; Suggs and Miracle 1993; Weston 1993

CHAPTER 7

Relatedness: Kinship, Marriage, Family, and Friendship

The key terms and concepts covered in this chapter, in the order in which they appear:

relatedness	marriage
kinship	
	exogamy
descent	endogamy
consanguineal kin	
adoption	monogamy
	polygamy
bilateral descent	polygyny
bilateral kindred	polyandry
unilineal descent	bridewealth
patrilineal	dowry
matrilineal	sororate
unilineal descent	levirate
groups	
patrilineage	family
matrilineage	
lineage	divorce
clan	
	friendship
kinship terminologies	
fictive kin	

People in all societies live in worlds of social ties. They consider themselves to be connected to other people in a variety of different ways and also consider that there are some people to whom they are not connected at all. Some anthropologists refer to these socially recognized connections as **relatedness**. There are many forms of relatedness that may be recognized in a given society, based on such categories as friendship, marriage, adoption, procreation, descent from a common ancestor, common labor, coresidence, sharing food, and sharing some kind of substance (e.g., blood, spirit, or nationality). Two of the most important forms of relatedness that have interested anthropologists since the birth of the field in the late nineteenth century have been **kinship** and marriage: the various systems of social organization that societies have constructed on principles derived from the universal human experiences of mating, birth, and nurturance. Members of Western societies influenced by the sciences of biology and genetics frequently believe that kinship relationships are (or should be) a direct reflection of the biology and genetics of human reproduction. Nevertheless, they are aware that, even in their own societies, kinship is not the same thing as biology.

7.1 KINSHIP VERSUS BIOLOGY

Europeans and North Americans know that in their societies, mating is not the same as marriage, although traditional Euro-American heteronormative assumptions anticipate, and encourage, mating between the partners (until recently presumed to be one man and one woman). Similarly, all births do not constitute valid links of descent; in some societies, children whose parents have not been married according to accepted legal or religious specifications do not fit the cultural logic of descent, and many societies offer few positions that they can properly fill. Finally, not all acts of nurturance are recognized as adoption. Consider, for example, the status of foster parents in the United States whose custody of the children they care for is officially temporary and can terminate if someone else clears the hurdles necessary to adopt those children legally.

Thus, mating, birth, and nurturance are ambiguous human experiences, and culturally constructed systems of kinship try to remove some of that ambiguity by paying selective attention to some aspects of these phenomena while downplaying or ignoring others. For example, one society may emphasize the female's role in childbearing and base its kinship system on this, paying little formal attention to the male's role in conception. Another society may trace connections through men, emphasizing the paternal role in conception and reducing the maternal role to that of passive incubator for the male seed. A third society may encourage its members to adopt not only children to rear but adult siblings for themselves, thus blurring the link between biological reproduction and family creation. Even though they contradict one another, all three understandings can be justified with reference to the panhuman experiences of mating, birth, and nurturance.

Every kinship system therefore emphasizes certain aspects of human reproductive experience and culturally constructs its own theory of human nature, defining how people develop from infants into mature social beings. Put another way, kinship is an *idiom*: a selective interpretation of the common human experiences of mating, birth, and nurturance. The result is a set of coherent principles that allow people to assign one another membership in particular groups. These principles normally cover several significant issues: how to carry out the reproduction of legitimate group members (marriage or adoption), where group members should live after marriage (residence rules), how to establish links between generations (descent or adoption), and how to pass on social positions (succession) or material goods (inheritance).

Collectively, kinship principles define social groups, locate people within those groups, and position the people and groups in relation to one another both in space and over time. While this set of principles may be coherent, it is also open to modification, negotiation, and even legal challenge as is shown by the ambiguities and questions raised by the consequences of *new reproductive technologies*—technologically mediated reproductive practices such as in vitro fertilization, artificial insemination, surrogate parenthood, and sperm banks (see chapter 6). New types of kin ties are also being created in the United States through the process of organ transplantation from brain-dead individuals to people who need organs to survive. To the surprise of some of the professionals who manage organ transplantation, the recipients and families of the donors not only want to meet one another but also have developed kin relationships (Sharp 2006). A man in his mid-60s who received the heart of a teenager now calls the donor's sister "Sis," and she calls him "Bro." The donor's mother, in her mid-50s, and the recipient, call each other "Mom" and "Son." Sharp found that for the people involved the transplanted organ was believed to carry some essence of the donor with it, and this powerfully connected the recipient to the kin of the donor. This was particularly true in the relationship of the donor's mother to the recipient. (See also chapter 11.)

7.2 DESCENT

Anthropologists traditionally use the term **descent** to refer to culturally defined relationships based on birth and nurturance. People related to one another by descent are what English speakers often refer to as "blood" relations and are socially relevant connections based on either parent–child relationships or sibling relationships. Anthropologists use the term **consanguineal kin** to refer to all those people who are linked to one another by birth as blood relations (the word comes from the Latin *sanguineus*, meaning "of blood"). In addition, however, a consanguineal kinship group may include individuals whose membership in the group was established not by birth but by means of culturally specific rituals of incorporation that resemble what Euro-Americans call **adoption**. Incorporation via adoption often is seen to function in a way that parallels consanguinity because it makes adopted persons and those who adopt them of the "same flesh." The transformation that incorporates adoptees frequently is explained in terms of *nurturance*: feeding, clothing, sheltering, and otherwise attending to the physical and emotional well-being of an individual for an extended period. Ethnographers have shown repeatedly that kinship bonds established by adoption can be just as strong as bonds established through birth. Indeed, in her study of adoption in Zumbagua, Ecuador, Mary Weismantel (1995) observes that many Zumbaguans are closer to their adoptive family than they are to their biological parents.

Because they are based on parent–child links that connect the generations, relations of descent have a time depth. In establishing patterns of descent, the cultures of the world rely on one of two basic strategies: either people are connected to one another through *both* their mothers and fathers, or they are connected by links traced *either* through the mother *or* the father but not both.

7.3 BILATERAL DESCENT

When people believe themselves to be just as closely related to their father's side of the family as to their mother's side, the term that is used is **bilateral descent** (this is sometimes also referred to as *cognatic descent*). Anthropologists have identified two different kinds of kinship groups based on bilateral descent. One is the *bilateral descent group*, an unusual form that consists of a set of people who claim to be related to one another through descent from a common ancestor, some through their mother's side and some through their father's; the other is the *bilateral kindred*, a much more common form that consists of all the individuals, traced through males or females, linked to one person or group of siblings.

The **bilateral kindred** is the kinship group that most Europeans and North Americans know. A bilateral kindred forms around particular individuals and includes all the people linked to that individual through kin of both sexes—people usually called *relatives* in English. These people form a group only because of their connection to the central person, known in the terminology of kinship as *Ego*. In North American society, bilateral kindreds assemble at events associated with Ego: when he or she is baptized, confirmed, bar or bat mitzvahed, married, or buried. Each person within Ego's bilateral kindred has his or her own separate kindred. For example, Ego's father's sister's daughter has a kindred that includes people related to her through her father and her father's siblings—people to whom Ego is not related. This is simultaneously the major strength and major weakness of bilateral kindreds. That is, they have overlapping memberships, and they do not endure beyond the lifetime of an individual Ego. But they can be widely extended, and they can form broad networks of people who are somehow related to one another. Marilyn Strathern (1996) has argued that these networks are ordinarily cut down to manageable size by practical factors such as the limitations of members' knowledge. At the same time, the logic behind the networks does not cease to operate, and always has the potential to reveal new links, and new relatives, that people did not know they had. The Internet has been a great help to people searching for lost or unknown relatives.

Kinship systems create social relationships by defining sets of interlocking statuses and roles (defined in chapter 5). Thus, a man is to behave in the same way to all his "uncles" and in another way to his "father"—and they are to behave to him as "nephew" and "son," respectively. (Perhaps he owes labor to anyone he calls "uncle" and is owed protection and support in return.) In anthropology, these are referred to as the *rights and obligations of kinship*. In a bilateral kindred, the "broad networks of people who are somehow related to one another" means that no matter where a person may be, if he or she finds kin there, the person and the kin have a basis for social interaction. This basis for interaction is different from the possible social interactions that the person might have with strangers (in this case, nonkin).

Organization in bilateral kindreds is advantageous when members of social groups need flexible ways of establishing ties to kin who do not live in one place. They are also useful when valued resources, such as farmland, are limited, and every generation must be distributed across available plots in an efficient and flexible manner. Bilateral kindreds become problematic, however, in at least four kinds of social circumstances:

1. when clear-cut membership in a particular social group must be determined;
2. when social action requires the formation of groups that are larger than individual families;
3. when conflicting claims to land and labor must be resolved; and
4. when people are concerned with perpetuating a specific social order over time.

In societies that face these dilemmas, unilineal descent groups are usually found.

7.4 UNILINEAL DESCENT

The second major descent strategy, **unilineal descent**, is based on the principle that the most significant kin relationships must be traced through *either* the mother *or* the father but not both. Unilineal descent groups are found in more societies today than any other kind. Those unilineal groups that are based on links traced through a person's father (or male kin) are called **patrilineal** (or *agnatic*); those traced through a mother (or female kin) are called **matrilineal** (or *uterine*). (Note that lineages are institutions—people do not choose whether they'd like to be patrilineal or matrilineal; these are the standardized, long-established social forms through which they learn about individuals and groups to whom they are related and how to interact with them.)

Unilineal descent groups are found all over the world. They are all based on the principle that significant relationships are created via links through one parent rather than the other. Membership in a unilineal descent group is based on the membership of the appropriate parent in the group. In a patrilineal system, an individual belongs to a group formed by links through males, the lineage of his or her father. In a matrilineal system, an individual belongs to a group formed by links through females, the lineage of his or her mother. "Patrilineal" and "matrilineal" do not mean that only men belong to one and only women to the other; rather, the terms refer to the principle by which membership is conferred. In a patrilineal society, women and men belong to a **patrilineage** formed by father–child links; similarly, in a matrilineal society, men and women belong to a **matrilineage** formed by mother–child connections. In other words, membership in the group is in principle unambiguous: an individual belongs to only one lineage. This is in contrast to a bilateral kindred in which an individual belongs to overlapping groups.

Talk of patrilineal or matrilineal descent focuses attention on the kind of social group created by this pattern of descent: the lineage. A **lineage** is composed of all those people who believe they can specify the parent–child links that connect them to one another through a common ancestor. Typically, lineages vary in size from 20 or 30 members to several hundred or more.

Many anthropologists have argued that the most important feature of lineages is that they are corporate in organization. That is, a lineage has a single legal identity such that, to outsiders, all members of the lineage are equal in law to all others. In the case of a blood feud, for example, the death of any opposing lineage member avenges the lineage member whose death began the feud; the death of the actual murderer is not required (feuding is defined in chapter 8). Lineages are also corporate in that they control property, such as land or herds, as a unit.

Finally, until the modern nation-state extended its reach, lineages were the main political associations in the societies that had them. Individuals had no political or legal status in such societies except through lineage membership. Members of lineages had relatives who were outside the lineage, but their own political and legal status derived from the lineage to which they belong.

Because membership in a lineage is determined through a direct line from father or mother to child, lineages can endure over time and in a sense have an independent existence. As long as people can remember their common ancestor, the group of people descended from that common ancestor can endure. Most lineage-based societies have a time depth that covers about five generations: grandparents, parents, Ego, children, and grandchildren.

When members of a descent group believe that they are in some way connected but cannot specify the precise genealogical links, they compose what anthropologists call a **clan**. Usually, a clan is made up of lineages that the larger society's members believe to be related to one another through links that go back to mythical times. Sometimes the common ancestor is said to be an animal that lived at the beginning of time. The important point to remember in distinguishing lineages and clans is that lineage members can specify the precise genealogical links back to their common ancestor ("Your mother was Eileen, her mother was Miriam, her sister was Rachel, her daughter was Ruth, and I am Ruth's son"), whereas clan members ordinarily cannot ("Our foremother was Turtle who came out of the sea when this land was settled. Turtle's children were many and for many generations raised sweet peas on our land. So it was that Violet, mother of Miriam and Rachel, was born of the line of the Turtle. . . ."). The clan is thus larger than any lineage and also more diffuse in terms of both membership and the hold it has over individuals.

Historically, anthropologists have shown how lineages might endure over time in societies in which no other form of traditional organization lasted, becoming the foundation of social life in the society. Lineages might be regarded as the foundation of social life; however, this does not mean that they are immovable and inflexible. People can use lineage and clan membership to pursue their interests. Because lineage depth frequently extends to about five generations, the exact circumstances of lineage origins can be hazy and open to negotiation.

Perhaps "Miriam" and "Rachel" from the preceding example have another sister whom everyone "forgot about" until someone appears who claims lineage membership as a descendant of the forgotten sister. If there are good reasons for including this person in the lineage, this claim might well be accepted.

By far the most common form of lineage organization is the patrilineage, which consists of all the people (male and female) who believe themselves to be related to one another because they are related to a common male ancestor by links through men. The prototypical kernel of a patrilineage is the father–son pair. Female members of patrilineages normally leave the lineage to marry, but in most patrilineal societies, women do not give up their membership in their own lineages. In a number of societies, women play an active role in the affairs of their own patrilineages for many years—usually until their interest in their own children directs their attention toward the children's lineage (which is, of course, the lineage of their father, the woman's husband).

By contrast, in a matrilineal society, descent is traced through women rather than through men. Superficially, a matrilineage is a mirror image of a patrilineage, but certain features make it distinct. First, the prototypical kernel of a matrilineage is the sister–brother pair—a matrilineage may be thought of as a group of brothers and sisters connected through links made by women. Brothers marry out and often live with the families of their wives, but they maintain an active interest in the affairs of their own lineage. Second, the most important man in a boy's life is not his father (who is not in his lineage) but his mother's brother, from whom he will receive his lineage inheritance. Third, the amount of power women exercise in matrilineages is still being debated in anthropology. A matrilineage is not the same thing as a *matriarchy* (a society in which women rule); brothers often retain what appears to be a controlling interest in the lineage. Some anthropologists claim that the male members of a matrilineage are supposed to run the lineage, even though there is more autonomy for women in matrilineal societies than in patrilineal ones; they suggest that the day-to-day exercise of power tends to be carried out by the brothers or sometimes the husbands. A number of studies, however, have questioned the validity of these generalizations. Trying to say something about matrilineal societies in general is difficult because they vary a great deal. The ethnographic evidence suggests that matrilineages must be examined on a case-by-case basis.

For Jews, Jewishness—membership in the Jewish people—has historically been passed matrilineally. A man or a woman whose father was Jewish but whose mother was not would have to go through a ritual that would incorporate them into the Jewish people, while such was not the case for people whose mother was Jewish (in the United States, the Reform movement of Judaism has recently moved to accept any person who has at least one parent who is Jewish as Jewish). This has led to interesting consequences in Israel as assisted reproduction has become more common. Israel is a pronatalist state, meaning that having children is encouraged; and the national health system in Israel supports access to reproductive technologies to all women, married or not, who wish to have children. Following the logic of Jewishness being passed matrilineally, then, means that the children of Jewish women who have been conceived through in vitro fertilization are automatically Jewish, and the religious background of the sperm donor is irrelevant. Indeed, due to a particular complication in Jewish family law, it may actually be better in certain instances if the sperm donor is *not* Jewish (Kahn 2000).

7.5 KINSHIP TERMINOLOGIES

People everywhere use special terms to address and refer to people they recognize as kin; anthropologists call these **kinship terminologies**. Consider the North American kinship term *aunt*. This term seems to refer to a woman who occupies a unique biological position, but it in fact refers to a woman who may be related to a person in one of four different ways: as father's sister, mother's sister, father's brother's wife, or mother's brother's wife. From the perspective of North American kinship, all those women have something in common, and they are all placed into the same kinship category and called by the same kin term. Prototypically, one's aunts are women one generation older than oneself and are sisters or sisters-in-law of one's parents. However, North Americans may also refer to their mother's best friend as "aunt." By doing so, they recognize the strength of this system of classification by extending it to include what many anthropologists traditionally called **fictive kin** (also discussed in chapter 5). In communities where formal kinship systems are still strong, speaking of fictive kin may be appropriate if it maps onto local distinctions between those considered formally to be relatives and those to whom kin terms are informally extended. But much recent kinship research has highlighted the flexibility of relatedness, and many anthropologists would argue that to presume that all people distinguish between "real" and "fictive" kin is a distortion.

Despite the variety of kinship systems in the world, by the middle of the twentieth century, anthropologists had identified six major patterns of kinship terminology based on how people categorized their cousins. The six patterns reflected common solutions to structural problems faced by societies organized in terms of kinship. They provided clues concerning how the vast and undifferentiated world of potential kin may be organized. Kinship terminologies suggest both the external boundaries and the internal divisions of the kinship groups, and they outline the structure of rights and obligations assigned to different members of the society. The major criteria that are used for building kinship terminologies are listed here, from the most common to the least common:

Generation. Kin terms distinguish relatives according to the generation to which the relatives belong. In English, the term *cousin* conventionally refers to someone of the same generation as Ego.

Gender. The gender of the individual is used to differentiate kin. In Spanish, *primo* refers to a male cousin and *prima* to a female cousin. In English, cousins are not distinguished on the basis of gender, but *uncle* and *aunt*, for example, are distinguished on the basis of both generation and gender.

Affinity. A distinction is made on the basis of connection through marriage, or affinity. This criterion is used in Spanish when *suegra* (Ego's spouse's mother) is distinguished from *madre* (Ego's mother). In matrilineal societies, Ego's mother's sister and father's sister are distinguished from each other on the basis of affinity. The mother's sister is a direct, lineal relative, and the father's sister is an affine; they are called by different terms.

Collaterality. A distinction is made between kin who are believed to be in a direct line and those who are "off to one side," linked to Ego through a lineal relative. In English, the distinction of collaterality can be seen in the distinction between mother and aunt or between father and uncle.

Bifurcation. Bifurcation distinguishes the mother's side of the family from the father's side. The Swedish kin terms *morbror* and *farbror* are bifurcating terms, one referring to the mother's brother and the other to the father's brother, respectively.

Relative age. Relatives of the same category may be distinguished on the basis of relative age—that is, whether they are older or younger than Ego. Among the Ju/'hoansi of Southern Africa, for example, speakers must separate "older brother" (*!ko*) from "younger brother" (*tsin.*)

Gender of the linking relative. This criterion is related to collaterality. The gender of the linking relative distinguishes cross relatives (usually cousins) from parallel relatives (also usually cousins). Parallel relatives are linked through two brothers or two sisters. *Parallel cousins*, for example, are Ego's father's brother's children or Ego's mother's sister's children. Cross relatives are linked through a brother–sister pair. *Cross cousins* are Ego's mother's brother's children or father's sister's children. The gender of either Ego or the cousins does not matter; the important factor is the gender of the linking relatives.

7.6 WHAT IS MARRIAGE?

The complexities and ambiguities of descent are many. The study of marriage and the family offers just as many complications, the first of which is how to define these terms. If we take the Euro-American heteronormative understanding of *marriage* as a prototype, we discover that all societies possess institutions that resemble heteronormative marriage. At the same time, the range of beliefs and practices associated with such institutions is broad, and the degree of overlap is not great. Nevertheless, we tend to classify all these institutions as *marriage* because of the key elements they do have in common. On these grounds, **marriage** prototypically involves a man and a woman, transforms the status of the partners, and stipulates the degree of sexual access the married partners may have to each other, ranging from exclusive to preferential. Marriage also establishes the legitimacy of children born to the wife and creates relationships between the kin of the partners.

We stress the prototypical nature of our definition because although some societies are quite strict about allowing females to marry only males, and vice versa, other societies are not. The ethnographic literature contains many examples of marriage or marriage-like relationships that resemble the prototype in every respect except that the partners may be two men or two women (as defined according to biological sex criteria) or a living woman and the ghost of a deceased male. Sometimes these marriages involve a sexual relationship between the partners; sometimes they do not. Apparently, the institution we are calling *marriage* has been viewed by members of many societies as so useful and valuable that they allow it to include partners of many different kinds—even though in all cases, the prototype people have in mind seems to be a union between a man and a woman. Thus, the ethnographic evidence demonstrates that claims that human marriage has always been between a man and a women are simply false.

Examining the definition of marriage just offered, we note that marriage is a *rite of passage* (see chapter 4). That is, the parties pass from one social status (unmarried persons) to a new social status (that of married persons). In every society, this transformation of status is accompanied by adoption of new roles, but the rights and obligations associated with these roles vary enormously from culture to culture. Prototypically, among the rights and obligations of spouses are socially sanctioned sexual relations with each other. But, again, the nature and exclusivity of these sexual relations vary from culture to culture: Sometimes partners are restricted to having sexual relations only with each other; in some cases, sexual encounters outside marriage are considered less serious for one partner (usually the husband) than for the other partner; and at least one documented society allowed the husband and wife to have sexual intercourse if they wish, but after spending one night together, they needed never see each other again.

In most cultures, it is assumed that the married partners will have children, and the institution of marriage provides the children with a legitimate ascribed social status, based on who their parents are. In some cases, it is as if the father's and the mother's statuses were plotted on a graph, allowing the status of their child to be placed precisely in the social space where the parents' statuses intersect; in other cases, the child's status depends solely on the position of one or the other parent. In addition, in most cultures, marriage creates formal relationships between the kin of the husband and the kin of the wife. By contrast, while mating may produce grandparents, it cannot produce in-laws or a formal relationship between the parents of the father and the parents of the mother. This aspect of marriage also has important social consequences.

7.7 WHOM TO MARRY AND WHERE TO LIVE

Societies use kinship systems to exercise control over the marriages contracted by their members. When marriage rules specify that a person is to marry outside a defined social group—extended family, lineage, clan, class, ethnic group, or religious sect, for example—anthropologists say that the society in question practices **exogamy** (or *out-marriage*). The opposite situation—in which a person is expected to marry *within* a defined social group—is called **endogamy**. These patterns may be obligatory (i.e., strictly enforced) or merely preferred.

Once married, the spouses must live somewhere. Anthropologists have identified several patterns of *postmarital residence*. *Neolocal* residence, in which the new partners set up an independent household at a place of their own choosing, should be familiar to people who have grown up in the United States, Canada, and most of Europe. Neolocal residence tends to be found in societies that are more or less individualistic in their social organization, especially those in which bilateral kindreds also are found. Neolocal residence exists throughout the world but is most common in nation-states and in societies bordering the Mediterranean Sea. Some societies with bilateral kindreds have *bilocal* residence patterns in which married partners live with (or near) either the wife's or the husband's parents. Despite this flexibility in allowing married partners to make decisions regarding where they might live, very few societies with bilocal residence have been described in the anthropological literature.

The most common residence pattern in the world, in terms of the number of societies in which it is practiced, is *patrilocal* residence in which the partners in a marriage live with (or near) the husband's father. (In older anthropological writing, the term *virilocal* is sometimes used to distinguish residing with the husband's kin from residing specifically with the husband's father, for which the term *patrilocal* was reserved.) Patrilocal residence is strongly associated with patrilineal descent systems—about 85 percent of societies in which postmarital residence is patrilocal are also patrilineal. If children are born into a patrilineage and inherit from the father or other patrilineage members, then there are advantages to rearing them among the members of the lineage.

When the partners in a marriage live with (or near) the wife's mother, anthropologists use the term *matrilocal* residence. (Again, in older anthropological writing, the term *uxorilocal* is sometimes used to refer to residence with the wife's kin, as distinct from living with the wife's mother.) Matrilocal residence is found exclusively in matrilineal societies (some matrilineal societies are patrilocal). Anthropologists who study matrilineal societies have observed that sometimes the married partners live with the husband's mother's brother. This is based on the logic of matrilineal descent in which the socially significant older male in a man's life is his mother's brother because he is a member of the man's matrilineage, while his own father is not. In these cases, anthropologists use the term *avunculocal* residence, building on the word *avuncular*, meaning "of uncles." As might be expected, avunculocal residence is found only in matrilineal societies, and in contrast to matrilocal residence, it emphasizes the inheritance and labor patterns linking men in a matrilineage.

7.8 HOW MANY SPOUSES?

You may have noticed that we use the phrase *married partners* rather than the more common *married couple*. This is because the number of people who may be married to one another at the same time also varies across cultures. A marriage pattern that permits a person to be married to only one spouse at a time is called **monogamy**. The term can also be used to refer to any marriage in which one person has only one spouse. The term **polygamy** is used to refer to marriage patterns in which a person may have more than one spouse at the same time, a practice also sometimes called *plural marriage*. Polygamy has two major forms: polygyny and polyandry. **Polygyny** is a marriage pattern in which a man may be married to more than one woman at a time. It is the most common of all marriage patterns in the world in terms of number of societies in which it is permitted. Polygyny enables a lineage, especially one with male children, to establish alliances with many other lineages through marriage.

In polygynous societies, it should be noted, not every man has more than one wife. In Islamic societies, for example, a man is permitted to have as many as four wives, but only on the condition that he can support them all equally well. Today, some Muslim authorities argue that "equal support" must be emotional as well as material. Furthermore, convinced that no man can feel exactly the same toward each of his wives, they have concluded that monogamy must be the rule. Other polygynous societies set no limit on the number of wives a man can marry. However, regardless of any limitations on the number of wives, polygynous societies are faced with a real demographic problem: because the number of men and women in any society is approximately equal, for every man with two wives, there is one man without a wife. To help solve this problem, men may be obliged to wait until they are older to marry, and women may be pressed to marry at a very young age; but even these practices do not completely eliminate the imbalance. As a result, polygyny is regularly connected with power in societies that practice it. That is, those men who are rich and powerful have multiple wives; those men who are poor and powerless either cannot marry, marry very late, have relationships outside of marriage, or marry women who are equally dispossessed.

Polyandry, a pattern in which a woman is married to more than one man at a time, is the rarest of the three marriage patterns. In some polyandrous societies, a woman may marry several brothers. In others, she may marry men who are not related to one another and who all will live together in a single household. The tendency in polyandrous societies—especially in those in which a woman marries a set of brothers—is to intensify the connections between lineages and to limit the number of potential heirs in the next generation because, no matter how many husbands a woman has, there is a limit to the number of offspring she can bear. This makes it easier for families to keep control of jointly held property, such as land.

7.9 MARRIAGE AS ALLIANCE

In most societies, a marriage is an alliance between two families or lineages, not merely between two individuals; and it frequently requires traditional exchanges of wealth to legitimize it. These are usually characterized as bride service, bridewealth (or bride "price"), and dowry. In some societies, the prospective groom must work for the family of the bride for a predetermined length of time before they may marry, a practice called *bride service*. Other societies solemnize marriages with an exchange of **bridewealth**: certain symbolically important goods that are transferred from the immediate family of the groom (or his lineage) to the family of the bride (or her lineage) on the occasion of their marriage. *Symbolically important goods* include those things that are considered to be appropriate for exchange at a marriage in a specific society—for example, cattle, cash, shell ornaments, cotton cloth, bird feathers, or household items. Bridewealth exchange is most common in patrilineal societies that combine agriculture, pastoralism, and patrilocal postmarital residence. Through their research in societies that exchange bridewealth, anthropologists have found that it is fundamentally incorrect to think of bridewealth as "buying" a wife. Rather, anthropologists view bridewealth as a way of compensating the bride's relatives for the loss of her labor and childbearing capacities. That is, when the bride goes to live with her husband and his lineage, she will be working and producing children for his people, not her own.

Bridewealth transactions create affinal relations between the relatives of the wife and those of the husband. The wife's relatives in turn use the bridewealth they receive for her to find a bride for her brother in yet another kinship group. In many societies in Eastern and Southern Africa, a woman gains power and influence over her brother because the cattle that her marriage brings allow him to marry and continue their lineage.

Dowry, by contrast, is typically a transfer of family wealth, usually from parents to their daughter, at the time of her marriage. It is found primarily in the agricultural societies of Europe and Asia, but it has been brought to some parts of Africa with the arrival of religions like Islam that support the practice. In societies in which both men and women are seen as heirs to family wealth, dowry is sometimes regarded as the way women receive their inheritance. Dowries often are considered the wife's contribution to the establishment of a new household to which the husband may bring other forms of wealth or prestige. In stratified societies, the size of a woman's dowry frequently ensures that when she marries, she will continue to enjoy her accustomed style of life. In some stratified societies, an individual of lower status sometimes marries an individual of higher status, a situation in which the children will take on the higher status. This practice is called *hypergamy*, and it is usually one in which the lower-status person is the wife and the dowry is seen (sometimes explicitly) as an exchange for the higher social position that the husband confers.

The ties that link kinship groups through marriage are sometimes so strong that they endure beyond the death of one of the partners. In some matrilineal and some patrilineal societies, if a wife dies young, the husband's line will ask the deceased wife's line for a substitute, often her sister. This practice, called **sororate** (from the Latin *soror*, "sister"), is connected with both alliance strength and bridewealth. That is, both lines—that of the widower and that of the deceased wife—wish to maintain the alliance formed (and frequently continued) by the marriage. At the same time, if a man marries the sister of his deceased wife, the bridewealth that his line gave to the line of the first wife will not have to be returned, so the disruption caused by the wife's death will be lessened. In many societies, if the husband dies, the wife may (and in rare cases be obligated to) marry one of his brothers. This practice, called the **levirate** (from the Latin *levir*, "husband's brother"), is intended, like the sororate, to maintain the alliance between descent groups. In some societies, it also functions as a kind of social security system for widows who might otherwise be destitute after the death of their husbands.

7.10 FAMILY

Kinship and marriage frequently are understood, both by scholars and by the people who marry, as creating families. *Family* is another term that seeks to label a practice that is apparently universal but so variable as to make definition difficult. One minimal definition of a **family** would be that it consists of a woman and her dependent children. Some anthropologists prefer to distinguish the *conjugal family*, which is a family based on marriage—at its minimum, a husband and wife (a spousal pair) and their children—from the *nonconjugal family*, which consists of a woman and her children. In a nonconjugal family, the husband/father may be occasionally present or completely absent. Anthropologists note that nonconjugal families are never the only form of family organization in a society, and, in fact, are usually rather infrequent. However, in some large-scale industrial societies, including the United States, nonconjugal families have become increasingly common. In most societies, the conjugal family is coresident—that is, spouses live in the same dwelling, along with their children—but in some matrilineal societies, the husband lives with his matrilineage, the wife and children live with theirs, and the husband visits his wife and children.

Families can be characterized according to their structure. The neolocal, monogamous family is called the *nuclear family* and is composed of two generations: the parents and their unmarried children. In the nuclear family, each member has a series of evolving relationships with every other member: husband and wife, parents and children, and children with one another. These are the principal lines along which jealousy, controversy, and affection develop in neolocal monogamous families.

The *polygynous family* is composed of the husband, his cowives, and their children. The polygynous family adds complexity in the older generation not found in the nuclear family—the relationships among the cowives and the relationship of the group of wives with the single husband. Additional complexity arises in the younger generation, as children have connections to half-siblings (the same father but a different mother) and full siblings (the same father and same mother), as well as an additional set of adults in their lives—their mother's cowives. These differences make the internal dynamics of polygynous families different from those of nuclear families.

The two family structures discussed so far are similar in that they are two generations in depth and involve one set of spouses (a man and a woman in the nuclear family, a man and his wives in a polygynous one). When families include a third generation—parents, married children, and grandchildren—anthropologists speak about *extended families*. When families maintain a two-generation depth but expand outward so that a set of siblings and their spouses and children live together, anthropologists talk about *joint families.* Simply put, a joint family is composed of several brothers and their wives and children or several sisters and their husbands and children. In societies in which they are found, extended and joint families are ideal patterns, which means that although people might want to live that way, not everyone is able to.

In recent years in the United States, anthropologists have observed the emergence of new family types. The *blended family* occurs when previously divorced people marry, bringing with them children from their previous marriages. The internal dynamics of the new family—which can come to include his children, her children, and their children—may sometimes have some similarities to the dynamics of polygynous families. Specifically, the relations among the children and their relations to each parent may be complex and negotiated over time.

A second new form is the *family by choice,* a term used by some LGBT people to refer to families that are not the product of heterosexual marriage. Derived from a model that resembles kinship based on nurturance (defined earlier in this chapter), some North American LGBT people argue that "whatever endures is real." As a result, the group of people that endures—which may include some or all of the kin of each member of the couple, their close friends, and children of either member or children who may be adopted—forms a family. Before marriage between gay or lesbian couples became legally possible in the United States, LGBT activists used this model as a resource in their struggle to obtain for long-standing families of choice some of the same legal rights enjoyed by traditional heterosexual families—such as hospital visiting privileges, partner insurance coverage, joint adoption, and property rights.

What new possibilities for families might appear in the twenty-first centuries? Anthropologist Jennifer Robertson describes a dream of the Japanese future promoted by Prime Minister Shinzo Abe in Japan, which relies on the roboticization of Japanese society not only to revive the Japanese economy but also to provide a technological solution that will reverse the growing demographic trend of young Japanese women who refuse to marry and have children. Supposedly, women will be more willing to be stay-at-home wives and mothers if they have humanoid household robots to relieve the burdens of housekeeping and child care. Robertson observes, however, that this vision of a future robotized Japanese society is better understood as "reactionary postmodernism" (2018, 49); that is, "the *renewal* of old values—especially those represented by the patriarchal extended family and wartime ideologies" (2018, 35). Many Japanese citizens, especially women, challenge this robotized vision of the Japanese future that is "premised on a future imagined as an improved and improvised version of the past" (2018, 79).

At the same time, in a cultural context where Shinto and Buddhist religious understandings recognize no sharp divide between human and nonhuman, living and nonliving, the Japanese find it much easier than Euro-Americans to imagine the "integration of robots into human (and specifically Japanese) society where they share familial bonds of kinship and perform familial roles"

(Robertson 2018, 131). Indeed, Japanese engineers are legally regarded as "fathers" of their robots, and such robots have been awarded Japanese citizenship, family membership, and residence permits (2018, 137–145.) "The dark irony remains that while Japanese 'familial civility'—epitomized by the household and corporate sector and codified by policy makers—embraces robots, the same is not freely extended to minorities, non-Japanese permanent residents, refugees, migrant workers, or foreigners" (2018, 145).

7.11 DIVORCE

Marriages do not always last, and almost all societies make it possible for married couples to **divorce**—that is, to dissolve the marriage in a socially recognized way, regulating the status of those who were involved with the marriage and any offspring of the marriage. In some societies, it is not merely the people who were married who are involved in the divorce; it may also include other family or lineage members of the divorcing parties whose relationships are also changed by the divorce. In societies in which bridewealth is part of the marriage ceremony, for example, divorce may cause difficulties if the bridewealth must be returned. In such societies, a man who divorces a wife or whose wife leaves him expects her family to return to him some of the bridewealth he offered in exchange for her. But the wife's family may well have exchanged the bridewealth they received when she married to obtain wives for her brothers. As a result, her brothers' marriages may have to be broken up to recoup enough bridewealth from their in-laws to repay their sister's ex-husband or his line. Sometimes a new husband will repay the bridewealth to the former husband's line, thus letting the bride's relatives off the hook.

Grounds for divorce vary from society to society as does which party may initiate divorce. Common grounds for divorce often include nagging, quarreling, cruelty, violence, stinginess, and adultery. Cross culturally, a frequent ground for divorce is childlessness.

Families break apart and new households form in other ways besides divorce. In joint families, for example, the pressures that build up among coresident brothers or sisters often increase dramatically on the death of the father. In theory, the eldest son inherits the position of head of household from his father, but his younger brothers may not accept his authority as readily as they did the father's. Some younger brothers may decide to establish their own households, and so the joint family gradually splits. Each brother whose household splits off from the joint stem usually hopes to start his own joint family; eventually, his sons will bring their wives into the household, and a new joint family emerges out of the ashes of an old one.

7.12 FRIENDSHIP

Anthropologists have devoted surprisingly little attention to **friendship**, and they have found that it is no easier to define it than it is to define other such forms of relatedness as kinship or marriage. Nevertheless, a useful definition might be the relatively "unofficial" bonds that people construct with one another. These tend to be bonds that are personal, affective, and, to a varying degree from society to society, matters of choice (Bell and Coleman 1999). A recent work on friendship (Killick and Desai 2010) argues that friendship evades definition and that it can best be understood, at least from the perspective of the people who use the term in a particular society, as a relationship that contrasts with other ways of relating to people. For instance, many anthropologists have traditionally highlighted the social obligations that require people to engage in certain activities with their kin, precisely because Euro-Americans tend to question the legitimacy of such obligations in their own societies, which emphasize the value of individual autonomy. However, more recent ethnographic work demonstrates that even where kinship or other social obligations are enforced, individuals still develop affective ties with one another that cannot be reduced to such obligations. You might go fishing with someone because that person is your cousin, and kin are obliged to work together on their family's boat; but you may also choose to fish with one *particular cousin* (or with someone who is not a relative at all) because you and that cousin have an unusually close bond. Killick and Desai claim that it is essential to retain the analytic distinction between friendship and kinship "since it is this aspect that appears to be of crucial importance in giving friendship its moral force in so many societies around the world" (Killick and Desai 2010, Kindle location 1%). In other words, when someone from the United States says that her husband is her best friend, she is perfectly aware of the difference between the affinal relationship of husband and wife, and that of the US definition of best friend, and she uses the difference to highlight the kind of relationship she has with her husband.

FOR FURTHER READING

Kinship   Carsten 2003, 2000, 2007; Collier and Yanigasako 1987; Parkin and Stone 2004; Schneider 1968, 1984; Stone 2014
Adoption   Weismantel 1998
New Reproductive Technologies   Kahn 2000; Strathern 1992
Reproduction and Power   Ginsburg and Rapp 1995
Gender   Brettell and Sargent 2013; Karkazis 2008; Lancaster and DiLeonardo 1997; Lewin 2006
Marriage   Hirsch and Wardlow 2006; Levine 1988; Padilla et al. 2007; Sacks 1979; Schuler 1987
Family   Ottenheimer 2006; Robertson 2018; Weston 1991
Friendship   Bell and Coleman 1999; Killick and Desai 2010

CHAPTER 8

Political Anthropology

The key terms and concepts covered in this chapter, in the order in which they appear:

state

political anthropologists

politics

power

agency

political ecology

political economy

raiding

feuding

mediator

negotiation

bloodwealth

warfare

egalitarian

bands

tribes

chiefdoms

social stratification

caste

class

wealth

prestige

complex societies

consensus

headman

big man

law

nationalism

nation

nation-states

imagined community

invention of tradition

domination

hegemony

biopower

governmentality

ideology

hidden transcripts

W hen nineteenth-century ethnologists from Europe and North America began to compare societies across space and over time, they noticed not only that members of different societies made a living in different ways but also that daily life in all these varied societies seemed to unfold in an orderly and predictable manner. The presence of apparent social order in societies of different sizes, organized according to a variety of diverse social principles, puzzled some observers because of their own assumptions about what made social order possible. These ethnologists lived in societies whose leaders assumed that individual human beings were naturally selfish and competitive and thus could live peaceably together only if they were compelled to do so by threat of physical force. That is, they believed that social order was not natural but could result only from the external imposition of power.

8.1 POWER

Power often has been understood first and foremost in terms of physical coercion, especially by European philosophers and social scientists, who traditionally define power in terms of one individual's ability to compel others to do what he or she wants them to do. This view of power seemed natural in societies like those of Europe and America that were organized into states. Anthropologists agree that states were not invented in Europe but first appeared several thousand years ago in half a dozen different regions of the world. Anthropologists group these states together, ancient and modern, because they appear to share certain prototypical features. That is, for anthropologists, a **state** is an independent political entity that controls a geographical territory with clear boundaries and that defends itself from external threats with an army and from internal disorder with police. States have specialized institutions to raise revenue by collecting taxes and to carry out other public duties such as maintaining roads and markets. All these tasks become possible because the state monopolizes the legitimate use of physical force.

Following the religious wars of the sixteenth and seventeenth centuries and the revolutions of the late eighteenth and nineteenth centuries, European history certainly seemed to prove that nothing less than deadly force in the hands of a strong state will keep people in line. As we saw earlier, according to seventeenth-century philosopher Thomas Hobbes, human life without the state was supposed to be "nasty, brutish, and short." And yet, historical and ethnographic materials suggested strongly that, elsewhere in the world, many societies not organized into states had long been able to conduct their external and internal affairs in an orderly fashion. Could it be that power was successfully institutionalized in these societies in forms other than the state?

These kinds of questions have traditionally been asked by **political anthropologists**. These scholars share with political philosophers and political scientists an interest in **politics**: the ways in which power relations (particularly unequal power relations) affect human social affairs. Political anthropologists have paid particular attention to how members of different societies go about making public decisions that affect the society as a whole. They also are interested in why people either accept these decisions as right and proper or criticize them as wrong and improper. Political anthropologists compare how leadership is understood and exercised, how competition between rivals is regulated, and how disputes are settled. In all these areas, people's cultural beliefs and practices clearly play a large role. In recent years, increasing attention has been focused on the ways in which larger regional and global power relations shape opportunities for the exercise of power by local groups (see additional discussion of global issues in chapter 10).

To encompass all these dimensions, many anthropologists prefer to define **power** as a generalized capacity to transform. This definition does not limit power merely to *coercion*, or the use of physical force. Rather, coercion is only one kind of power, and attention must be paid to all those other forms of influence that transform people's practical activities or their ideas about the world *without* relying on physical force. Forms of *persuasive* power range from the charisma of a religious prophet, to the formally proscribed but ubiquitous ability of weaker members of society to manipulate social rules to promote their own well-being, to the outright refusal of compliance shown by factory workers who go on strike. To speak of persuasive power draws attention to the power of individuals. But how much power can individuals exercise? The answer to this question depends on what an "individual" is understood to be. Unlike most other cultures from other places or times, Western capitalist culture exalts individuals and encourages (or forces) them to reject ties to other people, such as relatives, they have not freely chosen. This position, called *individualism*, is based on a view of human nature that sees individuals as the primordial "natural" units in the human world (see discussion of the *social contract* in chapter 5). Individuals are believed to be endowed by nature with the desire to pursue their own personal self-interest above all else. Individualism was well entrenched in the cultures to which the first social scientists belonged, but evidence from their reading and research caused many of them to question its universality. Some anthropologists have used ethnographic evidence showing the ways that individuals are molded by social, cultural, and historical processes to criticize extreme defenses of individualism used by Western elites to justify capitalist cultural practices.

At the beginning of the twenty-first century, anthropologists have mostly rejected the old-fashioned, extreme contrasts between "individual free will" and social, cultural, or historical "determinism." Although they remain critical of defenses of individualism that ignore culture and history, they nevertheless now widely agree that individuals are not just passively molded by their cultures to think and behave in prescribed ways alone. As discussed in chapters 5 and 6, contemporary anthropologists speak of individuals *enacting* or *performing* a range of cultural roles, rather than simply conforming to cultural rules; they also use the term **agency** to refer to individuals' abilities to reflect systematically on taken-for-granted cultural practices, to imagine alternatives, and to take independent action to pursue goals of their own choosing. Unlike deterministic accounts, this view recognizes degrees of individual freedom; but, unlike discussions of "free will," it accepts that people's ideas are always entangled with cultural practices characteristic of their own time and place, which restrict in some ways both the alternatives they are able to imagine and their abilities to act freely in pursuit of those alternatives.

8.2 POLITICAL ECOLOGY AND POLITICAL ECONOMY

As the earlier example of factory workers on strike suggests, for anthropologists, political issues do not develop in a vacuum but are intimately related to other dimensions of collective life, especially economic matters. And attention to economic matters, especially how people make a living, has regularly turned some anthropologists' attention to the relationships between particular societies and the wider environments in which they live. *Ecology* may be defined broadly as the study of the relationships among living organisms and their environments; *ecological anthropology* encompasses a number of anthropological approaches to the study of human populations in terms of the wider ecological contexts to which they must adapt to survive (see chapter 9 for further discussion of ecological anthropology).

In the middle of the twentieth century, Julian Steward and his followers developed the earliest version of ecological anthropology called *cultural ecology.* Cultural ecology focuses on the way specific, often small-scale, societies use culture to fashion adaptations to particular, local ecological settings. This approach resonates with the way anthropologists thought about "societies" and "cultures" at the time: as if they were naturally coherent, self-contained, sociocultural units responsible on their own for adapting (or failing to adapt) to particular kinds of natural environments. At the same time, even though human populations can call on culture to invent tools and forms of social organization that mediate their adaptations to local environments, cultural ecology approached human populations as if they faced the same kinds of adaptive challenges as populations of other species living in the same ecological setting. This approach was shared by other scholars who called themselves *human ecologists.*

But other anthropologists who have adopted ecological perspectives on the study of human populations have objected to the way in which traditional cultural ecology ignores history, especially the political history that links particular local populations with their neighbors. These anthropologists, who describe their approach as **political ecology**, draw attention to the ways in which human groups struggle with one another for control of (usually local) material resources. Although some political ecologists emphasize the ways in which ecological features of the local environment shape the political struggle for resource control, others emphasize the way in which the outcome of political struggles determines which groups will have access to how much of which resources. For example, in the nineteenth century, Eastern African pastoralists such as the Maasai moved their herds of cattle seasonally across large geographical areas in search of water and fresh grass and attempted to control access to permanent sources of water that could sustain herds in times of drought. But in the early twentieth century, after European colonial rule was established in Kenya and Tanganyika, much of the land that Maasai had traditionally relied on, together with its water sources, was taken away from them by the colonial government and allotted to farmers—either other Africans or European settlers. Despite the stated goal of the British colonial administration to increase cattle production,

Maasai found it increasingly difficult to maintain their herds on such limited resources. But the administration usually refused to acknowledge how their own policies of land and water management had severely altered the ecological conditions with which herders had to contend. They preferred to blame Maasai herders for trying to maintain herds that were too large to be supported on the land they had (Hodgson 2004).

A similar divide has characterized the work of anthropologists who have studied economic institutions in different cultural settings (*economic anthropology* is more fully discussed in chapter 9). On one hand, the first economic anthropologists, such as Melville Herskovits (1895–1963), tended to assume the existence of distinct, self-contained societies with varied cultural institutions, including economic institutions, the functioning of which it was the job of the anthropologist to describe and explain. Frequently, it was further assumed that these economic institutions had evolved "naturally" to solve the economic needs of those who used them. Other anthropologists interested in economic relations, however, have rejected the view that economic institutions in particular local societies can be understood on their own terms. Instead, they draw attention to the historical and political factors that have shaped a particular set of economic institutions into their current forms. These anthropologists often see their work as having as much to do with political anthropology as with economic anthropology; more specifically, they see their work as falling within the purview of what has been called **political economy**: that is, the focus is on the political creation (and consequences) of the division of labor in society. Political anthropologists studying non-Western societies that have been subject to colonial domination often find a focus on political economy useful. This perspective offers a framework for describing and explaining how capitalist colonialism disrupted indigenous precapitalist political and economic arrangements, reorganized relations of production, expropriated local wealth and power, and promoted the formation of new social classes.

8.3 DISPUTES AND DISPUTE RESOLUTION

One important focus of political anthropology has been on how the members of different societies, living within different kinds of economic and social institutions, handle their relations with their neighbors. Recall that a key task of the state as a political institution was to defend itself from external attack and from internal subversion. Anthropologists were curious about how societies not organized as states handled these matters. The ethnographic record shows that a variety of mechanisms, formal and informal, have been developed in different times and places. As they often have done when confronted with ethnographic variety, anthropologists invented classifications to sort out the patterns of dispute (and dispute resolution) about which they had information.

Scale is always important when considering these various mechanisms. Consider, for example, the issue of warfare. At the turn of the twenty-first century, when those of us who live in industrialized nation-states think about "warfare," we typically think of a conflict like World War I or World War II in which the professional armies of two or more nation-states clash using modern weapons (machine guns, tanks, bombs, and the like). The war ends when one side concedes defeat, lays down its weapons, and agrees to formal, written terms of surrender. To be sure, many of the armed conflicts being waged in the contemporary world cannot be easily reconciled with such a formal definition of warfare. But even contemporary forms of armed violence carried out by some nonstate actors (often called *terrorism* because of its aim of destabilizing states and generating fear among civilian populations) are rather different from the kinds of violent clashes that have more typically been found in smaller-scale, nonindustrial societies without states. Indeed, it seems quite clear that the kind of organized violence we associate with warfare first appears with the rise of the earliest state societies, some 5,000 years ago. As anthropologist R. Brian Ferguson observes, "By considering the total archaeological record of prehistoric populations of European and the Near East up to the Bronze Age, evidence clearly demonstrates that war began sporadically out of warless conditions, and can be seen, in varying trajectories in different areas, to develop over time as societies became larger, more sedentary, more complex, more bounded, more hierarchical, and in one critically important region, impacted by an expanding state" (2013, 116).

Using ethnographic, historical, and archaeological evidence, anthropologists worked out a set of categories that allowed them to distinguish modern warfare from these other kinds of conflict. For example, violent conflicts can be distinguished from one another in terms of how long they last and what goals they are expected to achieve. **Raiding**, for instance, is defined as a short-term use of force with a limited goal, such as stealing a few head of cattle or other material goods, usually from a neighboring group. Pastoral peoples commonly resort to raiding to recover animals they believe are owed them or simply to increase the size of their own herds at the expense of a nearby group of herders. Raiding can be contrasted with **feuding**, which describes ongoing, chronic hostilities between groups of neighbors or kin. Feuds are politically destabilizing because they are potentially endless. Often a feud begins when a member of one kin group takes the life of a member of a neighboring kin group. Relatives of the dead person feel obliged to avenge the death of their kinsman or kinswoman and so vow to take the equivalent of "an eye for an eye, and a tooth for a tooth." In this way, feuding can be seen as a form of negative reciprocity (defined in chapter 9). Feuding groups do not feel obliged to take the life of the specific individual who killed their relative; the death of any member of the group to which the killer belongs will restore the balance. But the group responsible for the first death will then feel obliged to avenge the death visited on them as repayment for the first death, and so on.

Peoples who engage in feuding are quite aware that this form of retaliation can escalate into a bloodbath. Therefore, some groups have invented cultural institutions that feuding groups can call on to achieve settlement, such as a **mediator**: a formally recognized, neutral third party to whom the disputing parties can appeal to settle their differences. Mediators have no coercive power of their own but instead rely on the persuasive power of **negotiation**—that is, of verbal argument and compromise—to induce the hostile parties to come to a mutually acceptable resolution of their dispute. Mediators play an exceedingly important role when the parties to a feud are close neighbors who must somehow find a way to coexist despite their mutual grievances. Often mediators appeal to traditional practices designed to mollify the aggrieved party, such as an offer by the offending party of a given amount of material wealth (e.g., in livestock or other valuables), a payment frequently referred to as **bloodwealth**. Some anthropologists view the invention of bloodwealth as a major cultural achievement that for millennia has managed to short-circuit feuds and restrain their destructive capacity.

Warfare, by contrast, involves violent conflict on a significantly larger scale. Entire societies mobilize against each other, trying to kill as many members of the other society as possible until one side surrenders to the other. Warfare occurs when persuasive means of dispute resolution, such as diplomacy, either do not exist or have failed or are ignored, and physical combat becomes the only avenue open to settle differences. Of course, none of these classificatory labels is airtight; all of them are designed to highlight what appear to be salient similarities and differences from a political point of view. Real-life cases are always more complex and ambiguous than the labels themselves might suggest. For example, feuding carried out on a grand-enough scale begins to look a lot like warfare.

8.4 FORMS OF POLITICAL ORGANIZATION

The contrast between feuding and warfare draws our attention back to an issue that has preoccupied many political anthropologists: societies that engage in warfare typically have some form of centralized political organization, whereas societies that engage in feuding typically do not. Prehistorians and political anthropologists have compared the different political systems known from archaeology, history, and ethnography. Like the nineteenth-century evolutionists, they recognize four broad types of political systems that appear to have developed over the 200,000 or so years our species has existed and that correlate broadly with other cultural attributes such as subsistence strategies and types of kinship organization (for discussion of subsistence strategies, see chapter 9; for kinship organization, see chapter 7). In the mid-twentieth century, anthropologists like Elman Service and Morton Fried offered new interpretations of cultural evolution that incorporated critiques of nineteenth-century schemes. Their work has influenced most subsequent anthropological discussions of comparative political systems.

The earliest political forms appear to have been **egalitarian**: that is, all (adult) members of the society had roughly equal access to valued resources, both material and social. The oldest human societies we know about archaeologically, which depended on foraging and on egalitarian forms of political organization, have been called **bands**. Foraging societies are small in scale; historically and prehistorically, they were few in number and widely scattered across the land. Bands of foragers typically number no more than fifty individuals coresident at the same time. Tasks are assigned on the basis of gender and age, but the division is not rigid. Kinship systems are generally bilateral (defined in chapter 7), and bands create alliances with one another through marriage. Relations of economic exchange are organized on the basis of reciprocity.

The domestication of plants and animals marked a major shift in the subsistence strategy, supporting somewhat larger egalitarian social groups that anthropologists call **tribes**. The major social change associated with those who took up *horticulture* (extensive agriculture) or those who began to herd animals is seen in the appearance of unilineal kinship groups (defined in chapter 7) that became the joint owners of property in the form of farmland or herds. New cultural forms such as age grades (defined in chapter 5) may create social links that crosscut kinship groups. Kin groups may compete with one another for resources, but they are not ranked hierarchically; indeed, within each kin group, the access of adults to communal resources remains broadly equal.

The erosion of egalitarian political forms is found in societies classified as **chiefdoms**. Chiefdoms make use of the same forms of subsistence and kinship as tribes, but distinctions among lineages emerge in terms of status or ranking. In particular, one lineage is elevated above the rest, and its leader (the chief) becomes a key political figure whose higher status often derives from his role in redistributive economic exchanges (defined in chapter 9). The chief's higher rank (and that of the lineage to which he belongs) gives him an increased opportunity to favor his kin and his supporters with material or social benefits, but he has very limited coercive power. Significant power remains in the hands of lineages, who continue to control their own communal wealth in land or herds. The social differentiation, ranking, and centralization that are incipient in chiefdoms are fully realized with the appearance of states. The state organization described previously (with its territory, army, police, tax collectors, etc.) did not appear until well after the invention of intensive agriculture approximately 10,000 years ago, which generated surpluses that could be used to support full-time occupational specialists such as potters, weavers, metalworkers, priests, and kings.

However, as we saw in Chapters 2 and 5, James Scott has recently argued that evidence traditionally interpreted to support an evolutionary sequence from bands to tribes to chiefdoms to states may tell a rather different story when read "against the grain" (Scott 2017). Situating his analysis within the framework of niche construction, Scott draws attention to the ways our ancestors entered into coevolutionary relationships with other species, and reshaped the nonliving landscape to accommodate these new relationships. Niche construction by states involved not only remaking the landscape by building irrigation canals and new fields but also by elaborating new social institutions capable of managing relations among plants, animals, and human populations. The "rise of the state" was not inevitable. Scott argues that "stateness . . . is . . . less an either/or proposition than a judgment of more or less" (2017, 23). The first social formations possessing the classic "strong definition of stateness" did not appear until the fourth millennium BCE in Mesopotamia (2017, 23–24). And in the face of epidemic disease, raiding and warfare, state institutions often broke down.

Scott emphasizes that those populations who were targeted to labor for the state regularly tried to escape from state control, or to avoid it altogether. The independent political arrangements and subsistence strategies that best allowed them to do this—living in "bands," "tribes" or "chiefdoms," and engaging in foraging, shifting cultivation or pastoralism in landscapes unsuitable for grain agriculture and inaccessible to state armies—have always been relegated to lower rungs on the ladder of civilization, according to the ideologies promoted by state rulers (and by nineteenth-century Western theorists of sociocultural evolution). But Scott rejects such linear evolutionary accounts, interpreting these alternative subsistence strategies and social arrangements as often successful responses to the negative features of life under state rule, even as they allowed other forms of cultural exchange with states to continue. Scott prefers to call these nonlinear entanglements and developments *deep history*, rather than prehistory or cultural evolution.

8.5 SOCIAL STRATIFICATION

As well as monopolizing physical force, state organization enforces **social stratification**, a permanent, inherited inequality between the various component groups of which the society is composed. Anthropologists frequently distinguish between **caste** societies, in which the individual members of distinct stratified groups are not allowed to move out of the stratum in which they were born, and **class** societies in which some individual social mobility up or down the class hierarchy may occur (see chapter 5 for details). At the very bottom of a class or caste hierarchy may be found a social category whose access to valued resources is so restricted that members do not even control their own labor. The degree and nature of such restrictions are variable across time and place, but they are regularly enforced by violent means, as in the case of *racial slavery* and its aftermath in the Americas, or the case of *dalits* in the Hindu caste system (see chapter 5).

Stratification means that some groups have disproportionate access to valued resources. For example, high-ranking groups may have *sumptuary* privileges: that is, they may be the only members of society entitled to wear certain fabrics or eat certain foods. In stratified societies, moreover, valued resources include not just material **wealth** (e.g., land or herds) or cultural **prestige** (e.g., esteem or respect) but also power itself. That is, those who rule the state are able to use their monopoly on coercive power to keep the lion's share of wealth and prestige and to perpetuate this inequality from one generation to the next. Because of the elaborate division of labor and its hierarchical organization in stratified castes or classes, state societies often are called **complex societies**, especially by archaeologists and prehistorians who contrast them with less elaborate and more egalitarian bands and tribes.

Those political anthropologists interested in the evolution of the state frequently have speculated on the processes that could have been responsible for transforming egalitarian political relations that had endured for thousands of years into unequal political relations. Many different single, unique causes, or *prime movers*, have been proposed to account for the emergence of political inequality and centralized hierarchy (e.g., population pressure, dependency on irrigation, conquest by neighbors, and environmental circumscription, to name but a few). The consensus among contemporary prehistorians seems to be that no single factor can explain all cases in which inequality and centralization emerged from egalitarian political arrangements. For example, archaeologists have uncovered the remains of many early societies organized as chiefdoms that never developed into states. It seems clear that although certain underlying factors must have been present, contingent historical factors also played an important role.

As Scott's work makes clear, anthropological preoccupation with explaining the "rise of the state" falls back into the analysis assumptions of unilineal evolutionism that had supposedly been eliminated long ago. Such a preoccupation can make a drive toward social complexity from band, to tribe, to chiefdom, to state seem inevitable and irresistible—even if the paths to complexity are varied and have not always been taken and even though human history is littered with the fall of states and the disintegration of empires. States and empires and other encompassing forms of social complexity are seen as powerful generators of inequality and oppression; moreover, the rise of state control will not necessarily be viewed as progressive, and the disintegration of an empire may be viewed as liberating. Scott's work offers a powerful demonstration of the insights that come from thinking "against the grain" and paying attention to "the art of not being governed "(Scott 2009). Such a perspective makes room to consider the open-ended unpredictability of future sociopolitical changes, as well as the ways in which societies organized with different degrees of complexity can coexist with and reshape one another.

8.6 FORMS OF POLITICAL ACTIVITY

The classification of political systems as bands, tribes, chiefdoms, and states can be useful even if one is not interested in their possible evolutionary relationships. Many political anthropologists have been intrigued by the striking contrast between egalitarianism and inequality, between diffuseness of power in egalitarian societies and centralized monopoly of power in stratified societies. As Meyer Fortes and E. E. Evans-Pritchard put it in 1940, centralized societies like chiefdoms or states have *heads* (chiefs or kings or presidents), whereas uncentralized societies do not; that is, they are *acephalous* (without heads). As Fortes and Evans-Pritchard noted, acephalous societies were not politically chaotic, but political order in such societies clearly seemed to be the result of cultural mechanisms rather different from the mechanisms on which centralized societies relied. Many anthropologists set about trying to identify just what those mechanisms were. To describe a band or tribe as "stateless" or "acephalous" is to describe it in terms of what it lacks: a state or a head of state. As indicated previously, however, some anthropologists prefer to describe bands and tribes in terms of what they possess, which (as Scott argues) is a high degree of political equality accorded to all adults (or, sometimes, to all adult males), as well as subsistence strategies that allow them to evade state control. People in the United States or Europe tend to equate political equality with forms of electoral democracy. But to do so is misleading because our forms of electoral democracy occur within the framework of a state, whereas the political equality found in egalitarian societies exists apart from the state.

To be sure, we find in bands and tribes many characteristics that might be justly described as "democratic"; for example, political decisions that affect the society as a whole must involve the consent of all adults (or adult males) in the society. But members of egalitarian societies typically do not go to the polls to vote formally for or against a particular policy with the understanding that whichever position gains the most votes wins. Instead, informal discussion and negotiation about alternatives take place among all adults who will be affected, a process that is feasible when the group is small as is typical in most band and tribal societies. Eventually, a decision that all adult members of the society accept emerges from this process—a result known as **consensus**. This does not mean that consensus is easy to achieve. Precisely because no adult in an egalitarian society can force any other adult to do anything, negotiations require enormous verbal skill. Successful negotiators often employ a range of techniques, ranging from indirectly suggesting, to cajoling, to shaming, to predicting dire consequences for failure to comply. In all cases, we are referring here to the exercise of persuasive, not coercive, power.

Not surprisingly, some individuals in egalitarian societies are more skilled, imaginative, and successful negotiators than others, and their achievements do not go unrecognized. Indeed, their achievements lead other members of their society to accord them great prestige. Individuals in bands or tribes who enjoy such prestige may be asked for advice or deferred to when decisions must be made because their past achievements—as hunters or ritual specialists, or fighters or diplomats—give their opinions greater weight than those of ordinary folk. Anthropologists have used the term **headman** to identify such individuals who may be the ones chosen by their fellows to deal with outsiders in ambiguous or threatening situations. In fact, outsiders (such as representatives of a colonial power) often have assumed that members of indigenous groups who mediated between their own group and the colonial administration were leaders with coercive power. As we have seen, however, this assumption was incorrect when applied to headmen in bands or tribes who have no capacity to force others to do their will. When colonial officials tried to incorporate "headmen" into their chain of command, expecting them to enforce compliance on the local level, they regularly discovered that, despite their prestige, headmen had no power to issue orders or force people to obey them. With the passage of time, under continued colonial rule, headmen often found themselves caught in an untenable position: expected by members of their own tribe to defend tribal interests against the colonial administration and expected by the colonial administration to extract compliance with colonial edicts from fellow tribesmen.

Another well-known anthropological example illustrating the exercise of persuasive power in egalitarian societies is that of the **big man**. Big men are "big" because of their ability to use their personal persuasive skills to arrange complex regional public events that involve kin and neighbors. In New Guinea, for example, big men gain personal prestige by organizing elaborate exchanges of valuables between their own and neighboring tribes. Such exchanges often begin as a kind of bloodwealth exchange: an end to hostilities is negotiated when the aggressors promise to present the aggrieved tribe with a quantity of wealth in the form of pigs, shells, money, and other valuables. Big men compete with one another to organize the collection and presentation of these goods, which is a major achievement given that they have no coercive means to compel other members of their tribe to participate. Moreover, the initial exchange that marks the end of hostilities is rarely the last one. If the tribe that has received wealth wants to maintain or enhance its own prestige, it must eventually reciprocate with a return gift. It falls to big men in the receiving tribe to plan and carry out the reciprocal exchange; and they always aim to return more than they received to enhance both their personal reputations and the reputation of their group.

8.7 SOCIAL CONTROL AND LAW

State societies function successfully because all the complex activities that take place within them are monitored by a more or less complex army of hierarchically organized public functionaries, each occupying a separate formal office with its own proper responsibilities and coercive powers. This form of public administration, or *bureaucracy*, illustrates another distinctive feature of states as forms of political organization: the *formalization* of a wide range of tasks (see also chapter 5). To formalize a bureaucratic or political office means to specify, explicitly and publicly, the rights and responsibilities of the officeholder. State societies formalize a wide range of tasks that are carried out by informal or barely formalized means in bands, tribes, and chiefdoms. For example, gossip is a very effective way to enforce conformity in small-scale societies without a police force. By contrast, state societies formalize not only leadership positions but also occupational qualifications and the public social rules that members of the society are expected to obey. Perhaps even more significantly, states formalize the *sanctions*, or penalties, to be meted out if social rules are broken.

Most anthropologists agree that in societies without states, including chiefdoms, proper social conduct is enforced largely by local groups using informal means. For example, in the modern nation-state of Indonesia, many local groups have sometimes resisted attempts by the national government to change the way they do things, insisting that compliance is forbidden by their own *adat*, or "custom." When, however, a centralized government publicly sets forth both explicit formal definitions of right conduct and explicit penalties for failure to observe such standards and backs these definitions with its monopoly on coercive power, anthropologists generally agree that it is appropriate to speak of **law**. In particular, they have been interested in comparing the ways in which law has developed or is administered in noncapitalist state societies.

The appearance of formal law in a state does not mean that informal means of social control disappear. Rather, formal law is ordinarily used to sanction only the most serious crimes such as theft, murder, or treason. Formal laws usually aim to be universal in scope, applying to all members of a society who possess certain attributes; and they usually focus on compliance (or lack thereof) with specific obligations (rights and duties) that all such individuals are expected to honor. Such a system of law is known as *substantive law*, and it is often the most interesting ethnographically because it encodes notions of right conduct that show much cross-cultural variation. Substantive law contrasts with *procedural law*, which describes how those accused of breaking the law are to be treated. Anthropologists who compare legal systems cross-culturally also often distinguish between *civil law*, the breaking of which affects only one or a few individuals, and *criminal law*, which regulates attacks against society or the state. Modern states have developed complex *law codes* in which explicit rules covering many areas of social, economic, and political life are articulated, together with the penalties incurred for breaking them.

Of course, members of any society when accused of breaking the law (informal or formal) often deny that they have done so. As we saw, egalitarian societies have developed their own informal ways of resolving such disputes, including mediation, feuding, and wealth exchange. In state societies, by contrast, formal laws and penalties are accompanied by formal legal institutions, such as *courts*, for resolving disputes. Informal dispute resolution remains in the hands of the affected parties: Recall that feuding kin groups, together with a mediator, must work out a resolution of their differences that satisfies the groups. Different disputants, however, might work out their differences in entirely different ways. It is this lack of uniformity in dispute resolution that a state tries to overcome in two ways. First, the state removes resolution of the dispute from the hands of the parties involved and puts it into the hands of a formal institution, the court; second, it evaluates the disputants' claims against the universal rights and responsibilities encoded in laws with uniform penalties. Because the court is supposed to be an impartial forum, care must be taken to ensure that the truth is told. Thus, all court systems develop rituals designed to achieve that end, such as the administration of oaths or ordeals to those who give evidence. In the end, the formal officers who preside in a court of law (i.e., judges) *adjudicate* the case before them: that is, based on the law code, they decide how a dispute will be settled.

Clearly, this entire apparatus can exist only in complex state societies producing sufficient surplus wealth to support the specialized formal court system with its law code, lawyers, judges, and punishments. In other words, a formal system of laws requires a formal system of punishments, or penal code, without which a full-fledged court system cannot function. Indeed, this system defines, for the society in which it is found, what formally counts as *crime* and what does not. New laws can be promulgated that turn formerly tolerated behavior (e.g., public begging) into a crime or that decriminalize formerly illegal behavior (e.g., when taxes are abolished, not paying one's taxes is no longer illegal).

Documenting changes in a legal system can offer important insights into the changing values and practices of the society to which the legal system belongs. One of the most powerful recent changes anthropologists have encountered all over the world involves attempts by citizens to petition their national governments or international institutions for legal rulings that will protect their *human rights* or their *cultural rights*. Often the petitioners are members of so-called traditional, or indigenous, groups who have learned how to operate successfully in regional, national, and international courts of law (see chapter 10 for a fuller discussion of anthropological studies of human rights and cultural rights).

8.8 NATIONALISM AND HEGEMONY

Much of the ethnographic data on informal dispute resolution were gathered in societies that once enjoyed political autonomy but at some time in the last 500 years came under the economic or political control of Western colonial powers. To be sure, capitalist colonialism did not affect all areas of the world at the same time or to the same degree; and many precolonial political institutions and practices survived, albeit under changed circumstances, well into the twentieth century. But the last two decades of the twentieth century exhibited an intensified push of capitalist practices into those areas of the globe that previously had been buffered from some of their most disruptive effects. And many political anthropologists in recent years have become less interested in local political particularities and more interested in global processes that increasingly shape the opportunities for local political expression.

Such anthropologists pay attention to political processes that began with the spread of European colonial empires. Political conquest and incorporation within one or another European empire destroyed many indigenous political institutions. However, colonial political practices stimulated colonized peoples to rethink and rework their understanding of who they were and how they should do politics. Much current anthropological investigation focuses on the paradoxical consequences of political independence in former European colonies.

The issues are complex and varied, but many anthropologists have been interested in the phenomenon of **nationalism**. Traditionally, anthropologists used the term **nation** as a synonym for ethnic group or tribe—that is, to identify a social group whose members saw themselves as a single people because of shared ancestry, culture, language, or history. Such nations/tribes/ethnic groups did not necessarily have any connection to political systems that we call states until the late eighteenth century, and especially the nineteenth century, in Europe. By the end of the nineteenth century, many Europeans believed that the political boundaries of states should correspond with cultural and linguistic boundaries—that is, that states and nations should coincide and become **nation-states**. In the latter half of the twentieth century, newly independent postcolonial states tried to realize the nation-state ideal by attempting to build a shared sense of national identity among their citizens, most of whom belonged to groups that shared few or no political or cultural ties in precolonial times.

At the same time, many groups that claim a common "national" identity on the basis of culture, history, or language find themselves encapsulated within a larger state or, worse, scattered across the territorial boundaries of more than one state. Following the nation-state logic, many of these groups see themselves as legitimate nations entitled to their own states. As the twenty-first century unfolds, the explosive potential built into these situations has created difficult political challenges for millions of people across the globe and seems to cry out for anthropological analysis.

Many anthropologists have borrowed Benedict Anderson's concept of the nation as an **imagined community** (also discussed in chapter 2), whose members' knowledge of one another does not come from regular face-to-face interactions but instead is based on their shared experiences with national institutions, such as schools or government bureaucracies, and the bonds created from reading the same newspapers and books. More recent anthropological work, however, highlights ways in which Anderson's original formulation of imagined communities "short-circuits all the labor that must take place for newspapers and novels to engender national, diasporic, or ethnic identities when these materials circulate among reading publics" (Gershon 2017, 23–24). Anthropologists have similarly been influenced by the discussion of the **invention of tradition** by historians Terence Ranger and Eric Hobsbawm. For example, many people believe that the kilt is a form of ancient dress that goes back centuries in the Highlands of Scotland. Although Highland plaids are known from at least the sixteenth century, they belong to a form of dress that originated in what is today Ireland, and the garment known as the kilt is a "tradition" that was in fact invented in the eighteenth century! The notions of imagined communities and invented traditions both highlight the fact that people in all societies exercise creative agency in every generation to fashion their collective identities and histories out of the accumulated cultural resources available to them. When new communities are successfully imagined and suitable traditions are invented for them; moreover, this cultural labor can make a genuine political difference.

The often violent postcolonial histories of aspiring nation-states, involving coups d'état and civil strife, have demonstrated to participants and observers alike that national identity cannot be imposed by coercion alone. Persuasive power must also be used, which is why anthropologists have drawn on the work of Antonio Gramsci (1891–1937). Reflecting on the reasons why the Italian nation-state was so much less successful in becoming unified than its European neighbors, Gramsci emphasized a contrast between the role of authoritarian domination (or coercive power) and hegemony (or persuasive power) that many contemporary social scientists have found useful. **Domination** can put a regime in power, but domination alone will not keep it in power. For one thing, it is expensive to keep soldiers and police on constant alert against resistance; for another, the people come to resent continued military surveillance, which turns them against the regime. This is why long-term stability requires rulers to use persuasive means to win the support of their subjects, thereby making a constant public show of force unnecessary. Gramsci used the term **hegemony** to describe control achieved by such persuasive means. Anthropologists have also been influenced by another approach to understanding politics in modern states that was developed by French historian Michel Foucault. Foucault and his colleagues identified a new form of state power that began to emerge in Europe after the Middle Ages and was fully developed by the nineteenth century. This form of power, which they called **biopower**, was concerned with managing the behavior of populations of living bodies—the living populations of citizens. Engaging in such management in ways intended to promote national policies is called *biopolitics* (see also chapter 6). Before the 1600s, according to Foucault, political thinkers like Machiavelli were mainly concerned with ways in which a ruler could maintain control of the state. By the seventeenth century, however, political thinkers began to ask new questions about how a ruler might govern a state in ways that preserved and protected its members. They likened governing a state to managing a household, but they realized that to achieve, this they would need more detailed information about the people, goods, and wealth of the state that needed to be managed. How many citizens were there—men, women, and children? How healthy were they? What kinds of goods did they produce, and in what quantities? Were there any ways in which the state could intervene to improve their health and increase the quality and quantity of goods they produced? To answer these questions, state bureaucracies invented the discipline of statistics to count and measure people and things subject to state control.

When European states began to govern their populations on the basis of such statistics, they began to exercise a form of what Foucault called **governmentality**, that is, policy interventions by a state (or other institution) designed to shape the conduct of those over whom it exercises authority. For example, statistics on population and production might indicate to bureaucrats that a famine was likely. Bureaucrats might then calculate both potential losses the state might suffer and a set of policies, based on these calculations, that suggested the best way to intervene to prevent or lower those losses. Using statistical information to manage populations in terms of this kind of governmentality is widespread today. The outcomes of particular forms of governmentality may be negative or positive for individuals: for example, statistical information can be used to plan mass immunization against communicable diseases, but it can also be used to identify all young people of a certain age to draft them into the military. In a globalizing world full of nation-states, anthropologists encounter different forms of governmentality (not only forms exercised by nation-states but also the capitalist market or nongovernmental organizations [NGOs], e.g.) as well as attempts by citizens to evade or manipulate them. (See the discussion in chapter 10 on anthropology of the environment.)

A variety of tactics can be used to build hegemony, including neutralizing opposition from powerful groups by granting them special privileges and articulating an explicit **ideology** that explains the rulers' right to rule and justifies inequality. If the ideology is widely promulgated throughout the society (e.g., in schools, through media), and if rulers make occasional public gestures that benefit large sections of the population, they may forestall rebellion and even win the loyalty of those whom they dominate. Because hegemony depends on persuasive power, however, it is vulnerable to the critical attention of the powerless, whose reflections on their own experiences may lead them to question the ruling ideology. They may even develop interpretations of their political situation that challenge the official ideology. Following James Scott (1992), some anthropologists use the term **hidden transcripts** to describe these alternative (or *counterhegemonic*) understandings because they are frequently too dangerous to be openly proclaimed. Because hidden transcripts offer an alternative, however, they offer openings to more sustained critiques of the status quo that eventually could lead to open rebellion.

Many anthropologists find the concept of hegemony to be useful because it offers a way of showing that oppressed groups that do not rise up in open revolt against their oppressors have *not* necessarily been brainwashed by the hegemonic ideology. Rather, such groups possess sufficient agency to create counterhegemonic interpretations of their own oppression. If they do not take up arms, therefore, this is probably because they have accurately concluded that rebellion would not succeed under current conditions. The concepts of hegemony and hidden transcripts help anthropologists demonstrate that political concepts such as "freedom," "justice," and "democracy" do not have fixed meanings but may be the focus of cultural and political struggle between powerful and powerless groups in a society.

FOR FURTHER READING

Power   Wolf 1999

Political Anthropology   Fried 1967; Lewellen 2003; Scott 2017; Sharma and Gupta 2006; Vincent 2002

Law   Harris 1997; Nader 1997

Nationalism   Anderson 1983; Hughey 1998; Tambiah 1997

Hegemony and Hidden Transcripts   Hobsbawm and Ranger 1992; Scott 1987, 1992, 1998, 2009

Political Ecology   Biersack and Greenberg 2006; Hodgson 2004

CHAPTER 9

Economic Anthropology

The key terms and concepts covered in this chapter, in the order in which they appear:

subsistence strategies
domestication
foragers
food producers
extensive agriculture
intensive agriculture
mechanized industrial agriculture

capitalism
market
economy
scarcity
original affluent society

modes of exchange
reciprocity
redistribution

proletariat

bourgeoisie
labor
means of production

mode of production
classes
relations of production

peasant
production for use
production for exchange
formal economy
informal economy
global assemblage
development
environmental anthropology

consumption

anthropology of food and nutrition

Since its formative years as a discipline, anthropology has been interested in the many and varied ways in which human beings in different societies make a living. In the late nineteenth century, anthropologists devoted much attention to the tools and techniques developed by various peoples to secure their material survival and well-being in a range of climates and habitats. Indeed, the objects people made for these purposes—spears, snares, fishnets, bows, arrows, hoes, plows, baskets, and the like—formed the collections of early ethnological museums in Europe and North America. Early anthropological theorists paid particular attention to the activities in which these objects figured, called the "arts of subsistence" by Lewis Henry Morgan (1818–1881).

9.1 THE "ARTS OF SUBSISTENCE"

Morgan focused on large-scale variation in patterns of the arts of subsistence in different human societies when he constructed his grand unilineal scheme of cultural evolution (a discussion of this approach is found in chapter 12). His key criterion for ranking subsistence patterns was technological complexity: the simpler the toolkit, the more "primitive" the society's arts of subsistence. Morgan's final scheme encompassed three great "ethnical periods"—Savagery, Barbarism, and Civilization—through which, he claimed, every human society either had passed or would pass as it evolved.

Morgan assumed that the society in which he lived had evolved further and faster than others on the globe and that, consequently, the arts of subsistence characteristic of those other societies could accurately be described in terms of not only what they possessed but also what they lacked. Thus, "savages" were all those peoples who had never domesticated plants or animals for their subsistence. Morgan subdivided them into lower, middle, and upper categories based on the complexity of the tools and skills they had devised for living off nature's bounty; "upper savages," for example, not only controlled fire and fished but had mastered the bow and arrow. The invention of pottery signaled for them the beginning of Barbarism. "Barbarians" herded animals and/or cultivated plants, and they also invented new subsistence tools and techniques such as iron implements and irrigated fields. All these advances were incorporated into the next ethnical period, that of "Civilization," which Morgan believed could be identified as soon as writing appeared.

Anthropologists have long since removed terms like *savage* and *barbarian* from their professional analytic vocabulary. They are well aware of how evolutionary schemes like Morgan's can be (and have been) used to rationalize the domination of the world by so-called civilized societies. But one does not have to accept these aspects of Morgan's analysis to recognize the importance of his classification of different arts of subsistence. He had collected information about a wide range of societies. He had hypothesized that variation in their arts of subsistence was systematic, showing up, for example, in correlations between particular technological developments and particular forms of social organization (especially kinship organization) in *domestic groups* (those whose members live in the same household). Karl Marx and Friedrich Engels (1820–1895) read Morgan and were persuaded that his ethnical periods documented changes in precapitalist modes of production. But again, one does not have to be a Marxist to be both impressed and puzzled by the patterns of subsistence to which Morgan drew attention.

9.2 SUBSISTENCE STRATEGIES

In early twentieth-century North America, Franz Boas and his students, having roundly rejected unilineal schemes of cultural evolution, were suspicious of grand explanations and unwilling to make far-reaching claims (for more on the

"Boasians," see chapter 12). But they were interested in documenting with great care how particular peoples went about making their living. As a result, throughout much of the first half of the twentieth century, anthropologists hesitated to do more than offer a loose categorization of the various subsistence strategies adopted by the peoples of the earth. The **subsistence strategies** identified—hunting and gathering (foraging), pastoralism, horticulture, and agriculture—reiterated the distinctions that Morgan had recognized and rested on a major divide based on the presence or absence of **domestication**: regular human interference with the reproduction of other species in ways that make them beneficial to ourselves. Many anthropologists continue to regard these strategies as representing the linear sequence of increasingly complex universal stages in the evolution of human economic arrangements—although as we will see, such a view is not accepted by everyone.

Hunter-gatherers—now usually called **foragers** or food collectors—are those who do not rely on domesticated plants or animals but instead subsist on a variety of wild foodstuffs. Their knowledge of their habitats is encyclopedic, and they manage to live quite well by roaming over large tracts of land in search of particular seasonal plant foods, returning to known water sources, and even occasionally setting fire to bush land to modify the habitat in ways that will attract their preferred game. By contrast, practitioners of the other three subsistence strategies are far more dependent on domesticated species and are sometimes referred to as **food producers** rather than food collectors. Pastoralists rely on herds of domesticated animals, such as cattle, camels, sheep, or goats, and regularly move these herds, sometimes over great distances, as water and forage in one area are used up. In many parts of the world, these movements are patterned in yearly cycles of *transhumance* as herders move from dry-season pastures to wet-season pastures and back again.

Horticulturalists cultivate domesticated plants by using human labor and simple tools and techniques to modify local vegetation or soil texture before planting their crops. In *slash-and-burn* or *swidden* cultivation, for example, hand tools are used to cut down all vegetation except large trees from an area to be planted. The vegetation is then burned, and the ash serves to fertilize the crops. But swidden farmers can use a particular field for only a few growing seasons before the soil is exhausted and must be left fallow for several years to regenerate. As a result, swidden farmers must move on to clear new fields every few years, which is why their practices are sometimes also referred to as *shifting cultivation*. Shifting cultivation is highly productive and energy efficient, but it functions well only when farmers have access to enough land to live on while old fields lie fallow long enough (often from 7 to 10 years or more) to regenerate. Shifting cultivation is thus sometimes also called **extensive agriculture** because so much land is required to support so few people.

Only with **intensive agriculture** do we find societies exploiting the strength of domestic animals by harnessing them to more complex tools like plows, and growing and harvesting crops with the help of irrigation and fertilizers. Intensive agriculturalists first appeared some 10,000 years ago in Southwest Asia. Their farming practices are intensive because the techniques they employ allow them to produce more than shifting cultivators could produce on the same amount of land while keeping their fields in continuous use. Contemporary intensive farming practices, often called **mechanized industrial agriculture**, rely on industrial technology for machinery, fertilizers, pesticides, and herbicides. This form of agriculture uses vastly more energy than does shifting cultivation, but it enables a few farmers to produce enormous amounts of food on vast expanses of land, their "factories in the field."

This sequence of categories provides a rough and ready classification of major differences in the way people have made a living over the course of human history. However, as James Scott suggests, reading evidence about subsistence practices "against the grain" reveals what is lost by highlighting only those practices that can be accommodated within a linear evolutionary framework. First, locating the development of human subsistence practices within the framework of niche construction (see chapter 2) makes it possible to recognize that for millennia, members of our species "had been deliberately rearranging the biotic world around itself with consequences both intended and unintended" (Scott 2017, 69). Scott describes the use of fire by foraging peoples as a form of "low-intensity horticulture" or "slow-motion forest 'gardening'" that affected the mix of plants available to them, many thousands of years before the appearance of "what many would consider 'proper' agriculture" (2017, 69–70). Second, locating the domestication of particular species within a niche construction perspective brings into view the many ways environments need to be remade to suit the needs of species that humans seek to manage—from weeding, harvesting, and storing crops to ways of managing mating and culling herds of domesticated animals. As Scott puts it, our species "has been domesticating whole environments, not just species" (2017, 70). Third, by removing the need to shoehorn a limited number of subsistence modes into a coherent evolutionary sequence, it becomes possible to acknowledge that people everywhere have always made their livings in ways that are more varied than these classic categories would suggest. "This is why . . . the conventional 'subspecies' of subsistence modes—hunting, foraging, pastoralism, and farming—make so little historical sense. The same people have practiced all four, sometimes in a single lifetime . . . and each of them bleeds imperceptibly into the next along a vast continuum of human rearrangements of the natural world" (2017, 71).

However, reliance on domesticated grains and animals (and the modified environments they required) eventually produced a qualitative change in human subsistence practices. This has traditionally been described by anthropologists as a move from forms of extensive agriculture like swiddening to forms of intensive agriculture incorporating fixed fields and the use of draft animals to pull plows. When this occurs, Scott argues, "the term 'domestication'—from 'domus,' or household—needs to be taken rather literally The domus was a unique and unprecedented concentration of tilled fields, seed and grain stores, people, and domestic animals, all coevolving with consequences no one could have foreseen" (2017, 73). Importantly, successfully managing the heterogeneous components on which intensive agriculture depended created the conditions for the development of more complex human forms of social life. What Scott calls "the late Neolithic grain and manpower module" became the base on which the first states were erected (2017, 116). In his view, if the key attributes of the first states were "territoriality and a specialized state apparatus: walls, tax collection, and officials," then such states were present in Mesopotamia by 3200 BCE (2017, 118).

One important consequence of the successful management of intensive agriculture was the new possibility of producing *surpluses* beyond what farmers required to survive from harvest to harvest and still save enough seed for the next year's crop. It is the appropriation of this surplus in the form of taxes (in the form of grain, livestock, or labor) that financed the projects undertaken by rulers of states (2017, 123). The first ancient civilizations are identified with new and complex forms of social organization, involving a specialized division of labor that promoted technical developments in all areas of material life. Early systems of inscription, or the knotted forms of record-keeping associated with the *quipu* in Andean civilizations, did not drive these changes, but they were extremely useful for various kinds of political, economic, and social record-keeping.

9.3 EXPLAINING THE MATERIAL LIFE PROCESSES OF SOCIETY

In general, fieldworking cultural anthropologists have left investigation of the origin of subsistence strategies and the rise of ancient civilizations to archaeologists and prehistorians. Given the pernicious use to which extreme and exaggerated unilineal evolutionary claims had been put in the nineteenth century, early twentieth-century ethnographers preferred to document the enormous amount of diversity still to be found in the material life of living societies. But this pursuit of cultural documentation, apparently for its own sake, struck later generations of anthropologists as unwarranted and pernicious in its own way. They sensed there were patterns to be detected and explained, and this required a professional willingness to develop theories that could generalize across particular cases. One attempt to reintroduce theory into the anthropological study of material life was made by Melville Herskovits (1895–1963) around the time of World War II. Herskovits urged anthropologists to borrow concepts and theories from neoclassical economics, the scholarly discipline rooted in Adam Smith's efforts in the eighteenth century to make sense of the new Western economic system later known as **capitalism**. Herskovits was persuaded that the concepts and theories of neoclassical economies had been refined to such a degree of scientific objectivity and formal precision that they could be applied to economies very different from the one they originally were invented to explain. Those anthropologists who decided to follow Herskovits's suggestion came to be known as formal economic anthropologists, or *formalists*. Perhaps the most obvious trace of neoclassical economic influence could be seen in their assumption that economic activity involved buying cheap and selling dear to maximize one's individual utility (or satisfaction).

Formalists took concepts that had successfully been used to analyze economic activity in capitalist market economies and searched for their analogues in noncapitalist societies. Most significant was their application of the Western concept of the **market**, understood as an abstract mechanism that determines *prices* of *commodities* (goods offered for sale), the basis of *supply* and *demand*. Furthermore, prices in the capitalist market are calculated (and paid for) in terms of *money*. However, although markets as material settings where people meet to exchange goods and services are found throughout the world, it was far from clear that the market mechanism central to capitalist economic would also be universally present. For example, many non-Western, noncapitalist societies had no system of coinage performing all the functions Western money performed. But formalist economic anthropologists noted that objects like iron bars or lengths of cloth or shells often seemed to be used much the way people in capitalist societies used money, as a medium of exchange or measure of value. And so formalists tried to use the ideas neoclassical economists had developed about money to make sense of, say, the way people in society X used shells. Or formalists might analyze customs in which a groom's family offered material valuables to the family of a bride to solemnize a marriage. This transaction looked very much like a "purchase" with something other than money being offered in exchange for a highly valued "good," the bride. Formalists thus tried to explain how much it "cost" to "pay for" a bride in the society. Adopting the assumptions of neoclassical theory, formalists assumed that each party to a marriage transaction would try to get as much as possible out of the transaction while giving as little as possible in return. Therefore, the number of cattle actually accepted in exchange for a bride would be subject to the forces of supply and demand, and the parties would agree on a "bride price" whereby supply and demand balanced.

Formalists did not view themselves as ethnocentric when they analyzed noncapitalist economic activities in this way. They thought that any culture-bound features of the concepts and theories they were using had long since been eliminated. But other anthropologists disagreed. These critics believed that, despite its sophistication, neoclassical economic theory still bore many traces of its origins in Western capitalist society. Critics pointed out that neoclassical economics, like capitalist society itself, subscribes to a particular view of human nature that sees isolated individuals as the only genuine human reality (see discussion of the *social contract* in chapters 5 and 8). That is, human beings are viewed as creatures who are by nature self-interested egoists who always act in ways that will increase their own individual well-being. Moreover, human beings all live under conditions of **scarcity**; that is, there will never be enough of all the material goods they desire to go around. As a result, the basic human condition consists of isolated individuals competing with one another, under conditions of scarcity, to obtain as much of what they want for as little as possible. Society might view such behavior negatively as selfish or greedy; but according to the neoclassical view, human society is artificial, secondary, and legitimate only to the extent that social rules do not interfere with each individual's pursuit of his or her own self-interest.

That is, in a world of isolated individuals competing for access to scarce goods, looking out for number one turns out to be a good thing—indeed, the *rational* thing to do—because putting others' needs first might interfere with maximizing one's own happiness.

Still, Adam Smith and others believed that when competition was carried out among individuals of more or less equal wealth and power, private vice could lead to public virtue. For instance, if you tried to cheat your customers, word would get around, and they would buy from other producers, causing you to lose money. Thus, you end up happier if you make your customers happy as well. Indeed, the price on which the two of you decide ideally ought to provide the best possible value either party might hope to obtain.

Only if such a view of human nature is accepted does neoclassical economic theory make sense. But anthropological critics were convinced that such a view of universal "human nature" could *not* make sense of the economic practices ethnographers had discovered in the *particular,* noncapitalist societies where they had done fieldwork. They pointed out that many economic systems were built on the assumption that human beings were, first and foremost, social creatures with legitimate obligations to other members of the societies in which they lived. Indeed, economic arrangements in such societies were shaped to the contours of other religious or political or kinship institutions in the society. That is, economic activities were *embedded* in the noneconomic institutions that made the society as a whole function properly. Rather than a measure of how individuals universally allocated scarce resources among alternative (presumably universal) ends, these anthropologists preferred to think of an **economy** as the concrete (and particular) way in which material goods and services were made available to members of a given society. Capitalism might allow individuals the freedom to pursue their own self-interest apart from the interests of others, but such an economic system was a recent and unusual addition to the ethnographic and historical record. Those anthropologists who defined economic systems in terms of their substantive institutional arrangements or provisioning their members came to be called *substantivists.* Substantivists argued that describing noncapitalist economic systems using neoclassical economic theory could only distort and misrepresent what was actually going on in those economies.

American anthropologist Marshall Sahlins (1972), a leading substantivist, set about debunking what he viewed as formalist misrepresentation of economic life in noncapitalist societies. After surveying a substantial ethnographic literature that described how foragers made a living, for example, Sahlins asked Westerners to reconsider how people might come to obtain more than enough of whatever they wanted—that is, become "affluent." Since the rise of industrial capitalism, many people assumed that the only path to affluence was by producing much; but Sahlins argued that a second "Zen road" to affluence consisted of desiring little. Foragers had very few material desires, and the habitats in which they lived were more than able to satisfy these needs. Thus, Sahlins concluded, the **original affluent society** was not industrial capitalism but foraging.

9.4 MODES OF EXCHANGE

Sahlins also drew on the work of economic historian Karl Polanyi, whose work showed just how misleading it was to suppose that all human economies, in all times and places, had been based on capitalist principles, given that the key components of market capitalism had come together only within the past few centuries in Western Europe. Polanyi distinguished among different **modes of exchange**—the patterns according to which distribution takes place—and argued that the capitalist mode of market exchange followed principles quite different from the principles that governed exchange in pre- or noncapitalist societies. He emphasized two particular noncapitalist modes of exchange: reciprocity and redistribution.

Sahlins borrowed Polanyi's classification of modes of exchange and tested them against a wide range of ethnographic data. He found that **reciprocity** governed exchange in small, face-to-face societies, especially those whose members lived by foraging. He also distinguished different forms of reciprocity. *Generalized* reciprocity involved no record-keeping, and parties assumed that exchanges would balance out in the long run. *Balanced* reciprocity required both that a gift be repaid within a set time limit and that goods exchanged be of roughly the same value. *Negative* reciprocity involved parties who repeatedly tried to get something for nothing from one another in a relationship that might continue over time, each trying to get the better of the other.

Redistribution as a mode of exchange requires the presence in a society of some central person or institution. Goods flow toward this central point and are then redistributed among members of the society according to their cultural norms of what is appropriate. Varieties of redistribution range from such non-Western institutions as the *potlatch* practiced by the indigenous inhabitants of the northwest coast of North America to the income tax and social welfare institutions of modern nation-states. To the degree that they exist, modes of redistribution act as *leveling mechanisms;* that is, they shrink gaps between rich and poor. In noncapitalist societies integrated by redistribution, the person responsible for amassing and then redistributing goods earned great prestige for generosity, but that person was often materially worse off afterward than most other members of the group. Polanyi pointed out that both reciprocity and redistribution may persist in societies organized along capitalist lines. In the United States, for example, exchange relations between parents and children ordinarily are governed by generalized reciprocity, and the collection of income taxes and the dispersal of government subsidies to citizens involve redistribution; but most goods and services are produced and exchanged by means of capitalist market mechanisms.

Similar ideas were developed by French anthropologist Marcel Mauss (1872–1950), one of Emile Durkheim's colleagues who contrasted *gift* economies of small-scale societies (based on reciprocity and laden with culturally significant noncommercial values) with *commodity* exchanges (in which a good's value is mediated by the capitalist market). A number of contemporary European anthropologists have developed Mauss's ideas to mount their own critique of market-centered analyses of noncapitalist economies.

9.5 PRODUCTION, DISTRIBUTION, AND CONSUMPTION

The debate between the formalists and the substantivists about the proper way to do economic anthropology became quite bitter in the late 1950s and early 1960s, with no resolution. Hindsight reveals that the divide between them was sharpened by the Cold War. In the Cold War years (which stretched from the late 1940s to 1989, when the Soviet Union broke apart), the ideological opposition between the Western "free market" (the First World) and Soviet "communism" (the Second World) was so strong that anyone in the United States who questioned neoclassical economic theory ran the risk of being labeled a "communist sympathizer," which was virtually synonymous with "traitor." Especially after the Cuban Communist Revolution in 1959, views of economic life in other societies that validated the assumptions of neoclassical theory were encouraged by members of the political elite in the United States. They hoped that, by showing a free-market route to economic prosperity, they could keep nations newly freed from colonial control (soon to be known as the Third World) from following Cuba's example. But in the late 1960s and 1970s, citizens in Western countries began to question publicly the official Cold War rhetoric; and some economic anthropologists began to study texts by Marx and his followers—and they tried to use Marxian analysis to make sense of their ethnographic data on non-Western economic life.

Although the debates among economic anthropologists can sometimes still become bitter, dialogue remains viable because all of them, regardless of perspective, largely agree that economic life can be divided into three phases: production, distribution, and consumption. Neoclassical economic theorists, dazzled by the power of modern capitalist markets, saw *distribution* to be key. After all, prices are set in the market when suppliers of goods and buyers of goods reach agreement about how much to offer for what. Historically, capitalist markets developed under circumstances in late-medieval European cities in which certain kinds of people—merchants, artisans—engaged in economic transactions free of the feudal obligations that controlled exchange between lords and peasants in rural areas. This freedom from obligations to others—the freedom to take one's chances buying and selling in the market—seemed to validate a view of human nature that eventually justified neoclassical economic theory in a society in which capitalism had triumphed. And it was a theory written primarily from the point of view of those who had engaged in free-market transactions and prospered.

Marx and his followers, however, paid attention to those whose participation in free capitalist markets kept them mired in poverty. These were the **proletariat**, the workers who toiled for wages in factories owned by the **bourgeoisie**, capitalists who sold for profit the commodities the workers produced. The very different positions of capitalists and workers were due to the fact that capitalists owned or controlled the means of production, whereas the workers owned nothing but their own labor power, which, to survive, they were forced to sell to the capitalist at whatever price that person was willing to pay. The unequal relationship between workers and owners under capitalism meant that when both met in the market to buy and sell, some of them (the capitalist owners) had considerably greater economic power than did others (the workers). The origins of that inequality required that attention be paid to the *production* phase of economic life.

Labor is a central concept for a Marxian analysis of economic production, especially social labor in which people work together to transform the material world into forms they can use. (Socialist feminist anthropologists have noted that the traditional Marxian account of *productive labor* ignores the *reproductive labor* performed by women in the household, which sustains economically productive workers and produces new workers; see chapter 6.) In noncapitalist economic systems, people ordinarily work with others to produce goods for their own use, using tools and materials that belong to them. Under industrial capitalism, all this changes. For example, workers might produce shoes in a factory: but shoes, along with the tools, technology, and materials used to make them—what Marx called the **means of production**—belong to the factory owner, not to the workers. Instead, workers receive money wages in exchange for their labor. With these wages, they are supposed to purchase in the market food, clothing, and other goods to meet their subsistence needs; that is, they become *consumers.* Because workers compete with one another for scarce wage work, they must put their individual self-interest first if they are to survive: thus, they come to view their fellows as rivals rather than comrades.

In all these ways, Marx argued, life under capitalism separates workers from the means of production, from the goods they produce, and from other human beings—a situation he called *alienation.* For Marxists, therefore, the isolated individual who is the hero of the capitalist version of "human nature" is actually an alienated social being forced into existence under the historically recent economic conditions of Western capitalism. Marx and most of his followers were interested in understanding how these socioeconomic conditions had developed in Western European societies. Like Marx, many also found the situation intolerable and believed that the point was not to understand society but to change it.

9.6 MODE OF PRODUCTION

Among those Marxian concepts that have been the most important in economic anthropology, we will emphasize here only one: the mode of production. A **mode of production** refers generally to the way the production of material goods in a society is carried out. Not only does it involve the tools, knowledge, and skills needed for production (the means of production), but it also depends on a particular division of social labor in terms of which different groups, or **classes**, of people are responsible for various productive activities, or the **relations of production**. Marx characterized European capitalism as a mode of production, and he contrasted it with the feudal mode of production that preceded it. In the feudal and capitalist modes of production, the central division of labor was between rulers and ruled: lords and peasants in feudalism and owners and workers in capitalism.

A key element in the Marxian analysis of modes of production concerns the nature of the relationship linking classes to one another in a particular society. Marx's point was that, although both classes had to work together for production to succeed, their economic interests were nevertheless contradictory because of their different relations to the means of production. Eventually, Marx predicted, these class contradictions would undermine the mode of production, leading to a revolution that would bring forth a new and improved mode of production.

Anthropologists studying economic conditions in different societies do not necessarily accept Marx's prophecies about revolution. But they have wondered whether the noncapitalist economic patterns revealed by fieldwork might usefully be understood as different modes of production. Some anthropologists working in Africa, for example, thought that the economic arrangements they observed among people who organized their societies (and their economic activities) on the basis of kinship might be framed as a *lineage mode of production*. That is, the opposed "classes" were elder and younger groups within particular lineages that owned important economic resources like agricultural land and implements (the *means* or *forces of production*). Like owners and workers under capitalism, the economic interests of elders and juniors were opposed and might lead to conflict: elders wanted to maintain their control over the forces of production, and juniors wanted to take it away.

Following the end of the Cold War in 1989, some economic anthropologists began to draw attention to the ways changes in manufacturing, transportation, and communication technologies had undermined the classic account of how capitalist production operated. Classic accounts located the production of goods for a mass market in bricks-and-mortar factories where workers labored on assembly lines (as pioneered by the Ford motor company). By the end of the twentieth century, however, these arrangements had been replaced by "post-Fordist" production practices involving more flexible forms of production aimed at specialty markets. New factories could be erected or dismantled easily and moved anywhere in the world where labor and other production costs seemed favorable, whereas full-time work in former industrial centers was replaced by part-time subcontracting, and labor union membership declined. The loss of income and other forms of support turned members of the classic proletariat into what many are now calling a *precariat*: that is, people who live with the imminent threat that the socioeconomic institutions and practices that once allowed them to make a living will be suddenly taken away. Members of such a precariat struggle with the consequences of job loss, the disintegration of industries or institutions where they once worked, and the collapse of community and kinship institutions on which they once were able to rely. As Hinkson observes, the processes engendering post-Fordist precarity are global in reach, and anthropologists working in many settings have come to think of precarity as "a pervasive experience of disenfranchisement and placelessness" (2017, 52). Making sense of such a condition of precarity—and understanding how people in different places attempt to cope with it—is an ongoing challenge for contemporary ethnographers.

9.7 PEASANTS

Other anthropologists have talked about a *peasant mode of production* observable in many Latin American societies. These societies are seen to be divided into classes, with peasants dominated by a ruling class of landowners and merchants. Anthropologists use the word **peasant** to refer to small-scale farmers in state societies who own their own means of production (simple tools, seed, and so forth) and who produce enough to feed themselves and to pay rent to their landlords and taxes to the government. Anthropologists have wondered how much autonomy peasants might have in particular societies and under what circumstances that autonomy might be undermined by changing political and economic conditions. For example, what happens to peasants who are forced to deal with the increasing penetration of capitalist market relations?

Many of the world's peasants were first introduced to capitalism as a result of European colonization. Colonized peasants continued to grow subsistence crops for their own consumption, but European colonizers regularly encouraged them to grow other crops that they could sell for cash. Sometimes these *cash crops* had been produced traditionally; in northern Cameroon in Africa, for example, peanuts were a traditional crop that local farmers began to sell on the market during the colonial period. Other times, cash crops were introduced from outside; in northern Cameroon, French colonial authorities introduced the variety of cotton now grown by local farmers and sold for cash. In this way, peasant **production for use** was pushed by colonial authorities in the direction of capitalist **production for exchange** in the capitalist market.

This form of agriculture (producing crops to be sold for cash rather than to be consumed at home) has had far-reaching effects on the economic life of peasants. To begin with, peasant farmers could continue to produce much of what they consumed, using the money they received for their cash crops to purchase imported goods or to pay taxes and school fees. Unfortunately, by using some of their land to plant cash crops, less was left to plant subsistence crops. In many cases, this led over time to increasing dependence on the money from cash cropping to buy necessities that could no longer be produced, or produced in sufficient quantity, to keep a peasant household going. Indeed, many ethnographers have documented situations in which members of ostensibly "peasant" households regularly leave the farm to perform wage work on plantations or in factories, or migrate abroad for work, sending part of their earnings home in the form of *cash remittances*. Without this additional income, many peasant households would collapse.

And this situation, in which members of the same household are alternately farmers and wage workers, has led anthropologists to wonder exactly how to describe and analyze what they are seeing. Are these peasants no longer truly peasants? Does their increasing reliance on wage work for survival mean that they have been "captured" by an expanding capitalist mode of production? Have they been transformed from peasants into a rural proletariat? Some anthropologists have argued that this is indeed the case, and some ethnographic materials support their arguments. In other cases, however, the situation looks more complicated. Although members of peasant households rely on wage work to keep their families going, they continue to farm, producing much of the food needed for household subsistence. Some anthropologists refer to these peasants who are also wage workers as members of an emerging "*peasantariat*."

From the perspective of neoclassical economic theory, members of this Third World peasantariat were understood to be "in transition" from "traditional" to "modern" (i.e., capitalist) economic practices. Neoclassical theory argued that capitalist economic institutions (those that paid taxes, obeyed government regulations, and otherwise adhered to rules set down by the state) belonged to sectors of the modern, national, **formal economy** into which other, so-called backward sectors of the **informal economy** eventually would be absorbed. In former colonies that had recently become independent states, the formal sector was often quite small, whereas the informal economy was very important, especially in urban areas. Many migrants supported themselves and their families by engaging in all sorts of unregulated, untaxed, and even illegal economic activities— from smuggling, to peddling, to selling cooked food. They also might move from a period of employment within the formal sector to a period in the informal sector and then back again. Moreover, anthropological fieldwork showed that many people active in the formal or informal economy of a city might also have ties to relatives in rural areas who engaged in agriculture and with whom they pooled economic resources.

Anthropologists working in many so-called Third World societies documented the seeming resilience of precapitalist economic arrangements confronted by more recent capitalist institutions. Such arrangements seemed to be delaying indefinitely the promised transition from "tradition" to capitalist "modernity." Anthropologists of a neoclassical bent might argue that the transition was still inevitable but would simply take longer than they originally predicted. Some anthropologists of a Marxian bent, however, argued that the situation was more complex. Rather than precapitalist institutions being replaced by capitalist institutions, they said, what had emerged in these settings was a new kind of social formation composed of two or more *articulating modes of production*. That is, in settings such as former European colonies in Africa, precapitalist modes of production and the capitalist mode of production, each organized according to different relations of production, appeared to have adapted to each other's presence. Under such circumstances, individuals and groups could turn to precolonial relations of production when participation in capitalist relations of production was too costly or did not suit them for other reasons.

The argument that two or more modes of production might articulate with each other, however, seemed to imply that individual modes of production were not bounded, self-contained sets of economic arrangements. As a result, the concept of mode of production met a fate similar to concepts of society or culture that at one time had also been conceived as bounded and self-contained. This has implications for the way peasants are conceived. James Scott argues that "a peasantry—assuming that it has enough to meet its basic needs—will not automatically produce a surplus that elites might appropriate, but must be compelled to produce it" (2017, 153). From this perspective, states have regularly faced "a constant struggle to compensate for the losses from flight and mortality by a largely coercive campaign to corral new subjects from among hitherto 'untaxed and unregulated' population" (2017, 155). Many of the latter are the foragers, pastoralists, and shifting cultivators whose complex and heterogeneous subsistence strategies have, until quite recently, allowed them to evade state control.

After 1989, the end of the Cold War ushered in worldwide changes in economic, political, social, and cultural relations. The boundaries that used to separate societies, nation-states, and cultural traditions from one another turned out to be far more porous than many anthropologists had assumed, and capitalism seemed to engulf the entire world. On one hand, it may be that, as a result of such changes, there will be no room in the twenty-first century for those people formerly known as peasants. On the other hand, different kinds of people (some of whom might have been considered peasants in the past) are now coming together in new ways, connecting a variety of heterogeneous cultural and material elements to one another, often in places far from their points of origin, to make possible brand-new kinds of economic, political, social, and cultural institutions. Some anthropologists use the term **global assemblages** (Ong and Collier 2005) to identify such newly articulated institutional arrangements, distinctive both for their unprecedented geographical reach and for the diverse nature of the people, objects, and meanings that they link together (see chapter 12 for more details on the concept of *assemblage*).

Global assemblages come in many varieties. One kind is the *commodity chain*, the series of linked moves that take commodities, such as garden vegetables, from farms where they are produced to sites where they are purchased by consumers. In the early twenty-first century, commodity chains that supply North American supermarkets with year-round fresh vegetables, for instance, stretch beyond the borders of the United States to growers in other parts of the world. For example, the commodity chain that ensures the regular delivery of fresh broccoli grown in rural Guatemala to supermarkets in various parts of the United States has many links. The producers and consumers of broccoli (as well as other participants in the chain) usually know only about those with whom they must deal to receive the commodity from the previous node and pass it successfully on to the next one. Different people and institutions that form links in the chain (farmers, buyers, truckers, airlines, distributors, supermarket consumers) often choose to participate in the commodity chain for local reasons that are unrelated to the reasons why others involved at different links have decided to participate. Some Guatemalan broccoli farmers, for example, are persuaded that growing a nontraditional export crop that they do not eat will earn them sufficient cash to build a better future for their families in the aftermath of a genocidal civil war. Some health-conscious North American consumers, by contrast, may know nothing about recent Guatemalan history but choose to purchase broccoli because they view it as part of a healthy diet (Fischer and Benson 2006).

As evident in the case of commodity chains, economic components are prominent in emerging global assemblages. Highlighting their links to other kinds of components in an assemblage, however, draws ethnographic attention to the labor needed not only to enable the movement of commodities such as food over long distances but also to maintain the complex infrastructure that makes such movement possible (see chapter 11). Other global assemblages come into existence for the purpose of economic "development" in one or another part of the world that has traditionally been considered "underdeveloped" from the perspective of Western societies. In the context of a neoliberal capitalist world economy, **development** ordinarily involves investment by governments and/or by outside donors in projects designed to change institutions and individual behaviors in impoverished local communities, such that poverty will be diminished. Development projects can aim to improve local health, education, and welfare in many ways; but overall, the goal is to enable people in targeted communities to escape poverty by adopting practices that allow them to make money in the formal capitalist market.

Another area of research into globalized development is in a field that some call **environmental anthropology**, which draws together insights from political ecology, science studies (see chapter 11), development studies, and studies of environmental social movements. Environmental movements have emerged in different parts of the world in efforts to protect the so-called natural environment from forms of industrial, capitalist "development" that are seen to destroy resources, engender pollution, and fail to relieve poverty. One of the more prominent forms of environmental movement has been directed at protecting rainforests from destruction.

In understanding the successes and failures of environmental developmental projects, many anthropologists draw on Foucault's concept of governmentality (see discussion in chapter 8). For example, anthropologist Arun Agrawal has shown how the British imported European forms of governmentality into India during the colonial period, using statistics to manage not only human populations but also populations of trees in Indian forests. In Kumaon, India, these attempts were initially resisted violently by the people who lived in the forests; so in the early twentieth century, colonial officials and forest communities worked out a new set of arrangements that allowed local communities to devise their own ways of undertaking the statistics-based management of their local forests. Participation of community members in these new institutions of forest management fostered a new local awareness of forests and the ways in which their resources were threatened. This new environmental awareness, acquired through practical involvement in forest management, led to the development of new forms of individual subjectivity in many local residents, who became supporters rather than opponents of governmental forest management and conservation. This entire process (the governmentalization of localities, the local development of regulatory communities to manage forests, and the subsequent development of environmentally sensitive subjectivities in the managers) is what Agrawal calls *environmentality* (2005). Agrawal's findings provide an encouraging contrast to the results of research on other kinds of global alliances that have dispossessed indigenous peoples and appropriated their lands and resources (Brosius, Tsing, and Zerner 2005).

The emergence of heterogeneous assemblages in many different domains of life, across sometimes vast geographical distances, is a prominent feature of contemporary processes of globalization (see chapter 10). In the twenty-first century, global assemblages that manage to stabilize their newly articulated parts into established institutions are likely to play important roles in the social, cultural, political, and economic lives of people in many parts of the world.

9.8 CONSUMPTION

The final phase of economic activity is **consumption**, when the goods or services produced in a society are distributed to those who use them up, or consume them. Most economists, whether of neoclassical or Marxian persuasion, traditionally have had little to say about why it is that *these* goods and *these* services (as opposed to other goods and services) get produced and distributed. Either consumption preferences are reduced to the idiosyncratic, unpredictable, and inexplicable choices of individuals (as in neoclassical economics), or they are reduced to basic biological needs (as when Marx stated that human beings need first to eat and drink before they can make history). Some anthropologists have made similar arguments. Bronislaw Malinowski, for example, wanted to show that "primitive" peoples were in fact no less human than their "civilized" counterparts. He argued that, although all viable societies must satisfy their members' universal *basic human needs* for food, shelter, companionship, and so forth, each society has invented its own cultural way of meeting those needs. Malinowski's approach, however, failed to address the question of *why*: for example, Trobriand Islanders satisfied their need for food with yams and pork rather than with, say, sorghum and beef.

One way to answer such a question is to point out that yams and pork are locally available for consumption in the ecological setting to which Trobriand Islanders have become adapted. Answers of this form to questions about consumption were developed in the 1950s by *cultural ecologists*, some of the early practitioners of ecological anthropology. *Ecological anthropology* studied the ways in which human populations relate to other populations of living organisms in a particular material environment. As we saw in chapter 8, the kinds of societies studied by ecological anthropologists tended to be small-scale units understood as responsible on their own for adapting (or failing to adapt) to particular kinds of local environments. Although these populations might be connected with other neighboring populations through trade relationships, ecological anthropologists generally assumed that the diet and other basic material resources of any population depended largely on what their local environment afforded. Thus, it is not surprising that desert-dwelling herders of camels or cattle do not depend on saltwater shellfish to meet their basic subsistence needs, nor that people who hunt and gather for a living in the rainforest do not depend on fast-food hamburgers. At the same time, research in ecological anthropology has revealed the unusual range of local foods on which some populations come to depend, as well as the impressive varieties of food that can be collected and consumed even by people with very simple technologies, such as those who gather and hunt for a living.

Not all ecologically oriented anthropologists agree about the importance of culture in human evolution and ecological adaptation. Some (but not all) anthropologists who practice what is called *behavioral ecology* have been heavily influenced by the ideas of sociobiology, a school of evolutionary thought that assigns culture little or no role in human adaptation but instead argues that genetically driven and/or environmentally driven necessity keeps culture "on a short leash." Other anthropologists influenced by cultural ecology, such as *culture inheritance theorists*, find sociobiological accounts inadequate. They argue that symbolic culture has played a key mediating role in human evolution and that it continues to exert powerful influences on contemporary human ecological adaptations.

Culture appears to play an important role in consumption patterns for at least two reasons. First, consumption preferences often are more closely linked to one's membership in a particular social group than to the ecological setting in which one lives. Second, the consumption preferences people share often involve goods and services that are not easily explained with reference to basic human biological needs. A good illustration is the pattern found in capitalist societies that sociologist and economist Thorstein Veblen (1857–1929) labeled conspicuous consumption. *Conspicuous consumption* involves the purchase and public display of goods known to be costly and unnecessary for basic survival. For example, many people who live in the suburban United States find it necessary to own an automobile for transportation. Getting from home to work to the supermarket to the shopping mall in no way requires the extra speed and power of a sports car, but many suburban residents nevertheless spend tens of thousands of dollars for sports cars. Veblen suggested, and cultural anthropologists agree, that people who drive these cars do so not for practical reasons but to display them as *indexes* (see chapter 3) that point to their economic success. That is, they want to show other people (especially those whom they want to impress) that they are so prosperous, they are not limited to purchasing goods for purely practical reasons; rather, they can "waste" cash on nonnecessities, on luxurious, ostentatious extras.

Even though our continued existence requires a minimal level of food, water, shelter, and human companionship, ethnographic research has powerfully demonstrated that it is virtually impossible to separate people's indispensable *needs* from their discretionary *wants*. This is because all human groups attach cultural meanings to the goods and services they consume. For this reason, Veblen's pattern of conspicuous consumption within the capitalist mode of production constitutes only one end of the continuum of consumption practices documented for different societies with different modes of production. In all cases, what people consume makes a statement about who they are, what they value, and where their loyalties lie.

The anthropological study of consumption has contributed greatly to a critique of approaches to consumption that would reduce it to biological necessity or individual idiosyncrasy. Anthropologists have shown how consumption patterns associated with such seemingly unproblematic foods as meat or sugar have been shaped by cultural beliefs and practices in different times and places. In particular, they have shown what happens when consumption goods are turned into commodities under capitalism. This process has been under way now for several centuries and continues to affect the consumption choices of people throughout the world. For example, fast food becomes highly valued when capitalist production draws into the paid workforce those household members who previously had the time, energy, and resources to prepare meals from scratch. And the particular kind of fast food people come to prefer increasingly is shaped by expensive media campaigns designed to persuade consumers using the same tactics Veblen described a century ago.

Many anthropologists have begun to examine the way consumption practices in non-Western societies are changing as a result of these processes, however, and they have been able to show that non-Western consumers of Western-made products are not simply the dupes of advertisers and marketers. Daniel Miller, in particular, helped redirect the focus of studies of commodity consumption by anthropologists. Under conditions of globalization, Miller has argued, mass-produced commodities are on offer to people everywhere, and anthropologists should not automatically assume that choosing to consume such commodities signifies the triumph of Western imperialism or the loss of cultural authenticity. Rather, members of many societies in the world have selected some Western material goods and rejected others based on how well they think those goods will enhance or enrich their own traditions. Thus, Otavalan weavers in Ecuador purchase television sets to entertain weavers producing traditional textiles in locally owned shops, with the result that production increases, enabling Otavalan merchants to more successfully compete in an international market for indigenous products. Under such circumstances, the consumption of television strengthens, rather than diminishes, Otavalan tradition (Colloredo-Mansfeld 1999). Indeed, the recent successful participation in the institutions of international capitalism by non-Western peoples—from Otavalan textile producers to Japanese, Chinese, and Korean businessmen—suggests that there is perhaps nothing intrinsically "Western" about capitalism or consumption. These cases suggest that consumption of goods sold in capitalist markets need not mean that consumers are being obediently programmed to replace their own traditions with Western consumerism; instead, they are *indigenizing* and *domesticating* capitalist practices and consumer goods as they create their own alternative versions of modernity.

9.9 THE ANTHROPOLOGY OF FOOD AND NUTRITION

Food makes up an important proportion of the commodities that people all over the world are increasingly purchasing in the market; and the way in which foods are produced, distributed, and consumed in global capitalist markets has altered health and dietary practices everywhere. As a result, some anthropologists have turned their attention to the consequences of these changes, especially in societies where people used to grow most of their own food, harvest crops or butcher animals using local methods and cook and serve meals according to traditional cuisines. (See also chapter 11.) Anthropologists in this field also study how culturally variable attitudes toward food and eating affect local understandings of fatness and thinness, as well as the connections people make between food and cultural identity. Such work has led to the emergence of a new area of specialization, the **anthropology of food and nutrition.**

One prominent example of the commodification of food consumption involves the expansion of fast foods into communities across the globe. Coca-Cola and McDonald's hamburgers are regularly deplored as prime examples of Western (or US) cultural imperialism, responsible for the destruction of local cuisines and their replacement with commodified foods. Anthropologists have shown, however, that this interpretation is incomplete and misleading. For instance, Daniel Miller (1998) challenged this view with his study of Coca-Cola, which has been sold in Trinidad since the 1930s. Because Coca-Cola spreads through franchises, the bottling plant that originally produced Coke in Trinidad was locally owned; because the plant needed to import only Coca-Cola concentrate from the US corporation, the local owner purchased all other necessary ingredients locally in Trinidad. Eventually, this bottling company was exporting soft drinks throughout the Caribbean, becoming an important local economic force. It bottled other soft drinks in addition to Coca-Cola and competed with other local bottling companies, which shaped company decisions about new flavor lines. The Trinidadians Miller knew did not associate drinking Coke with attempts to copy people in the United States. Not only had the industrial production of Coke and other soft drinks been indigenized, the consumption of Coke was incorporated into a set of local, Trinidadian understandings about beverages that divides them into two basic categories: "red, sweet drinks" and "black, sweet drinks." In this framework, Coke is simply an up-market black, sweet drink used as a mixer with rum, which is also locally produced.

Anthropologists who have studied the multiplication of McDonald's fast-food restaurants all over the world echo Miller's observations. McDonald's, like Coca-Cola, spreads through franchises, which allows every local McDonald's restaurant to be locally managed and to develop a menu customized to local tastes. Like Coca-Cola in Trinidad, McDonald's must also find a place for itself in the food and dining landscape of every community where a restaurant is located. In the early 1990s, for example, when it first arrived in Beijing, China, McDonald's was associated with the United States, and the food was not especially appealing to adult Chinese who ate there. At the same time, the "Americanness" of the restaurant meant that Chinese customers experienced the fantasy of visiting a foreign country every time they walked into McDonald's. In addition, Chinese clients associated America with modernity, and they were positively impressed by the modern industrial efficiency showcased by the restaurant space, including its kitchen, and by its smiling, disciplined workers. Customers were also attracted to the clean, open, egalitarian, family- and woman-friendly ambiance of the dining experience, with clean bathrooms, which contrasted starkly with traditional Chinese institutions and practices associated with meals taken outside the home. The restaurant space also provided a setting where newly affluent workers could celebrate milestones (including birthday parties) in new ways that seemed appropriate in an urban Chinese setting remodeled by capitalist economic practices (Yan 2005).

During the same period, McDonald's also opened a restaurant in Moscow, Russia, and similarly attempted to accommodate itself to local tastes, securing local sources of beef for the hamburgers and of potatoes for the French fries and emphasizing these local sources in their advertising. As Russian consumers became more familiar with hamburgers and French fries, they began to incorporate them into their own domestic food practices. As in Beijing, however, the restaurant buildings themselves were especially attractive to Russian consumers, who indigenized them by holding private celebrations there, including birthday parties for their children. In both cities, people who visited McDonald's were not interested in eating quickly and leaving, and local employees did not push them to do so. These "slow" dining practices reflect the fact that, outside the United States, fast-food restaurants regularly attract economically better-off customers who linger over their meals; these establishments are not regarded as low-status eateries designed to feed working-class or poor people quickly and cheaply. At the same time, McDonald's employees in Moscow allowed visitors to the city to use the clean restrooms to bathe and wash their clothes and permitted homeless children to finish the food customers left behind on their trays. All these practices permitted Muscovites to indigenize McDonald's so thoroughly that many of them forgot that McDonald's was "foreign" and began to think of McDonald's as just another local restaurant (Caldwell 2005). Surprising ethnographic findings of these kinds inform ongoing work by anthropologists on the complexities of production, marketing, and consumption of food in a global capitalist economy.

FOR FURTHER READING

Economic Anthropology   Carrier 2006; Gudeman 2016; Hann and Hart 2011; Wilk and
  Cliggett 2007
Peasants   Netting 1993
Consumption   Colloredo-Mansfeld 1999; Miller, 1998; Mintz 1996
Money   Weatherford 1997
Food and Nutrition   Counihan 2004; Counihan and Van Esterik 2008; Miller 1998; Mintz
  1985; Watson and Caldwell 2005; Williams-Forson and Counihan 2011

CHAPTER 10

Globalization

Anthropologists have specialized in taking seriously the ways of life of people in "remote" parts of the world—remote, that is, from the activities and concerns of most people in the Western capitalist nations from which the anthropologists traditionally came. Until very recently, limitations rooted in the technologies of transportation and communication meant that, even when political or economic ties linked territories at some distance from one another, the movement of people or goods or ideas from one place to another was slow and cumbersome. By 5,000 years ago, the growth of states and their expansion into empires drew peoples in several regions of the world into intensified contact with one another.

At the beginning of the twenty-first century, however, economic or political events whose consequences used to be felt only within restricted geographical regions regularly affected people living in regions of the world that used to be considered distant from one another. It was only a little over five centuries ago that European explorers began to make contact and then to conquer indigenous groups on all continents, eventually establishing far-flung colonial empires that lasted until the middle of the twentieth century. The relationships established by European colonial domination created the conditions for the emergence, by the end of the twentieth century, of a network of capitalist economic relations that spanned the globe.

10.1 THE CULTURAL LEGACY OF COLONIALISM

Colonialism can be defined as political conquest of one society by another, followed by social domination and forced cultural change. Since the rise of the first states in antiquity, regions of varying sizes have been brought together in different parts of the world as a result of imperial expansion—and what is today Western Europe was marginal to most of them. None of those earlier empires, however, ever attained the scope of the European colonial empires, especially during their period of greatest expansion, which stretched roughly from the end of the nineteenth century until shortly after World War II when European colonies began to gain their independence. At that time, many observers hoped that the relationships of subjugation between colonizer and colonized would dissolve. They hoped that different geographical regions of former empires would regain the kind of autonomy that had so often followed the break-up of empires in the past. Such hopes were dashed, however, when the ties between former colonies and their former imperial rulers not only did not disappear after independence but instead often reappeared in the form of "consultancies" to the new governments. These persisting relationships in the absence of imperial political domination have often been called **neocolonialism**, and social scientists have struggled to explain why they are so resilient. Many scholars, anthropologists included, decided that neocolonial ties were basically economic in nature and that their strength came from an international division of labor, which colonialism itself had established. Once certain geographical regions within an empire became specialized in specific economic tasks within the imperial economy, the argument went, those relationships became very difficult, if not impossible, to dislodge, even when the empire itself no longer existed. Much evidence was collected to document the forced social and cultural change wrought on the economic, social, and cultural lives of colonized peoples to create this international division of labor during the period of European colonial rule.

The European empires of the last two centuries were, by and large, not made up of settler colonies. Except for select areas like Southern or Eastern Africa for the British or Morocco and Algeria for the French, European soldiers and administrators were always relatively limited in number; the colonizers relied on superior military technology, rather than sheer numbers, to impose their will. They were neither able nor, in most cases, interested in remaking colonized societies from top to bottom, but they did institute certain changes that would make it easier for them to achieve the economic goals that were their primary motivation. Thus, large tracts of land were regularly appropriated from colonized peoples for the purpose of resource extraction (e.g., mining) or for growing cash crops valued in Europe (see chapter 9 for further discussion of cash crops), displacing indigenous farmers and herders from their lands and turning them into wage workers forced to seek employment on plantations, in mines, or in the growing cities. Economic efficiency further required the building of infrastructure (roads, ports, etc.) by which cash crops or minerals could be transported out of colonies and back to Europe. Colonists regularly relied on the labor of colonized peoples to build such infrastructure, sometimes resorting to the use of *corvée,* or forced labor, in which laborers were required to work a given number of days on a given project or risk fines or imprisonment.

As colonial economic control increased, colonized peoples became familiar with European economic practices such as the use of money to purchase commodities or the production of goods for exchange. Adopting wage work and purchasing goods to meet subsistence needs increasingly became a necessity as people were deprived of the land on which they formerly had grown subsistence crops or as their traditional artisanal production of pots, cloth, or farm implements was supplanted by manufactured items produced in and imported from Europe. Over time, indigenous peoples had to come to terms with these cultural practices, and the way they did so has varied from time to time and place to place. They were coping with what many scholars have called **cultural imperialism**, a situation in which the ideas and practices of one culture are imposed on other cultures, which may be modified or eliminated as a result. Western colonialism appeared to produce a distinctive kind of cultural imperialism, frequently called **westernization**, in which the ideas and practices of Western European (or North American) culture eventually displaced many of the ideas and practices of the indigenous cultures of the colonies. In places where European settler colonies eventually broke from Europe, as in North, Central, and South America, anthropologists often speak of **internal colonialism** imposed on indigenous peoples within the borders of independent states.

10.2 ANALYZING SOCIOCULTURAL CHANGE IN THE POSTCOLONIAL WORLD

The contradiction inherent in most colonial policies urging cultural assimilation, however, was that even the most highly "assimilated" members of colonized societies could never hope to be treated as equals by their colonial masters. This realization by growing numbers of educated members of **subaltern** (lower-ranked, marginalized) groups helped fuel the movement for independence from colonial control, which gained momentum after World War II. By virtue of their shared colonial history and their shared rejection of domination, independence leaders argued that they and their followers had developed a distinct sense of themselves as "a people" or "nation," an orientation that came to be called **nationalism**.

Nationalist leaders in colonies claimed that colonized peoples, like other "nations" of the world, had a right to political self-determination: that is, they were entitled to become independent nation-states (see also chapter 8).

In the postcolonial world of the 1950s and early 1960s, the leaders of many newly independent nation-states were hopeful that their countries could escape the impoverished status they had occupied under colonial rule. Although such leaders rejected the notion that their citizens needed to become "civilized," they were committed to the idea that their societies needed "development" and "modernization." Many economists in Western nations agreed with them. In a manner reminiscent of Lewis Henry Morgan, these economists subscribed to a unilineal theory of economic development, often referred to as **modernization theory**. They studied the economic histories of the first nations in the world to "develop" or to "modernize"—that is, to create economies based on industrial production and capitalist business practices. Some economists believed that they had discovered a universal recipe for modernization, "a technological fix" that would guarantee economic development in any new nation that followed their advice. (For more on modernism, see chapter 1).

Modernization theory did not view industrial capitalism as a distinctive cultural system but rather as the most highly developed economic system yet produced on the face of the earth. It assumed that "nations" were units that passed naturally through stages of economic growth at different rates, and that the more "mature" nations ought to assist the "young" nations to attain maturity. However, economists from Western industrial nations insisted that the leaders of new nations carefully follow their recipe for development. Like parents dealing with sometimes unruly adolescent children, they worried that young nations eager to modernize might resist disciplined evolution through the stages of economic growth and look for a shortcut to economic prosperity.

During the Cold War years when modernization theory developed, the tempting shortcut was seen as socialist revolution. The twentieth century has been marked by a series of revolutions all over the globe, the best known being those in Mexico, Russia, China, Vietnam, Algeria, Cuba, and Nicaragua. In 1969, anthropologist Eric Wolf characterized all but the Nicaraguan revolution (which would take place 10 years later) as wars waged by peasants to defend themselves from the disruptions caused in their societies by capitalist market penetration. Following the Russian Revolution, opponents of the capitalist system elsewhere in the world also formed *revolutionary movements* whose explicit aim was to throw capitalists out of the country by force. Although many rank-and-file members of the revolutionary movements had modest dreams of return to a more prosperous status quo ante, their leaders often hoped to replace capitalism with some locally appropriate form of socialist society. After the successful Cuban Revolution in 1959 when Fidel Castro and his supporters openly committed themselves to socialism and allied with the Soviet Union, modernization theory became the foreign policy option of choice in the United States, a potentially powerful approach to economic development that might woo potential revolutionaries elsewhere away from the Marxist threat. The Marxist threat was real because Marxists argued that the factor responsible for the impoverished econo-mies of postcolonial states was precisely what the modernization theorists were offering as a cure, namely, capitalism. A key feature of capitalism is the way it creates separation, or *alienation*, of workers from the tools, raw materials, and technical knowledge required to produce goods. When, for example, peasants are pushed off the land and forced to work for wages in mines or on commercial farms, they are caught up in a process sometimes called *proletarianization*: a pro-cess of class formation that transforms people deprived of subsistence resources into workers at the bottom of the capitalist political economy (see chapter 9 for more on these issues).

Once these transformed relations of production are well entrenched, political independence alone will not make them go away. For example, successful com-mercial plantations will not automatically be dismantled so that peasants can reclaim lands to farm because the landlords (whether outsiders or locals) will be unwilling to give up the wealth that can be accumulated by using wage laborers to produce cash crops for the international capitalist market. This, it is argued, is why political independence brought neocolonialism rather than economic inde-pendence to so many parts of the world. The economies and cultures of colonized peoples had been so thoroughly remade under capitalist colonialism that cutting off all ties to former masters would have resulted in economic catastrophe. In the 1960s, Latin American economists and sociologists were trying to understand why their nations, free of official colonial domination for over a century, were no better off than the newly independent states of Africa. Articulating an analytic framework that came to be called **dependency theory**, they argued that poverty and "underdevelopment" were a *consequence* of capitalist colonial intervention in otherwise thriving independent societies, and not some original lowly state in which colonized territories had been languishing until the colonizers arrived. Capitalist colonialism *reduced* colonies to a state of underdevelopment in which their economies came to depend on decisions made outside their borders by co-lonial rulers who were promoting their own interests and not the interests of the colonies. Indeed, they argued, the "development" of rich countries depended on the deliberate impoverishment of other parts of the world. From this perspective, capitalist recipes for economic "development" could hardly be the solution to "underdevelopment" because capitalism had created the underdevelopment in the first place.

Modernization theory and dependency theory both see "development" as a process that is a natural part of all social life, but they differ in their under-standing of the forces that encourage it or block it. Modernization theory not only views capitalist entrepreneurship as the key to self-sustaining economic growth but also personifies nation-states as primordial sociocultural units, each of which is individually responsible for its own successful modernization. In recent years, the individualism at the center of modernization theory has reap-peared in the guise of **neoliberalism** in which international institutions like the World Bank and the International Monetary Fund urge individual nation-states to pursue their own economic self-interest in competition with one another.

Neoliberalism replaces the goal of achieving prosperous national self-sufficiency with the goal of finding a niche in the global capitalist market. State bureaucrats have had to divert funds away from state institutions that subsidized poor citizens to invest in economic enterprises that would earn income in the market.

Dependency theory, by contrast, rejected the individualistic analysis along with its conclusions. Nation-states were viewed not as primordial entities, but as historical creations; and some nations of the world were able to become powerful and rich only because they forced other societies into weakness and poverty. The fates of a rich country and its poor colonies (or neocolonies) were thus intimately interrelated. Social–scientific perspectives that take this observation as their starting point usually are said to pay attention to an **international political economy** (see chapter 8). In recent years, many anthropologists interested in the international political economy have become sharp critics of neoliberalism.

An ongoing struggle between anthropologists favorable to modernization theory and those critical of it was a feature of the Cold War years of the 1950s and 1960s. By the 1970s, critics of modernization theory were active in anthropology, many of them influenced by dependency theory. By the 1980s, however, many anthropologists agreed that dependency theory was too simplistic to account for the complexities of the postcolonial world. Many anthropologists thus adopted the broader perspective of **world system theory**, an analytical framework first suggested in the 1970s by sociologist Immanuel Wallerstein.

World system theory expanded on and strengthened the Marxist critique of capitalist colonialism inherent in dependency theory. Wallerstein's most original idea was to apply a functionalist analytic framework (see chapter 12) to the capitalist world system, which was, in his opinion, the only social system that came close to being self-contained and self-regulating in the structural–functionalist manner. Wallerstein stressed that capitalism was a *world* system—not because it included the entire world but because the system incorporated territories scattered across the globe to maintain itself and to grow. Unlike empires, which in the past had united far-flung territories under a single political authority, the capitalist world system united far-flung territories *by economic means alone* through the capitalist market.

Modernization theorists, as we noted, conceive of nation-states as autonomous actors ranked in various positions along a continuum from "backward"/ "underdeveloped"/"less developed" and so on to "developed" industrial economies. By contrast, analysts who adopted a world system perspective use a different terminology, classifying nation-states and other political entities in terms of the role they play within the world system's international division of labor. Thus, those countries that are fully industrialized, monopolize technological expertise and innovation, control financial decision-making for the system as a whole, and pay relatively high wages to skilled workers are said to belong to the *core* of the world system. Core nations today would include the former European colonial powers, the United States, and Japan. By contrast, those countries whose main contributions to capitalism are raw materials for industries in the core and expanding markets for manufactured goods are said to belong to the *periphery* of the world system. The ranks of peripheral nations are dominated by former colonies. Finally, some countries are said to belong in the *semiperiphery*; these nations either were once part of the core or look as though they might someday be able to move into the core. In recent years, China, India, Brazil, and Indonesia often have been considered semiperipheral by world system theorists; arguably, China is well on its way to being an important member of the core.

Thinking in terms of world systems, rather than empires, changed the way historians and social scientists approached world history outside Europe prior to the rise of capitalism. For example, geographer Janet Abu-Lughod (1989) made a persuasive case for the existence of a thirteenth-century world system centered in India that organized trade by land and sea from Southeast Asia to Western Europe and from China to East Africa. Some anthropologists have been inspired by Abu-Lughod's work because it not only provides a fuller historical context for understanding the development of cultures they study in the lands that formerly belonged to this world system but also shows that the capitalist world system is not the only world system ever to exist and that Western cultural hegemony is not inevitable.

Following the end of the Cold War in 1989, cultural anthropologists were among the social scientists who observed a series of far-reaching and intensifying global changes. From one point of view, it looked as though the fall of socialism in the former Soviet Union and the adoption of capitalist economic practices in China was making it possible for the capitalist world system to swallow up the entire world. From another point of view, however, the forces that were responsible for these new interconnections appeared to be so powerful that they were undermining key features of the world system.

For example, world system theory rests on the assumption of an international division of labor in which people in different geographical regions specialize in different economic tasks. This makes it both possible and meaningful to distinguish core from semiperipheral from peripheral nations. However, the vast improvements in transportation and communication technologies in recent decades have permitted a breakdown in the link between economic role and territory. Anthropologists have described massive movements of peoples, objects, and activities from their former locations in one or another region of the world system, together with complex struggles of those migrants, objects, and activities to find places themselves elsewhere in the world. Anthropologists today often carry out fieldwork among people whose ancestors may have been rooted in a single territory but who themselves may be living in a **diaspora** (or scattering) of migrant populations located in many different places.

Today demand for certain kinds of workers in core countries has promoted migration, both legal and illegal, of people from periphery to core. At the same time, technology-dependent manufacturing activities that used to take place exclusively in the core have been relocated in peripheral nations to take advantage of low wage rates. Wage work in manufacturing formerly enabled citizens of core nations with little formal education to earn middle-class incomes; the cost and inconvenience of moving factories out of the core meant that workers could bargain for higher wages and greater benefits with some success. Today's cutting-edge manufacturing plants, however, can be shipped to peripheral countries and quickly set up. They can also be quickly dismantled to move them elsewhere in the periphery where labor costs are lower. Increasingly, jobs that require knowledge of computerized technology are also moving to peripheral or semi-peripheral locations: workers' salaries can be lowered with no decrease in work efficiency, thanks to modes of high-tech electronic communication such as the Internet. Although the manufacturing jobs that have been moved out of the core are welcome in poor peripheral countries, the loss of such jobs in core countries has caused severe hardship and dislocation for the newly unemployed, swelling the numbers of the precariat. Indeed, increasing numbers of manufacturing jobs are being replaced everywhere by robotic technologies—another dimension of the post-Fordist transformation of capitalist production (see chapter 9).

10.3 GLOBALIZATION

The intensifying flow of capital, goods, people (tourists as well as immigrants and refugees), images, and ideas around the world has come to be called **globalization**. For example, over the past quarter century, tourism has become an important target of anthropological interest. This is not surprising since it is one of the largest industries in the world, moving nearly a billion people annually. *Tourism* is any activity that involves the self-conscious experience of another place (Chambers 2010, 6). As might be expected, anthropologists focus on how tourism is experienced, not just by tourists, but by the local communities that receive tourists. Here, there is a great deal of variation, and generalizations are difficult. For some communities, tourism is an excellent source of income, local identity, and pride; while for others tourism has brought pollution, inequality, and unemployment. Some anthropologists have been concerned with the issue of *authenticity* as something tourists seek; intermediaries like tour operators, travel writers, and travel agents promise; and local hosts may provide. There seems to be a popular view of authenticity as connected with traditions that have been maintained from an autonomous, premodern past. While there have been sharp arguments within anthropology about whether authenticity is possible, Chambers reasonably argues that "the authentic occurs under conditions in which people have significant control over their affairs, to the extent that they are able to play an active role in determining how changes occur in their social settings" (2010, 101). Under that definition, the tapestries based on graphics by Dutch artist M. C. Escher that Lavenda and Schultz observed for sale in the indigenous textile market in Otavalo, Ecuador, in 1978 were authentic because the weavers themselves had chosen to weave those designs, despite the objections of the Ecuadorian textile experts who were trying to convince them to weave ancient designs from Otavalo itself.

In the last decades of the twentieth century, many ethnographers documented global flows and their consequences, revealing transformations of a world once characterized by relatively firm national borders and localized populations. Examples like that of the Otavalan merchants reinforced the concern of many anthropologists that ethnographers should not presume that, all things being equal, people everywhere would prefer to stay put and to live exactly as their ancestors did. In the twenty-first century, as unprecedented numbers of migrants and asylum seekers have risked (or encountered) death in the deserts of the American Southwest or in the waters of the Mediterranean Sea, this concern has produced new approaches to understanding human population movement. One example is the work of Jason De Léon and his collaborators, as we saw in chapter 1. Another example directly addresses the traditional social scientific understanding that human population movement is a passive response, either to "push" factors that drive people away from one place, or to "pull" factors that draw them elsewhere, or to both. Anthropologists, who acknowledge the role of human agency, are aware that people may reconsider their options under changing circumstances and may set out on their own in pursuit of what they have decided is a better life. Nicholas de Genova and others who have studied immigration issues in Europe, for example, argue that freedom of movement is basic to human existence. This perspective, emphasizing the *autonomy of migration*, argues that "the movement of people around the world, and hence across these border zones, came first. The multifarious attempts to manage or control this autonomous mobility have always come as a response " (De Genova 2017, 6). Research by anthropologists and other scholars of border studies, who begin with the autonomy of migration, provide evidence to show that national borders (in Europe and elsewhere) must be understood as outcomes of ongoing struggles between people who insist on their right to move in search of a better life and those who insist on restricting that movement (De Genova 2017; see also Kotef 2015).

Other ethnographic research taking human mobility as a focus draws attention to importance of features of the built environment that enable or restrict mobility. Examples include studies of the building of roads and waterways (e.g., Raffles 2002), the installation and management of infrastructure such as running water (e.g., Anand 2017; Von Schnitzler 2016), or the provision of transportation in urban settings (e.g., Sopranzetti 2018). While this research is not always cast in the framework of niche construction, it resonates with that perspective. Indeed, in his studies of struggles between lowland states and hill peoples in Southeast Asia, James Scott points out that it was precisely the remoteness and difficulty of access to the settlements of highland people that allowed them to keep the state and its armies at a safe distance. This form of self-protection, which involved deliberately enlisting what he calls the "friction of terrain" (2009, xi), began to erode after World War II: "Since 1945, and in some cases before then, the power of the state to deploy distance-demolishing technologies—railroads, all-weather roads, telephone, telegraph, airpower, helicopters, and now information technology— so changed the strategic balance of power between self-governing peoples and nation-states, so diminished the friction of terrain, that my analysis largely ceases to be useful" (2009, xii). Since that time, he argues, states have employed such technologies to enact "strategies of 'engulfment'," encouraging supposedly reliable citizens to move into remote hills or rainforests, securing these territories for the state and extracting the resources they contain (2009, xii).

As Scott's analysis shows, people need not ever leave their homes to be buffeted by the forces of globalization. The explosive recent development of computer technology, the Internet, and social media has also enabled many kinds of links among people who have never seen one another, creating global networks, or *virtual communities*, that reach beyond the boundaries of nation-states. Many anthropologists have become interested in the growth of *cyberculture*: the distinct beliefs and practices developing in connection with the growth of computer-mediated communication (see also chapter 6). The cultural possibilities that might be produced by unbridled cyber exchanges on a global level remain limited, however, because access to computer-mediated communication is still largely the preserve of middle-class users with mastery of computer technology and literacy in English. In addition, even as various national governments continue to try to restrict their citizens' access to cybercommunication, with varying degrees of success, these technologies have also been used to interfere in the social media practices of other countries. (See chapter 3 for more on virtual worlds.)

Globalization and its consequences—especially the way it appears to have overcome traditional limits of time and space—are an excellent illustration of what many anthropologists and other scholars describe as the *postmodern condition*. This term refers to the situation in which human beings find themselves at the dawn of the twenty-first century: time is compressed; distances are annihilated. Under these conditions, the supposed benefits of "rational scientific modernity"—prosperity, equality, peace—appear more elusive today than ever and have increasingly been called into question (see chapter 1).

After 1989, for example, the certainties of the Cold War years gave way to bewilderment for many citizens of the United States: Who were our enemies? Who were our friends? Indeed, who are "we" and who are "they"? Since a terrorist attack destroyed the World Trade Center in New York City on September 11, 2001, many Americans have been persuaded that "terrorists" have stepped into the slot that used to be occupied by "communists." But this has hardly led to unanimity in the United States regarding how "terrorists" are to be identified or how they should be fought. Some terrorist groups might be international, but both the United States and Europe have experienced attacks by terrorist groups that were home-grown.

The struggle to manage situations of uncertainty and insecurity of this kind has given rise to a phenomenon sometimes called **identity politics**: struggles by groups to create and sustain exclusionary political alliances defined more narrowly than and often in opposition to a common identity as citizens of a nation-state. Although neither the nation-state nor citizenship has disappeared, many groups and individuals clearly refuse to accept them as overriding standards beneath which all other communities and identities should be subordinated or eliminated. Identity politics exposes the fact that societies and cultures that have been portrayed, either by their members or by outsiders, as homogeneous and harmonious are more often characterized by **cultural pluralism**. That is, they are made up of a multiplicity of heterogeneous subgroups whose ways of thinking and living vary, whose interests may be opposed, and whose cooperation is not automatic. Coercion by ruling elites may give the appearance of cultural uniformity. It may seem that members of heterogeneous subordinate groups have willingly adopted the hegemonic majority culture, a process called *assimilation*. When coercion weakens, however, pluralism often reemerges. It becomes apparent that some members of a society have serious reservations about the values and practices they have been pressured to accept. Rather than assimilating, therefore, they have simply refrained from challenging openly the cultural practices of the majority, a process called *accommodation*.

Cultural heterogeneity becomes even more complex in societies that have experienced recent immigration, producing a situation that is often called **multiculturalism**. The nation-states of Western Europe, for example, have all received large numbers of new immigrants from all over the world in recent decades. Citizens who already have differences with one another are challenged to make room for various groups of new arrivals while each set of migrants is faced with constructing a place for itself among a variety of other contending groups with different cultural backgrounds. Living permanently surrounded by cultural heterogeneity regularly produces struggles over pressures to assimilate and disputes about how much the members of each group ought to accommodate to each other or to the norms of the wider society.

10.4 THE CULTURAL EFFECTS OF CONTACT

Anthropologists probably have always been aware that the non-Western societies in which they were doing fieldwork had been heavily affected by imperialist forces of one kind or another. This awareness was surely responsible at least in part for the relativistic defense of bounded, internally harmonious "cultures" so important in the early twentieth century. It was only after World War II, however, and especially after the achievement of political independence by former European colonies, that the colonial contact situation itself became an explicit focus of ethnographic study.

When anthropologists began to address the consequences of cultural contact, they invented a new vocabulary to try to describe the processes that seemed to be at work. In the United States, Herskovits and his colleagues spoke of *acculturation*: a process by which cultures in contact borrow ideas and practices from one another, thereby modifying or replacing traditional ideas and practices. The study of cultural borrowing had always been important in North American anthropology, and anthropologists pointed out that the process often involved reshaping the borrowed item to make it fit into preexisting cultural arrangements. When viewed by an outside observer, the result often was described as *syncretism*: a mixing of elements from two or more traditions. For example, a syncretistic religion emerges when missionary Christianity and a traditional indigenous religious system both contribute to new shared spiritual practices that are neither wholly "Christian" nor wholly "traditional" (see chapter 4).

Frequently cited examples of religious syncretism are the so-called *cargo cults* that developed in Melanesia and New Guinea in the decades after colonial conquest, many of them stimulated by contact with the US military during World War II. The *cargo* refers, in general, to the abundant manufactured goods brought to the islands by Western missionaries, traders, and soldiers. Although cargo cults differed in many specifics of belief and practice, they had in common the mixture of Christian religious doctrine and traditional indigenous beliefs about ancestors. A key feature was the belief that the ancestors would return on ships or planes, bringing for their kin the cargo that Europeans possessed in such abundance. In some places, members of the cargo cult even constructed models of airplanes or control towers that had the ritual function of enticing the ancestors and their cargo. (See the discussion about religious change in chapter 4.)

Acculturation theorists realized that processes of cultural borrowing and modification might be mutual—with the partners involved taking from and giving to one another on an equal, unconstrained basis—or that they could be skewed in one direction only as a result of unequal power relations. The latter situation could often be found under colonial rule. For example, children in colonies frequently were taken from their home villages and taught the colonizer's language and culture in boarding schools deliberately designed to cut off children from the influence of their families' traditional way of life. In such cases, the goal was often explicitly to "civilize" the children, which in the circumstances meant to replace the children's culture with that of the colonizer. That is, the colonizers wanted these children to assimilate to colonial society and culture, to cut off identification with their culture of origin and become totally absorbed in the ways of Europeans. Pressure to assimilate is not unique to colonial situations; it is commonly encountered by refugee or immigrant groups moving into societies dominated by cultural traditions very different from their own. In both cases, however, the goal of assimilation is the same: the disappearance of distinctive cultural features that set the lower-ranking and less influential subaltern groups apart from those privileged and powerful groups who dominate them.

Struggles over multiculturalism at home and charges of cultural imperialism abroad forced anthropologists to reexamine the processes that ensue when people of different cultural backgrounds come into contact. Their field research showed that the realities of cultural exchange were much more complex than the struggles of identity politics or the worries about cultural imperialism would lead one to imagine. Their efforts were complemented by the actions of individual members of different subaltern groups who refused to assimilate to a hegemonic culture, asserted their right to pick and choose from global culture the customs they wanted to follow, and resisted attempts by other members of the groups to which they belonged to police their beliefs and behavior (see chapter 2).

The charge of Western cultural imperialism—that Western cultures were dominating and destroying other cultures, producing global cultural homogenization—did not hold up to scrutiny. The notion of cultural imperialism denies agency to non-Western people who make use of Western cultural forms. It also ignores the fact that many non-Western cultural forms have been adopted by members of Western societies (e.g., sushi). Finally, it ignores the fact that cultural forms sometimes bypass the West entirely as they move from one part of the world to another (e.g., movies from India have been popular in Africa for decades). These are all examples of the active reconciliation of cultural practices from elsewhere with local practices to serve local purposes: that is, they are examples of indigenization—sometimes also called *domestication* or *customization* (see Inda and Rosaldo 2007; see also chapter 2).

The rate of cultural borrowing followed by indigenization has speeded up enormously under conditions of globalization. This has led many social scientists to describe the process as **cultural hybridization**. The emphasis in discussions of cultural hybridization is on forms of cultural borrowing that produce something completely new from the fusing of elements of donor and recipient cultures. Rather than speaking of dependency and cultural loss, this discourse emphasizes creativity and cultural gain. It acknowledges the agency of those who borrow and helps discredit the notion that "authentic" cultural traditions never change. This approach offers a new angle from which to consider such phenomena as cargo cults. Rather than being viewed simply as curious products of culture contact, cargo cults begin to look like creative attempts by colonized groups deprived of the promised benefits of capitalist colonialism to make sense of their deprivation and to overcome it by innovative religious means.

But the concept of cultural hybridization is not without problems. Cultural hybridity implies the mixture of two or more nonhybridized, "pure" cultures, which are not supposed to exist. Furthermore, hybrid identities are not always liberating if they are not freely adopted. In fact, anthropologists have been able to show that cultural hybridization is experienced differently by those with power and those without power. Those with power are the ones more able to pick and choose as they please from the offerings of global culture. Indeed, cultural hybridity has been commodified, on display and for sale at international music festivals and ethnic art markets. Those who can consume these multicultural offerings on their own terms experience cultural hybridity very differently from those who have hybridity thrust on them. These latter are often members of poor and marginal migrant groups who feel unable to protect themselves from forms of cultural hybridization they have not chosen and that threaten their own fragile survival structures. When cultural hybridity becomes fashionable, the experience of hybridized elites is highlighted, and the class exploitation and racial oppression that hybridized nonelites continue to experience often disappears from view. To ignore these alternative ways of experiencing hybridity is misleading and dangerous.

10.5 GLOBALIZATION, CITIZENSHIP, AND HUMAN RIGHTS

Identity politics practiced in a context of globalization has led to the development of a variety of new understandings about the nature of the nation-state and citizenship that anthropologists have begun to study. For example, in the contemporary world, migrants from one part of the world to another regularly keep in touch with those they left behind, and this can lead to their continuing support of nationalist struggles in their homeland, a phenomenon called **long-distance nationalism**. Sometimes those left behind in the homeland try to create a *transborder state* by reaching out to those who have migrated elsewhere, claiming them as citizens of their nation of origin even if they are also citizens of the state to which they have migrated. Such *transborder citizenship* may be written into laws granting dual nationality or extending voting rights in the country of origin to migrants who are citizens elsewhere (Schiller and Fouron 2002).

The emergence of transborder states exposes the fact that some formally recognized nation-states in fact cannot meet the needs of all their citizens, some of whom they must send abroad as migrants. The emergence of transborder citizens calls into question traditional beliefs about citizenship in a nation-state. It becomes clear that *legal citizenship*, granted by the state, is often at odds with the *substantive citizenship* in which migrants engage in their new homelands as they take action to build better lives for themselves and their families. Indeed, given the unparalleled opportunities for mobility that globalization offers those with the right connections and resources, the very idea of citizenship in a single nation-state is undermined. For example, elite overseas Chinese families with business interests all over the world have created a kind of *flexible citizenship* that allows them, with multiple passports and ample funds, to move from one nation-state to the next or to settle family members in different nation-states, depending on which regime serves their family interests best. Cultivating the ability to reap the advantages or to circumvent the obligations connected with citizenship in any particular nation-state, these elite Chinese have developed a *postnational ethos* in which the very concept of nationalism has lost meaning (Ong 1999). Under these circumstances, struggles over policies managing the status of immigrants and refugees have become perhaps the most acute political struggles in the contemporary world, and anthropologists are actively engaged in research on their effects.

In a globalized world, people in many peripheral countries have become familiar with the ideology of individual **human rights**: rights to which all humans everywhere are entitled, by virtue of being human. The concept of human rights originally developed in powerful core cultures, but today local groups in other parts of the world also may claim that they have been deprived of their natural rights to life, liberty, or property. They often find allies in core nations who support their demands that their human rights as individuals be respected. Such claims frequently have been made by citizens of nations whose leaders signed the United Nations Declaration on Human Rights but who find their own rights being violated by those same leaders.

On one hand, asylum seekers may attempt to cross international borders because they are looking for a place to settle where their human rights will be respected. On the other hand, minority groups living within the boundaries of a nation-state who are subjected to coercive attempts at cultural assimilation may resist and demand that the wider society respect not only their individual human rights but also the shared **cultural rights** of the group to which they belong. The argument has been made in recent years, in international forums like the United Nations, that cultural groups have rights of their own, distinct from the rights of their individual members. Such cultural rights usually include whatever is seen as necessary to keep the group's culture viable, such as adequate economic and political resources to preserve their values and practices, including their language, and pass them on to future generations. Indeed, international debates over human rights—individual versus group rights, political and civil rights versus socioeconomic rights, rights as defined by nation-states versus the right of self-determination by indigenous and other minority groups within their borders—show that defining human rights is an ongoing multicultural project of global proportions.

Some anthropologists suggest that a culture of human rights has emerged under globalization, such that individuals and groups of many different kinds, in many different parts of the world, resort to courts of law to receive redress when they believe their human rights have been violated. (See chapter 8 for discussion of law.) One of the most striking consequences of this development has been the ways in which *filing* a human rights claim itself shapes the kind of claim plaintiffs can make. That is, plaintiffs must craft their cases using the categories that human rights law recognizes. If these legal categories are at odds with categories that are meaningful to the plaintiffs, plaintiffs often have no choice but to tailor their case to match the categories that the law recognizes. Plaintiffs may be forced to portray themselves or their culture in ways that contradict their own self-understandings or else give up the opportunity to have their day in court. Even if they win their case—perhaps especially if they win—these experiences are bound to affect their views of themselves and their culture in ways they may not have intended but cannot easily reverse. At the beginning of the twenty-first century, there is probably no place on earth where the discourse of human rights has not penetrated—and global networks established by human rights treaties and courts of law make it possible for a local case to gain international attention with great rapidity.

Claims for cultural rights, as well as individual rights, are taken seriously in the twenty-first century. However, sociopolitical entities like nation-states still depend for their legitimacy on their being run by representatives of the "nation." The pressures to assimilate recalcitrant minorities may range from *ethnocide*, or the deliberate destruction of a cultural tradition, to *genocide*, or the mass murder of an entire social or cultural group whose presence is seen as threatening to those who run a state, as has been documented in Nazi Germany, Cambodia, the former Yugoslavia, Rwanda, and elsewhere. (See the discussion of ethnocide and genocide in chapter 5.) In the face of such intergroup violence, anthropologists and other social scientists have struggled to define ways of dealing with the differences that divide cultural and political groups that cannot avoid having to deal with one another.

One recent suggestion has been that the contemporary multicultural challenges may be met if we find a way to promote among all the value of cosmopolitanism. **Cosmopolitanism** refers to being at ease in more than one cultural setting. It was promoted by the Stoic philosophers of ancient Rome and revived by the philosopher Emmanuel Kant during the Enlightenment. For Kant, to be a cosmopolitan meant to be experienced in the ways of Western Europe, and it was applied to elites only. Those who would promote cosmopolitanism today, however, want to extend the concept to include the alternative "cosmopolitanisms" of nonelites such as poor migrants who manage to deal gracefully with the culturally hybrid experiences they encounter and the multiple perspectives they must juggle whenever they find themselves answerable to different groups of people with different values and practices.

To cultivate this kind of cosmopolitan awareness is often difficult. For one thing, it requires more than simply being open to or inclusive of other cultures. Many anthropologists would argue that it also requires acknowledging the legacy of inequality bequeathed on many of the world's people by colonialism. In addition, it requires recognition that the cosmopolitanism of the future must involve active input from individuals and groups whose views have not been acknowledged in the past. For example, it may well be that a Western concept like "human rights" will become widely accepted, but a cosmopolitan understanding of human rights will need to pay attention to the understandings of human rights that grow out of struggles by non-Western peoples who have indigenized the concept to make it better reflect their own experiences. In the best of circumstances, both Western and non-Western contributors to cosmopolitan projects may be able to offer each other the tools they need to achieve less polarized ways of living simultaneously in multiple worlds. This is a form of cultural hybridization that many anthropologists, and those among whom they work, would very much endorse.

At the same time, cosmopolitan thinking is challenged by ongoing violence and persecution around the world, often made most visible by the plight of growing numbers of refugees seeking to escape violence and persecution in their countries of origin by migrating to the European Union, the United States, or other nation-states. French anthropologist Didier Fassin has observed that, until the 1980s, political persecution was generally considered a human rights violation entitling victims to enter countries like France. After that time, however, political asylum seekers were increasingly lumped together with victims of earthquakes and tsunamis and addressed by a new form of governmentality (see chapter 8), which he calls **humanitarianism**, "a mode of governing that concerns the victims of poverty, homelessness, unemployment, and exile, as well as disasters, famines, epidemics and wars—in short, every situation characterized by precariousness" (2012, x). Humanitarian thinking is based on recognition of a universal humanity, but it also emphasizes "humaneness," the feelings that draw human beings to help other humans who are suffering. However, Fassin points out that the discourse of humanitarianism has come to replace the discourse of human rights: today, outside observers are encouraged to regard all crises as equal and to experience empathy for the suffering victims rather than indignation at the violation of their human rights. According to Fassin, humanitarian reason involves a constant balancing act between compassion for asylum seekers and repression in the form of strict immigration policies. He concludes that, for good or for ill, humanitarian reason "bridges the contradictions of our world, and makes the intolerableness of its injustices somewhat more bearable. Hence its consensual force" (2012, xi).

10.6 NEW GLOBAL INSTITUTIONS

In recent decades, a large number of new institutions have become involved in working with national governments and other communities located within their borders. Members of these **nongovernmental organizations (NGOs)** provide forms of expertise that apparently qualify them to advise state officials and members of local communities on how best to address particular challenges they face, often in relation to social or economic development. Many NGOs began as institutions designed to bypass national or local governments, which were seen to be corrupt or ineffectual. Today, NGOs have become major players in all sorts of development projects—and a focus of much ethnographic fieldwork. Sometimes NGOs are donors who fund development projects; sometimes NGOs propose projects of their own in a competition for donor funding. Ultimately, local and national government representatives, target populations, NGOs, and donors become stakeholders invested in the successful outcome of the development projects in which they are involved. But additional groups and institutions may assert their own stakeholder status and be drawn into the development project as it unfolds.

Before the 1970s, for example, outside development experts usually insisted that proper forest management involved the conservation of resources, and forest dwellers were often seen as threats to conservation. Since the 1970s, however, the need to take into account the effects of forest management on the people who were living there has become more prominent. One development model that combines conservation with poverty reduction has been attempted in a number of forests in recent years, with mixed results. For example, local people may earn money as forest rangers or from tourists who pay to visit the forest; unfortunately, this income is often insufficient to reduce poverty in any substantial way. Even when such projects look promising, they may not be sustainable, due to a variety of complications, including the funding cycles of donors.

But local people are not passive, and they have often been able to find allies to support their efforts to defend their interests. For example, anthropologists have documented cases in which local and international environmental activists have worked with indigenous social movements and NGOs to defend ownership of their traditional resources, sometimes by nontraditional means. For example, they may create maps of their traditional territories and use these in lawsuits that are sometimes decided in their favor. In Ecuador, for example, some indigenous communities have been granted full control and authority (or *sovereignty*) over traditional lands that are located within the boundaries of the nation-state. Anthropologist Juliet Erazo writes about how the indigenous Amazonian Kichwa territory of Rukullakta has dealt with the challenges and opportunities that accompany these changes. On one hand, with territorial sovereignty comes the responsibility of figuring out how to persuade those who live in Rukullakta to start thinking of themselves as territorial citizens willing to take on responsibility for running the territory; that is, leaders are learning how to fashion a new form of governmentality appropriate to territorial citizenship. On the other hand, managing their own development requires funding that they must secure from nongovernmental donors, so territorial leaders are obliged to fashion projects that donors find attractive. During the Cold War, this meant being willing to turn their land into a ranching cooperative; but since the end of the Cold War, donors have become more interested in funding projects that protect the environment and promote sustainable development. Recognizing these new opportunities, Rukullakta's residents gave up their previous legal designation as a cooperative; highlighted their indigenous identity; began to speak of their lands as an indigenous territory; and elected a *kuraka*, or chief. Much of their land is now part of a UN Biosphere reserve for purposes of conservation. Erazo emphasizes that these changes do not reflect a romantic view of their past but represent pragmatic efforts to represent themselves to donors in ways that will allow them to obtain outside assistance under changed circumstances, and to retain control of their lands (2013).

NGOs are not the only organizations advising local actors or intervening in local policymaking. For many years, organizations such as the United Nations, the World Bank, The World Trade Organization, and others have become important players in the lives of people on many continents. According to Ronald Niezen and Maria Sapignoli these **global organizations** are hard to define, because they embody paradoxes: although they are active around the world, the interests of particular nation-states affect how much they are able to achieve. As in the case of Rukullakta, a global organization like the UN often defends the claims of indigenous groups seeking official recognition, not only of their distinctive identities but also of their rights to development; and yet, the UN's mandate also goes beyond the mandates of NGOs. A global organization like the UN, Niezen and Sapignoli conclude, "is a distinct kind of institution, situated in intersections of the 'local,' the 'national,' and the 'global,' in which globality emerges as the central point of reference (although as much in the realm of ideals as in reality)" (2017, 2).

Ethnographic research in global organizations has increased in recent years, as anthropologists have encountered representatives of such organizations in the course of traditional fieldwork. Some ethnographers eventually chose to make global organizations their primary field site. Research in a global organization requires long-term commitment and traditional participant-observation (in this case, sometimes working for the organization on selected projects). It also challenges academic anthropologists to work collaboratively with interlocutors who are themselves highly educated, cosmopolitan experts. Frequently, this kind of ethnography is most successful when carried out by teams of researchers.

According to Niezen and Sapignoli, a key feature of global organizations like the UN are the way they "conceal the uses (and abuses) of power that take place through the initiatives they sponsor, downplaying their deeply rooted value judgments as they apply their policies and programs" (2017, 11). This is accomplished by using technical, managerial discourse that avoids mentioning politics, as well as by using numbers as apparently objective forms of evidence and measurement. At the same time, refusing to formally acknowledge power inequalities has advantages for global organizations like the UN that have no ability to impose their projects on states, but must rely on diplomacy, persuading state institutions to collaborate with them to institute change (Niezen and Sapignoli 2017, 12). "If the behavior of non-compliant states cannot always be influenced by compulsion, and if directly invoking the wrongs of the state are likely to produce no other result than defensive denial and justification, then other means of persuasion must be found, means that do not cause offense but that at the same time communicate concerns and offer avenues to reform without losing face" (2017, 13).

In the face of these tensions, contradictions, and paradoxes, Niezen and Sapignoli conclude that global organizations are best understood as "palaces of hope." Their goals "are sometimes not only hopeful and ambitious, but willfully and blindly impossible"; and yet "almost miraculously, there continue to be impressive numbers of NGOs that participate in UN programs" (2017, 19). Those who work within the bureaucracies of these institutions regularly become disillusioned, as they are aware of the gap between hopeful ambitions and the practical impossibility of realizing them. Even so, Niezen and Sapignoli conclude that "hope . . . still often lies hidden behind the sordid reality of humans in conflict . . . behind all the ills of the world that together make up the agendas of global organizations" (2017, 21).

FOR FURTHER READING

Overview   Inda and Rosaldo 2007; Kearney 1995; Robbins 2004
Colonialism   Dirks 2006; Pels 1997; Stoler 2002
Refugees, Genocide, and Human Rights   Daniel and Knudsen 1995; Goodale 2009; Malkki 1995; Merry 2006; Messer 1993; Nagengast 1994
Globalization   Abu-Lughod 1989; Appadurai 1996; Featherstone 1990; Fischer and Benson 2006; Hannerz 1996; Lewellen 2002
Tourism   Chambers 2010; Gmelch 2010; Smith 1989
Dependency and Development   Edelman and Haugerud 2005; Lewellen 1995
Migration and Long-distance Nationalism   De Genova 2017; Schiller and Fouron 2002
Citizenship   Ong 1999
Cosmopolitanism   Breckenridge, Pollock, Bhabha, and Chakrabarty 2002
Global Institutions   Brosius, Tsing, and Zerner 2005; Erazo 2013; Fassin 2012; Li 2007; Niezen and Sapignoli 2017; Ong and Collier, 2005

CHAPTER 11

The Anthropology of Science, Technology, and Medicine

The key terms and concepts covered in this chapter, in the order in which they appear:

science studies

technology
science and technology studies
cyborgs

health
medical anthropology
biomedicine
disease
suffering
sickness
culture-bound syndromes
illness
cosmopolitan medicine

ethnomedical systems
medical hegemony

adaptation

critical medical anthropology
biology of poverty
subjectivity
trauma
structural violence
biologization
medicalization
biosociality
health activism
biological citizenship

We observed in chapter 1 that the discipline of anthropology was founded as a scientific study of human beings. Science is still central to the work of many contemporary anthropologists. By the beginning of the twenty-first century, however, it had become clear that not all anthropologists understand science in the same way. In the course of the past 50 years, historians, philosophers, and other scholars (including scientists themselves) have reconsidered traditional assumptions about what science is and how it works. **Science studies** is the overall umbrella term under which scholarly research exploring these issues has come to be known, and anthropologists have become active contributors to science studies.

In the 1970s and 1980s, some scientists criticized science studies research, concerned that their work was being unfairly maligned by outsiders who had no understanding of science. By the 1990s, however, it had become clear that much of this controversy was misplaced. Even in the early years, science studies scholars regularly collaborated with working scientists in fields like physics and biology, and this kind of cross-disciplinary cooperation has increased over time. Science studies research has led to widespread agreement across many disciplines that science in practice often does not conform to the idealized images of science often presented to nonscientists.

In the twentieth century, most discussions of science centered on concerns about scientific *theories*: Did they build incrementally on one another over time, or was the history of science characterized by a series of revolutionary theoretical shifts? For instance, was Einstein's theory of relativity a natural outgrowth of Newtonian physics, or did it mark a break with Newtonian thinking? Did modern genetics develop smoothly out of earlier theories about inheritance in biology, or did it mark a sharp shift away from such thinking? For a long time, debates about these matters remained confined to disputes about relationships among conceptual systems in science. The impasse was broken, however, when science studies scholars began to produce studies showing how the making of scientific concepts and theories articulates with specific *laboratory practices* that rely on particular forms of *scientific apparatus* (e.g., Galison 1987, 1997). Awareness of the need to describe this articulation between theoretical concepts, actions by living organisms, and the manipulation of material objects led science studies scholars like Bruno Latour, Michel Callon, and others to speak of *actor-networks* in which agency was *distributed* over interconnected living and nonliving components, which they called *actants*. Among other things, this implied that nonliving actants (like scientific apparatus) possessed their own forms of material agency, above and beyond the agency exercised by human scientists. *Assemblage* is another concept, usually associated with the work of French theorists Gilles Deleuze and Félix Guattari, that some anthropologists prefer to use when describing the process of the fitting together of heterogeneous elements to produce new hybrid entities that nevertheless retain traces of their heterogeneous origins and are liable to disassemble over time and space.

Debates continue among anthropologists and others about the similarities and differences, advantages or disadvantages, of using actor-networks or assemblages to guide their analysis of processes that work themselves out over time and space. However, both sets of concepts are attractive to some anthropologists insofar as they permit them to address *processes* of emergence or dissolution of entities (entities in the making) that other analysts assume to be fixed and unchanging (entities as made). For instance, classic Enlightenment accounts of knowledge-making begin by marking out unchanging ancient boundaries between entities with fixed essences—for example, "nature" and "culture." As Bruno Latour argued many years ago, however, the ozone hole in Earth's atmosphere is best understood as a hybrid product of both "nature" and "culture"—of activity in the nonhuman world and of human activity together. Reasoning about natural-cultural hybrids like the ozone hole or glacial melting or air pollution has been central to the development of science-studies-grounded arguments about the Anthropocene that directly implicate human activities in global climate change.

Finally, science studies research has shown that it is misleading to speak of "science" in the singular. Instead, we need to acknowledge the existence of different scientific disciplines whose claims about different facets of the world rest on different kinds of experimental practices, different kinds of material evidence, and different theoretical frameworks. However, the conclusions of science studies scholars do not amount to a rejection of science or a denial of scientific achievements; on the contrary, it would be more accurate to say that the result has been a richer understanding of the many complexities involved in scientific research.

11.1 SCIENCE AND ANTHROPOLOGY

One science studies innovation important for anthropology was *laboratory ethnography*. Ethnographers followed scientists as they went about their everyday laboratory practices, discovering (among other things) the range of embodied skills that scientists in certain fields must master if they are to effectively operate the often-elaborate technical apparatuses that makes successful research possible. Ethnographers like Bruno Latour also revealed the significance of a range of "nonscientific" institutions and individuals *outside* the laboratory, whose support was essential if "strictly scientific" research projects *inside* the laboratory were to continue. Successful directors of laboratories, for example, had to wear many hats: not only did they need to be able to secure proper working conditions for their scientific staff, they also had to cultivate good relationships with university administrators, laboratory instrument makers, and government funding agencies. Pioneers of science studies in anthropology include Sharon Traweek (1992), who explored these sorts of issues in the world of high-energy physicists, and anthropologist Emily Martin (2001), who brought a science studies perspective to the study of reproduction in the United States, situating the views of medical science alongside women's understandings of their own bodily processes.

Scientists themselves, of course, had long been aware of the nonscientific factors that were essential to scientific success. Wider public awareness of these factors, however, called into question popular images of scientists as individual geniuses isolated in their laboratories, exclusively concerned with pushing back the frontiers of knowledge. Frank acknowledgment that research priorities and funding could be shaped by sociocultural, economic, and political interests challenged idealized views of science as a pure, disinterested search for universal, objective truth. Together with many anthropologists, many scientists value science studies for having provided a more accurate, if less exalted, view of the complex alliances and entanglements that produce scientific outcomes. Historian of science Steven Shapin encapsulates the science studies perspective in the title of a recent collection of his essays: *Never Pure: Historical Studies of Science as If It Was Produced by People with Bodies, Situated in Time, Space, Culture, and Society, and Struggling for Credibility and Authority* (2010). By the end of the first decade of the twenty-first century, research in the anthropology of science, technology, and medicine was well established in anthropology, and theoretical insights derived from science studies were being adopted to address an increasingly wide range of research topics of interest to anthropologists and other scholars.

11.2 ANTHROPOLOGY, SCIENCE, AND TECHNOLOGY

The power of Western science has been furthered for several centuries by innovations in technical apparatuses used in laboratories. The Industrial Revolution owed a great deal to the technological innovations to which scientific research contributed, and contemporary industries rely on scientists and engineers to continue to innovate in ways that allow them to compete more successfully in the capitalist marketplace. But what is technology? At the most general level, **technology** is usually thought to refer to material objects shaped by human beings to increase their ability to act on the world and reshape it for their own purposes. Stone tools made over 3 million years ago in Africa by our ancestors are the oldest evidence of human technology, which long predate the emergence of our own species, *Homo sapiens*, some 200,000 years ago. Technologies became much more elaborate and diverse a few thousand years ago, when humans began to settle down, domesticate animals and plants, and create the first complex societies. It has been only within the past 300 years or so that the Industrial Revolution in Europe marked a new burst of technological creativity with far-reaching consequences for all human societies everywhere.

At times, the power of technology has seemed so enormous that humans have seen it as almost a living entity, pushing human beings and their concerns aside, bending us to its will, and determining the direction our societies will develop. There is no question that some technologies are indeed powerful: from steam engines to atomic weapons to computers, the profound consequences that followed their incorporation into human societies are undeniable, and often frightening. But technology is not an autonomous force. **Science and technology studies** (sometimes called STS) is an offshoot of science studies that has been able to demonstrate that technologies, like science itself, require support of various kinds if they are to be effective. Technologies, from electrical power grids to cell phones, help to stabilize new forms of human sociocultural arrangements, but they must in turn be supported by other forms of technology, as well as sociocultural institutions and practices, if they are to be successfully adopted and maintained. Smartphones, for example, are ubiquitous and extremely useful, until there is a break in service and people have to find different methods of staying in touch, reading the news, checking bank balances, and so on. Controversial technologies may be denied funding; and controversial forms of scientific research may be stifled because of social, political, or ethical opposition. These factors become visible in complex ethnographic accounts of infrastructure development involving transportation or other utilities in different parts of the world (e.g., Sopranzetti 2018, Anand 2017, Von Schnitzler 2016).

In common with other scholars who study science and technology, anthropologists have come to think of many features of culture and social organization as being, themselves, technologies. Anthropologists influenced by the work of French theorist Michel Foucault may have been the first to think and speak about technology in this way (see chapters 6 and 10). In his historical studies, Foucault highlighted the ways in which practices characteristically associated with social institutions (clinics, madhouses, hospitals, and prisons) act on their inmates in ways very similar to the way a material artifact (such as a whip) might act on them, directing their movements and enforcing discipline. Indeed, those who think about technology this way may agree with feminist science studies scholar Donna Haraway, who argued some years ago that human beings are **cyborgs**, hybrid entities that are part living organism, part machine, living in worlds that are simultaneously material and symbolic, living and nonliving, human and nonhuman. It is not necessary to think of science fiction when thinking about cyborgs—a cataract operation that inserts a plastic lens into a human eye turns that human into a cyborg (see chapter 6).

Many contemporary anthropologists have been attracted to science and technology studies. Some anthropologists who study processes of globalization explore the way technology intervenes in a variety of ways to reorganize social ties across the globe (see chapter 10). Anthropologists who study computer technology analyze not only the economic and business sides of this phenomenon but also the transformations of individual identities and social ties that accompany individuals' increasing involvement with various forms of online social networking (Kelty 2008). Other anthropologists explore the way that online platforms open up possibilities for the creation of new art forms, such as massively multiplayer, online, role-playing games like World of Warcraft. (See chapter 3 on media anthropology.) A recurring feature in many anthropological studies of technology is recognition of the uneven way in which different human communities are (and are not) incorporated into computer-mediated forms of social interaction. Access to this technology is highly skewed in favor of wealthy, educated members of powerful states with strong economies, although Internet cafés have reduced some of that disparity. Success in the cyberworld depends not only on literacy in a written language (usually English) but also on mastery of the machines themselves and the software that runs on them. At the same time, some forms of cybertechnology (such as cell phones and now smartphones) have spread quickly throughout the world and are rapidly being customized to meet the needs of users of many kinds, at all income levels.

In recent decades, programs of science studies and STS have become widely institutionalized in university departments throughout North America, Europe, and elsewhere. Anthropologists are often members of these departments, working alongside scholars trained in a range of other scientific and social scientific disciplines. Science studies is now well entrenched within anthropology, and its findings are increasingly being incorporated into a number of anthropological specialties, including the anthropology of the environment (see chapter 10) and medical anthropology.

11.3 THE ANTHROPOLOGY OF MEDICINE

Members of the same society who share an understanding of what it means to be healthy are also likely to agree about what symptoms indicate an absence of health. Many people in the United States are likely to understand **health** as a state of physical, emotional, and mental well-being, together with an absence of disease or disability that would interfere with such well-being. But anthropologists recognize that what counts as wellness or its opposite is very much shaped by people's cultural, social, and political experiences and expectations. This means that measuring health (or its reverse) in a straightforward way can sometimes be challenging. Increasing numbers of anthropologists now apply insights and practices of the various subfields of anthropology (including science studies) in efforts to understand and find solutions to health challenges faced by members of the many communities where they work. This area of specialization is generally called **medical anthropology**.

Medical anthropologists have been deeply influenced by (as well as critical of) findings by Western physicians and medical scientists that claim to describe normal human biological functioning, the causes for impairment of such functioning, and the scientifically developed therapies available to cure or manage such impairment. These traditional scientific forms of knowledge and practice are often called **biomedicine**, and forms of biological impairment identified and explained within the discourse of biomedicine are those to which medical anthropologists often apply the term **disease**. However, medical anthropologists regularly deal with systems of belief and practice in relation to human health that developed outside the influence of biomedicine. This is why they have developed a technical vocabulary that does not presume the universality of biomedical understandings of health and disease. For example, many medical anthropologists prefer to use the term **suffering** to describe the forms of physical, mental, or emotional distress experienced by individuals who may or may not subscribe to biomedical understandings of disease or that do not fall under the categories of suffering recognized in biomedicine. One of the earliest discoveries made by Western anthropologists was that people with different cultural traditions often had particular ideas of their own about the sources of human suffering and how it might be healed. As a result, medical anthropologists have often used the term **sickness** to refer to classifications of physical, mental, and emotional distress recognized by members of a particular cultural community. Sometimes such sicknesses may bear a close resemblance to diseases recognized by scientific biomedicine; but other times, the sickness (and therapy to relieve it) may be unique to a particular cultural group: such sicknesses been called **culture-bound syndromes**. Finally, some medical anthropologists contrast both the biomedical understanding of disease and local cultural categories of sickness with a suffering person's own understanding of her or his distress, which is called **illness**.

Anthropologists have long been intrigued by the range of explanations people in different cultures offer to explain why people get sick and how they may be cured. While knowledge of medicinal plants and other treatments resembling biomedicine often plays a role, many ethnographers have been impressed by explanations that attribute sickness to the breaking of taboos, punishment by ancestors, witchcraft, or sorcery. Evans-Pritchard's celebrated study of witchcraft, oracles, and magic among the Azande, for example, demonstrated how sickness and death (but also healing) could be explained in mystical terms, even while the Azande accepted that the material causes recognized by Western biomedicine also were implicated. For example, Evans-Pritchard found that the Azande understood the material causation involved when a person trips over a root and cuts his foot in the same way as a Western scientific observer understands it; nevertheless, the Azande might also invoke witchcraft to explain why the cut fails to heal. (See discussion of the Azande in chapter 4.)

By the 1960s, the anthropology of medicine had expanded. Inspired by the work of Clifford Geertz, whose contemporary work in interpretive cultural anthropology focused on the systemic features of cultural domains like religion and common sense, Charles Leslie and his associates urged that non-Western medical beliefs and practices be understood as cultural systems (Leslie 1976). Leslie was particularly interested in "great tradition" medical systems that developed over centuries in the civilizations of South Asia and China. Recognizing the sophistication of fully fledged alternative medical systems (like Ayurvedic medicine in India) helped to relativize Western biomedicine. Leslie also pointed out that Western exploration, colonial expansion, and industrialization had fostered the spread and adoption of Western biomedical practices around the world. Because scientific biomedicine has become incorporated into medical systems throughout the world, and is no longer the exclusive property of "the West," Leslie argued that it was more accurately characterized as **cosmopolitan medicine**. Around the world, cosmopolitan medicine enjoys high status, but it coexists with a range of alternative **ethnomedical systems** based on the practices of local social groups—a state of affairs known as *medical pluralism*. Under conditions of medical pluralism, people seeking medical care develop *hierarchies of resort*: first, they consult local practitioners whom they know and trust, and who treat them with respect; if they fail to receive satisfaction, they will seek out practitioners associated with other ethnomedical systems. In the United States, biomedicine enjoys **medical hegemony**: it is the most highly valued medical system and the standard against which others are regularly compared. But medical pluralism means that residents of the United States who are dissatisfied with biomedical treatments, or who cannot afford to pay for them, are able to choose from a range of alternative ethnomedical systems such as acupuncture, herbal medicine, or visits to a shaman. Indeed, they may consider biomedicine to be just another ethnomedical system.

11.4 HUMAN HEALTH IN EVOLUTIONARY CONTEXT

Medical anthropologists who study patterns of sickness and health in different human populations may have training in evolutionary biology or medicine and may regularly become skilled in disciplines like demography, the statistical study of human populations, or *epidemiology*, which collects information on the distribution of disease in human populations and seeks explanations for such distributions. They learn to distinguish *epidemic* diseases that spread quickly over a short period of time from *endemic* diseases that are always present in the population. Demography and epidemiology were originally developed to collect information in large settled populations in nation-states, which means that medical anthropologists who carry out fieldwork in other kinds of human populations need to adapt demographic and epidemiological techniques accordingly. Research by ethnographers working in small, isolated communities requires such modification, for example, as does research by archaeologists and biological anthropologists who attempt to calculate demographic patterns characteristic of past human populations, a field called *paleodemography*. Some archaeologists use evidence from the biological remains of human populations to reconstruct patterns of sickness and health in past societies, a field called *paleopathology*. However, contemporary medical anthropologists work in complex societies all over the world, regularly collaborating with biomedical scientists to solve health problems in particular communities. The ethnographic insights cultural anthropologists can bring to such collaborations is increasingly recognized and valued.

The anthropological perspective has always emphasized that human biological adaptations to physical environments are mediated by cultural practices. How this relationship is understood, however, varies among medical anthropologists, depending on the subfields within which they were trained and the particular theoretical orientations that prevail within those subfields at particular points in time. Some anthropologists (including some medical anthropologists) are comfortable speaking of both biological and cultural evolution, and they focus on the biological and cultural evolutionary contexts of human sickness and health. This approach tends to accept the traditional Western modernist distinction between "biology" and "culture" and conceives of both biological and cultural evolution as processes shaped by natural selection on units of "information." (See chapter 2 on cultural inheritance theorists.) Units of biological information are associated with "genes," and biological evolution is measured by changes in gene frequencies over time (in conformity with the modern synthesis that is the foundation of contemporary evolutionary biology). Cultural evolution is measured by changes in the frequencies of particular units of cultural information across space and time, as these are acquired and passed on by means of social learning (Boyd and Richerson 1985; Durham 1991).

For medical anthropologists who seek to understand human sickness and health in an evolutionary context, a key concept is that of **adaptation**: an adjustment by an organism (or group of organisms) that helps it cope with environmental challenges of various kinds. Most evolutionary biologists tend to restrict their attention to *biological adaptations*: modifications of anatomical or physiological attributes of organisms, produced by natural selection, that better adjust organisms to the environmental settings in which they live. Examples would include the wings of birds, the heightened sense of smell in mammals active at night, and the fact that humans walk upright on their hind limbs. Anthropologists, however, are also committed to the view that human adaptation to any environ-ment is always mediated by culture. As a result, medical anthropologists who adopt an evolutionary perspective are also on the lookout for *cultural adaptations* that help human individuals or groups adjust to the demands of their environ-mental settings. Human populations began to rely on cultural adaptations long ago. Major cultural adaptations included not only the manufacture of tools out of stone, bone, and other materials; they also included the domestication of plants and animals and the modification of landscapes to create farms and pastures and dwellings of various kinds. It is important to recognize that such cultural adaptations do not free humans from the pressures of natural selection; rather, they *change* the nature of the selective pressures human populations face. For example, populations that shift from hunting and gathering food to tending do-mesticated crops may be able to produce more food for more people on less land, which can be viewed as an adaptation. At the same time, living together in a settlement means that infectious diseases pass easily from person to person and become endemic in the population, which can be viewed as a *maladaptation.*

As theoretical biologists begin to pay increasing attention to phenotypic plasticity and the consequences of developmental processes for human health and illness, medical anthropologists, as we saw earlier, have become increasingly sensitive to the kinds of social arrangements that may appear adaptive for some individuals or groups but highly maladaptive for others. This recognition led medical anthropologist Margaret Lock to coin the term *local biologies* to refer to "biological difference among people that results from bodily responses to differ-ing environments over time and across space. Such differences are not genetically determined, and a great number are of no consequence, although some bear pro-foundly on health and illness" (Lock 2017, 5).

11.5 HUMAN HEALTH AND NUTRITION

The concerns of medical anthropology were not always central to traditional ethnographies, but many ethnographies nevertheless contributed to medical anthropology by showing connections between particular subsistence strategies (e.g., hunting and gathering or farming) and particular forms of social organiza-tion (i.e., a particular division of labor), explaining how these shaped human diets and were related to local patterns of sickness and health. In fact, many medical anthropologists are concerned with *nutrition* (the content and quality of the diet regularly consumed by members of particular human communities) and the re-lationship between human cultural practices and nutritional adequacy. Anthro-pologists have long known that foraging groups who gathered or hunted in their traditional territories regularly enjoyed adequate caloric intake and a varied and balanced diet, despite occasional periods of food scarcity, even in challenging environments. They also protected their health by regularly moving away from their own waste, and they could walk away from diseases that people in settled communities could not escape. Traditional hunters and gatherers also did not suffer from high blood pressure and other chronic complaints endemic among their settled neighbors. Unfortunately, this state of affairs began to change when hunters and gatherers adopted sedentary lifestyles themselves, together with diets that relied on a narrow range of domesticated species, processed foods, and alcohol (Lee 2013). These changed diets were less varied and often lacking in key nutrients, creating the conditions for *malnutrition*. Often, the amount of food was also inadequate, creating a situation of *undernutrition*.

The health profiles of communities all over the world have been affected in recent centuries by changes in nutrition that resulted when large-scale socioeconomic and political changes affected the traditional subsistence practices (and hence the diets) of local communities. These changes were associated with global processes such as the expansion of Western colonial empires, the eventual dismantling of those empires, and the integration (often on unequal terms) of newly independent nation-states into a global capitalist economy. (See chapter 10.) In the 1930s, British social anthropologist Audrey Richards was already drawing attention to problems of hunger and work among indigenous groups in Africa whose traditional forms of subsistence had been disrupted by British colonial economies. In the 1940s, American anthropologists like Margaret Mead were concerned about problems of diet and nutrition both in the United States and abroad and stressed the importance of understanding culturally shaped food practices of the groups whose nutrition the government was trying to improve. Access to adequate, nourishing food has regularly been a challenge for many cultural groups that have been marginalized by social, political, or economic changes that undermine their traditional livelihoods. Matters have gotten worse in recent decades, when more recent political, economic, and social changes have created large populations of displaced persons and refugees who struggle to survive in a context of violence, often living in camps that are poorly supplied with food, water, and basic shelter. (See also chapter 9 on the anthropology of food and nutrition.)

11.6 HEALTH AND HUMAN REPRODUCTION

Good nutrition is not only essential for individual survival; it also is a requirement for healthy biological reproduction. Women have always been expected to integrate their reproductive labor with productive economic labor in their households and communities. Ethnographic work that recorded information connecting the level of women's reproductive health with particular subsistence strategies and particular gendered divisions of labor provided a useful comparative framework for later medical anthropological research. Medical anthropologists have drawn attention to a range of factors that affect women's health and fertility and their ability to care for their children. Many formal studies of *fertility* by government agencies or biomedical authorities have exclusively been concerned with the challenges of population growth in many poorer societies and have pressured families to reduce the number of offspring they produce. Medical anthropologists have been instrumental in drawing attention to the challenges that *infertility* poses for individual women living in societies with particular gender and family structures. In societies like China, where descent is traditionally traced through males, and property and status move through lineages of related men, women who fail to produce sons for their husbands may be regarded as extra mouths to feed and may find themselves isolated when their husbands die and they have no son to take care of them in old age. In addition, the spread of global capitalism may undermine traditional sources of livelihood and social organization, which in turn erode traditional supports for reproductive health. In many countries, landless peasants who are forced out of the countryside into cities in search of work often live under extraordinarily difficult circumstances that have a serious negative impact on pregnant and nursing women and their children (Scheper-Hughes 1992).

11.7 SICKNESS AND HEALTH IN THE GLOBAL CAPITALIST ECONOMY

As these examples suggest, susceptibility to health risks often has less to do with genetics, biology, or even with culture than with the unequal social and political circumstances under which people must live. **Critical medical anthropology** draws attention to the ways in which many forms of physical, mental, and emotional suffering correlate with forms of socioeconomic and political inequality. For example, people who live in low-income neighborhoods in large cities—with inadequate housing, high unemployment, and a lack of nourishing food—may also be exposed to a high level of violence, drug and alcohol dependence, and other environmental assaults on their health. Diseases such as AIDS (acquired immune deficiency syndrome) or tuberculosis thrive among poor people whose health is compromised by poor housing, poor nutrition, inadequate clothing or shelter, and insufficient or nonexistent access to regular medical attention. Critical medical anthropologists often refer to this set of health conditions as the **biology of poverty**.

In recent years, anthropologists have examined how individual psychological functioning is affected by the biology of poverty. Suspicious of concepts like "self" or "personality" that are closely associated with Western notions of individualism (see chapter 6), many anthropologists prefer to speak of individual **subjectivity**: interior experiences of persons that are shaped by their locations in a particular field of power relations. To focus on subjectivity in an anthropological analysis is to acknowledge the way in which individuals are to some extent initiating subjects, or *agents*, of their own actions. However, subjects are never absolutely free to act as they choose. Our action is circumscribed by various forms of social, economic, and political inequality that we encounter in the societies in which we live. That is, we occupy various *subject positions* in society and are subject to the institutional forms of power in which those *subject* positions are embedded.

Social and cultural patterns are sometimes overturned by unpredictable experiences that leave enduring marks on the subjectivities of individuals who live through them. Unfortunately, such experiences are increasingly common in the early twenty-first century as societies in many parts of the world experience violent conflicts. Armed conflict and war regularly produce **trauma**, severe suffering caused by forces and agents beyond the control of the individual. Large-scale violence aims to destroy not only individuals but also the social order. Both individual and cultural factors contribute to the trauma and are equally implicated in recovery from trauma. Anthropologists have also drawn attention to less dramatic forms of violence that cause considerable human suffering. Medical anthropologist Paul Farmer, for example, speaks of **structural violence**, which is the outcome of the way that political and economic processes structure risk differently for different subgroups within a population, such that some groups are more vulnerable to infectious disease or domestic violence than are other groups (Farmer 2003).

Biomedicine has difficulty coping with notions like the biology of poverty. For biomedicine, diseases are located exclusively within the physical bodies of individuals, and attempts by scientists to locate more and more forms of suffering within the body are sometimes called **biologization**. Once suffering is biologized, it is *reduced* to just those attributes of an individual physical body that are accessible to biomedical science. Biologized conditions are turned into diseases and become candidates for **medicalization**—that is, the development of biomedical therapies designed to cure individuals diagnosed with a disease. Medicalization can certainly lead to positive outcomes, when the medical therapy relieves symptoms, perhaps indefinitely. At the same time, critical medical anthropologists highlight the fact that biomedicine leaves untouched the socioeconomic and political factors responsible for ill health and suffering in the first place—factors that may well contribute to the recurrence of the disease when treated individuals return to their old environments.

Critical medical anthropologists are sometimes able to show how people's health improves when their socioeconomic circumstances improve. For example, biomedical treatment in the form of antiretroviral medications can turn AIDS into a manageable condition. However, if people who live with AIDS must struggle to survive in conditions of poverty—homeless, jobless, under- or malnourished, and without a family, friends, or neighbors to look out for them—the support system that enables them to continue taking their medicine as prescribed is undermined, sometimes fatally (Biehl 2007). Many critical medical anthropologists are concerned that in the contemporary world, more and more forms of human suffering are being medicalized, despite widespread agreement by many observers that relief is likely to come only from social, economic, or political solutions, not from medication alone. At the same time, some prominent critical medical anthropologists, like Paul Farmer, are also medical doctors. By combining biomedical practices with sociocultural and political innovations, they, their allies, and the people they serve have worked to improve access to high-quality health care in a number of poor and marginalized communities.

Research by some critical medical anthropologists has begun to focus on public policies that influence practices of health care—work that relies on insights from science studies. One area of interest concerns biomedical technologies that make possible health care interventions such as organ transplantation and assisted reproduction. Such biotechnologies hold great promise, and access to them is desired by people all over the world. But access to them is skewed by inequality, and the outcomes they promise are often oversold. Their availability and desirability also can generate new complications and ethical dilemmas: in some parts of the world, a poor person will sell organ traffickers a kidney that will then be transplanted into a rich person's body (Scheper-Hughes and Wacquant 2003). The organ sellers hope the cash they receive will get them out of debt, but often it does not. The transplant recipients sometimes prefer to purchase organs from strangers to protect the well-being of close kin who might be a closer tissue match. Is this exploitation of the poor by the rich? Or do poor people own their own bodies and, therefore, have a right to sell their organs if they wish? But the very idea that a person's body is separate, self-contained, and autonomous is deeply rooted in Western philosophy. Does export of such an understanding of the body along with the biomedical technology ride roughshod over alternative views of bodies as well as turn a blind eye to exploitation?

Critical medical anthropologists have also become interested in the global spread of other biomedical commodities such as pharmaceuticals, whose impact they study from several perspectives. For example, pharmaceutical manufacturing is a big business that makes enormous profits, and the search for profit in new markets has been promoted by the spread of neoliberal economic practices as a result of globalization. The way pharmaceuticals and the companies producing them find a place for themselves in the medical institutions of different societies is complex and often problematic, and ethnographic research is often able to tease apart the many factors involved. Some critical medical anthropologists have studied the way in which pharmaceutical companies are now looking for fresh populations to test the effectiveness of new drugs in poor countries where health care is often meager (Petryna 2009). They expose the contradiction of testing pharmaceuticals on people who will never be able to afford to buy the successful drug once it is manufactured. They expose the paradox of governments that will supply drugs for free to people suffering from diseases like AIDS, but that simultaneously allow the public health care infrastructure of their societies to crumble. They have also explored the consequences that follow when people with a shared biomedical diagnosis find one another and develop a shared identity based on this diagnosis, a form of biological identity that anthropologist Paul Rabinow has called **biosociality**. People who share a biosocial identity may become involved in **health activism**, banding together and organizing politically to demand that the state acknowledge the existence of the disease and provide funding for research to seek a cure, actions generating a phenomenon sometimes called **biological citizenship**.

All these forms of research are increasing the prominence of contemporary medical anthropology as an applied anthropological subfield with a rich and diverse history. Some of the more recent directions in medical anthropology, moreover, rely heavily on research in science and technology studies; indeed, medical anthropology actively contributes to the ongoing development of science and technology studies. In many ways, the anthropology of science, technology, and medicine offers a promising model of new and valuable ways in which the subfields of North American anthropology are supporting one another in the twenty-first century.

FOR FURTHER READING

Studies of Science and Technology   Galison 1987, 1997; Hackett et al. 2008; Haraway 1991, 1997; Kelty 2008; Kuhn 1996; Labinger and Collins 2001; Latour 1987; Latour and Woolgar 1986; Martin 2001; Pickering 1995; Shapin 2010; Traweek 1992
Collected Essays in Medical Anthropology   Good et al. 2010
Medical Anthropology and Human Adaptation   Boyd and Richerson 1985; Durham 1991; Lee 2013; McElroy and Townsend 2008; Wiley and Allen 2009
Critical Medical Anthropology   Baer et al. 2003; Biehl 2007; Farmer 2003; Fassin and Pandolfi 2010; Kiefer 2007; Lock and Nguyen 2017; Scheper-Hughes 1992; Singer and Baer 2007

CHAPTER 12

Theory in Cultural Anthropology

The key terms and concepts covered in this chapter, in the order in which they appear:

theory

empirical

fact

unilineal cultural evolutionism

biological determinism

races

diffusion

culture traits

historical particularism

culture areas

functionalism

structural functionalism

superorganic

ethnoscience

emic

etic

structuralism

agency

symbolic anthropology

ecological anthropology

cultural ecology

multilineal evolutionism

behavioral ecology

cultural materialism

historical materialism

political ecology

the ontological turn

Originally, anthropology aimed to be a science of culture. Its early practitioners modeled themselves on the most successful scientists of their day—the physicists, chemists, and especially the biologists. As much as possible, they aimed to adopt the methodology of science and described their activities using scientific terminology. Thus, important late nineteenth-century scholars like Lewis Henry Morgan and Herbert Spencer were most explicit about the fact that their work involved a search for the laws of society and culture and that discovering such laws would permit them to describe the relationships of material cause and effect that underlay social and cultural phenomena.

Since their day, the applicability of the scientific method to the study of human social and cultural life has been debated. In recent decades, as we saw in chapter 11, work in the multidisciplinary field of science studies has reconfigured scholarly understandings of how science works. Not all anthropologists are comfortable with the findings of science studies research and continue to hold views about science that are more or less continuous with their nineteenth-century predecessors. Many sociocultural anthropologists, however, are actively involved in research programs (e.g., in medical anthropology and political ecology) that take the insights of science studies for granted. In what follows, we will indicate where these different understandings have had an impact on anthropological theories.

12.1 ANTHROPOLOGY AS SCIENCE

Why did early anthropologists think that culture could be studied scientifically? If we believe E. B. Tylor, it was because culture was patterned, orderly, *lawlike.* As Tylor famously said, if law is anywhere it is everywhere. Like physical scientists and social scientists such as Herbert Spencer (1820–1903) and Emile Durkheim (1858–1917), Tylor and other early anthropologists believed that the phenomena of culture—languages, customs, techniques, rituals, and so forth—were real phenomena that existed in the world, were tangible and measurable, and could be registered by the senses. The current shape of these phenomena, therefore, had to be understood as the effect of other tangible, material causes at work in human society rather than the result of intangible metaphysical or spiritual causes. Durkheim echoed this when he later argued that social facts could be explained only by other social facts. Much of culture seemed resistant to rapid change, but when it did change, it did so in a patterned and lawlike manner. Thus, Tylor, Spencer, and Lewis Henry Morgan described culture as evolving rather than changing unpredictably or randomly with the passage of time.

In anthropology, as in science, a **theory** is a formal description of some part of the world that explains how, in terms of cause and effect, that part of the world works. Anthropology followed the lead of scientific theorizing in other fields in which the aim was to explain a complex phenomenon by *reducing* it to a set of simpler elements whose interactions were both necessary and sufficient to produce the phenomenon in question. Because human culture in general and individual cultural traditions in particular are enormously complex phenomena, anthropologists hoped that they might discover those simpler elements and laws that *determined* the direction of cultural evolution.

Early scientists, and anthropologists who wanted to imitate their method, also argued that the plausibility of any theory depended on the evidence used to defend it, and they were universal in urging that only solid empirical evidence be allowed. To be **empirical** means that the evidence used to support a theory is the product of hands-on experience and can be inspected and evaluated by observers other than the original researcher. Only evidence that could meet this standard could be considered scientific **fact**. Scientific investigation has always stressed the importance of empirical research, arguing that the evidence of one's senses is a surer foundation for reliable knowledge than speculation unsupported by direct experience and that the objectivity of one's evidence must be tested against the critical observations of others before it is granted.

12.2 NINETEENTH-CENTURY APPROACHES

The nineteenth century was the century of evolutionary thinking in Western scholarship. In nineteenth-century biology, evolutionary thought is ordinarily associated with Charles Darwin (1809–1882). Ideas about cultural evolution, however, actually predated Darwin's 1859 publication of *On the Origin of Species* and was already well developed in the work of Darwin's contemporary Herbert Spencer (1820–1903). Spencer thought that human societies could usefully be compared to living organisms; and he stressed that, over time, like living organisms, societies increased in both size and internal complexity. Spencer's ideas had parallels with the work of his contemporary, Lewis Henry Morgan. Morgan is best remembered for two key contributions to the development of anthropological theory: his emphasis on patterned variation in kinship terminologies, which led him to speculate about the different forms human families might assume in different societies, and his attempt to connect these patterns of family organization to patterns of subsistence in a universal evolutionary sequence. The sequence he proposed drew together many contemporary ideas about the evolution of culture, including the idea that all cultures everywhere either had evolved or would evolve through the same sequence of stages: Savagery, Barbarism, and Civilization (also discussed in chapter 9). Nineteenth-century **unilineal cultural evolutionism** is generally regarded as the first theoretical perspective to take root in the discipline of anthropology.

Morgan recognized that his scheme was tentative in places and required more evidence to sustain certain claims. Nevertheless, like other cultural evolutionists in this period, he was convinced that he had discovered underlying laws of cultural change and that better empirical evidence collected by future researchers would refine the patterns he had exposed.

Theories of cultural evolution were challenged by other theories that claimed to explain the diversity of human social life in different ways. One of the strongest competitors in the late nineteenth century was the argument that biological differences between different human populations explained their different ways of life—or, put another way, that a group's way of life was determined by its distinct, innate biological makeup. This approach, called **biological determinism**, is also known as *scientific racism*, for it claimed to have empirical evidence that supported both the existence of biologically distinct human populations, or **races**, and the relative rankings of these races on a scale of superiority and inferiority. Not surprisingly, this Eurocentric framework assumed that light-skinned European races were superior to darker-skinned African, Asian, or Native American races because the latter had been conquered and dominated by the former (see also chapter 1 and chapter 5).

Late nineteenth-century evolutionary anthropologists never fully separated themselves from the biological determinists. Even though their defense of a universal set of cultural evolutionary stages presupposed a common humanity and common destiny shared by all the peoples of the world (which they sometimes described as the *psychic unity of mankind*), they believed that this common potentiality had not been equally developed in all living human populations and that its actual degree of realization was indicated by the stage of cultural evolution a particular society had achieved. Thus, although the descendants of people whose way of life was classified as "savage" might one day achieve the same level of sophistication as a contemporary people classified as "barbarian," there was no question of considering them equal at the present time. People living at a more highly evolved level of culture were simply viewed as more highly evolved *people* than those living at lower levels. Not until the twentieth century and the work of North American anthropologists like Franz Boas and his students would scientific racism be rejected as an explanation of human cultural diversity (also discussed in chapter 2).

12.3 EARLY TWENTIETH-CENTURY APPROACHES

Although unilineal evolutionary schemes were built on valid observations about changes in human subsistence strategies and incorporated empirical evidence about kinship that has proved reliable over time, these schemes also included (as all scientific theories do) considerable speculation. As the twentieth century began, German anthropologists were offering a very different universal theory of culture change, based on the supposedly regular spread of various cultural items from group to group by **diffusion**, or borrowing. Some proponents of both views were becoming increasingly extreme in their claims. In the face of this extremism, Boas in the United States denounced both theories. In the best scientific fashion, he used empirical ethnographic and historical evidence to expose the inadequacies of both forms of reductionism. Boas agreed that cultures changed over time, but such change could not be confined to passage through a single sequence of progressive evolutionary stages. Rather, historical evidence showed that cultures sometimes simplified over time, instead of becoming more complex, and in any case could easily skip stages by borrowing advanced cultural inventions from their neighbors. Similarly, although cultures are full of cultural items or activities, called **culture traits**, borrowed from neighboring societies, anthropologists go too far if they assume that most human groups are incapable of inventing anything on their own and must await the innovations that spread from a few favored sites of cultural creativity. Boas pointed out that some social problems—how to organize kinship, for example—have only a few possible solutions and are likely to be independently discovered again and again by widely separated peoples.

Boas and his students rejected both extreme evolutionary schemes and extreme diffusion schemes, preferring to focus on the distinct histories of change in particular human societies, an approach that came to be called **historical particularism**.

By comparing the culture histories of neighboring peoples, they were able to trace the limits of diffusion of many cultural traits, eventually producing maps of **culture areas** far smaller and more complex than the vast maps of the German diffusionists.

The theoretical extremism that Boas rejected was also rejected in England and France at about the same time. Although not ruling out the possibility of one day being able to construct a theory of cultural evolution, anthropologists like Bronislaw Malinowski (1884–1942) and A. R. Radcliffe-Brown (1881–1955) in England and sociologist/anthropologist Emile Durkheim and his colleagues in France declared a moratorium on speculations about cultural evolution unsupported by empirical evidence. All urged that research focus instead on living societies to collect precisely the kind of detailed empirical evidence that might one day enable the construction of a plausible theory of cultural evolution.

Malinowski set an example with his own field research in the Trobriand Islands. Not only was he a pioneer in modern participant-observation field methods, but he also set standards for the collection of ethnographic data that had a lasting influence on subsequent generations of anthropologists. His approach was to classify the customs and beliefs he learned about in the field in terms of the function each one performed in the satisfaction of what he called *basic human needs* (also discussed in chapter 9). For this reason, his research program became known as **functionalism**. Malinowski's main goal in much of his ethnographic writing was to debunk contemporary stereotypes of "savage" peoples as irrational, compulsive slaves to their passions; and so he emphasized repeatedly how orderly and well organized Trobriand life was and how customs that appeared irrational to ignorant outsiders could actually be shown to play important functions in meeting the Trobriand Islanders' basic human needs.

The theoretical response of other British and French anthropologists was to focus not on the function of particular customs in meeting the needs of individual human beings but rather on their function in preserving the structure of the society itself. Hence, this school of thought came to be called **structural functionalism**. Heavily influenced by the writings of Durkheim, Radcliffe-Brown was its most tireless promoter in Britain. Structural functionalists were concerned with what kept societies from falling apart (see chapter 5), and they could demonstrate that a variety of social practices described by ethnographers—witchcraft accusations, kinship organization, myths, and the like—performed this function.

In the mid-twentieth century, an antagonism developed between structural-functionalist British social anthropologists (as they called themselves) and North American cultural anthropologists. In retrospect, the antagonism seems rather trivial, but for many anthropologists at the time the issue was whether anthropology would be taken seriously as an empirical science. As we have seen, British social anthropologists, via Radcliffe-Brown, who was influenced by Durkheim, took *society* as their defining concept. To them, human bodies arranged in space in particular configurations constituted the unquestionable empirical reality that must be shaped by material laws of cause and effect operating in the social realm. North American anthropologists, however, focused on the concept of *culture*—the ideas, beliefs, values, and meanings that different groups of people developed to express their understanding of themselves and to adapt to their material environments.

For a British social anthropologist, nothing could be less material and thus possess less causal power than ideas, beliefs, and values. For the most outspoken of them, culture was a by-product, or a rationalization of material social arrangements that had nothing to do with culture but were instead the inevitable outcome of the operation of universal social laws (the necessity of maintaining social solidarity so that the social group endures over time) that automatically forced living human organisms into particular social configurations in particular circumstances. But North American cultural anthropologists countered such arguments by emphasizing the power of culture to shape all aspects of people's lives, including the ways they organized their societies. For example, A. L. Kroeber (1876–1960), one of Boas's students, argued that culture was a **superorganic** phenomenon (to be contrasted with inorganic matter and organic life). That is, although culture was carried by organic human beings, it existed in an impersonal realm apart from them, evolving according to its own internal laws, unaffected by laws governing nonliving matter or the evolution of living organisms, and essentially beyond the control of human beings whom it molded and on whom, in a sense, it was parasitic.

The views of these early twentieth-century anthropologists were so extreme in part because they were struggling to block any explanation of society or culture that would locate its origins either outside human individuals in some unseen, immaterial, personalized force like God, within human flesh as part of a purported racial essence, or in the innate psychological structure of human minds. Durkheim, Radcliffe-Brown, and Kroeber, each in his own way, struggled to defend the view that sociocultural beliefs and practices constituted a distinct scientific subject matter that had to be explained in its own terms by specialists who understood how it operated—that is, by social (or cultural) scientists like themselves.

In North America, cultural anthropologists developed a series of theoretical perspectives based on their conviction that culture shaped human behavior, including the construction of particular forms of social structure. In the early twentieth century, Ruth Benedict applied what was understood about the configuration of individual human personalities to the *configurations of entire cultures*. Anthropologists influenced by Freudian psychoanalysis carried out ethnographic studies of child-rearing practices, hoping to explain differences in values and practices that distinguished adults with different cultural backgrounds. These efforts gave rise to what came to be called the *culture-and-personality school*.

12.4 MID-TWENTIETH-CENTURY APPROACHES

Developments in the study of language inspired other cultural anthropologists to borrow insights from linguistics in attempting to explain how culture worked. One outcome of this was the development of **ethnoscience**, a movement in cultural anthropology that involved borrowing the techniques perfected by descriptive linguists to elicit information about culturally relevant domains of meaning by studying how the members of a particular group classified objects and events in their environments. Ethnoscientists were extremely concerned that the taxonomies they elicited not be contaminated by the imposition of their own cultural perspectives. Therefore, they went to great pains to preserve the boundary between the culturally relevant categories of their informants, called **emic** categories, and the categories that were the product of anthropological theory, called **etic** categories (also discussed in chapter 3).

Another rather different attempt to apply insights from linguistics to cultural analysis was developed by French anthropologist Claude Lévi-Strauss. Inspired by the so-called structural linguistics of Swiss scholar Ferdinand de Saussure (1857–1913; see chapter 3), particularly its analysis of phonemic structures, Lévi-Strauss tried to see whether the same kinds of structural patterns might be found in other domains of culture. Lévi-Strauss first applied his structural analysis—later called **structuralism** or *French structuralism*—to the study of kinship systems, but he gained an international reputation both inside and outside anthropology for his structural studies of myth (myth is discussed in chapter 4).

Lévi-Strauss collected multiple variants of numerous myths from indigenous societies in the Americas and appeared to be, on the surface at least, as interested in explaining cultural diversity as other contemporary cultural anthropologists. But he parted company with those anthropologists, such as ethnoscientists, who used linguistic methods to produce more detailed and accurate descriptions of culture but who still thought of culture as a historically contingent set of learned beliefs and practices. Instead, Lévi-Strauss saw surface diversity as the by-product of much simpler underlying processes of thought rooted in the structure of the human mind itself. Lévi-Strauss argued that, because all human beings were members of the same species, they possessed the same innate mental structures. The most obvious of these structures, he asserted, was the tendency to classify phenomena in terms of binary oppositions, like male–female, night–day, up–down, or mind–body. Lévi-Strauss argued that the diversity of cultural phenomena around the world was a surface diversity, the output produced by people with identical mental structures who were working with different kinds of natural and cultural resources. All people thus were engaged in a kind of cultural tinkering, or *bricolage*, in which they combined and contrasted elements of their experience in complex constructions rooted in a universal set of human mental structures. Structuralism was immensely influential inside as well as outside anthropology. Literary critics, in particular, seized on structuralism as a theoretical toolkit that could help them dissect the structure of literary or artistic work. But Lévi-Strauss and other structuralists also had their critics. Early criticism mostly concerned the validity of particular structural analyses of myths or other cultural phenomena. Different analysts, using what they thought were the same structuralist methods, frequently produced different analyses of the same cultural materials, leading critics to raise the question of just how "scientific" structural analysis actually was and how much it depended on the analysts' own interpretive style.

Later criticisms pointed out that structuralists (not unlike the Chomskyan linguists mentioned in chapter 3) assume that cultures are closed and monolithic and that cultural products, like myths, can have only a single "correct" reading. Structuralists wanted their readings accepted as objectively valid, like scientific discoveries; but their critics argued that the attempt to reduce all the variants of a myth to a single underlying structure ignored the possibility that the variants themselves contained important information about the social, political, or historical self-understanding of the myth tellers. Rather than simply being the vehicles through which myths worked themselves out across time and space, perhaps the members of each society who recounted the myth were agents attempting to use the resources of myth to make sense of specific concrete social experiences. By reducing all cultural forms to the innate structures of the human mind, structuralism appeared to some observers to be merely a new kind of biological determinism.

Structuralism is only one of a series of theoretical perspectives in contemporary cultural anthropology that have come under fire because of their apparent denial of human **agency** (defined in chapter 9). An ongoing struggle in anthropology concerns the relationship of culture to the individual. While most contemporary parties to the struggle agree that culture is learned, they disagree concerning how much is learned, how important it is for human survival, and how far individuals can go in modifying or rejecting aspects of their cultural heritage.

A different and very influential approach to human action developed in anthropology in the 1960s. This is referred to as **symbolic anthropology**, or sometimes *interpretive anthropology*, because of its emphasis on systems of meanings rather than on innate structures of mind or on the material dimensions of human life. For symbolic anthropologists, human culture is a system of symbols and meanings that human beings create themselves and then use to direct, organize, and give coherence to their lives. The most prominent symbolic anthropologists of the last part of the twentieth century were Mary Douglas, Victor Turner, and Clifford Geertz.

The work of Mary Douglas (1921–2007) combined a commitment to Durkheimian functionalism with an emphasis on the ways in which cultural symbols both reflect and shore up particular social orders. In her most famous book, *Purity and Danger* (1966), she explored widespread beliefs about purity and pollution in different societies, arguing that pollution was best understood as "matter out of place" within a particular symbolic order. Douglas drew attention to the ways in which a particular society's ideas about purity and pollution were regularly based on a metaphoric connection between the human body and society (see chapter 6). She argued, for example, that symbolic practices that appeared to be concerned with protecting vulnerable human bodies from pollution were actually concerned with keeping vulnerable social structures from falling apart. Social vulnerabilities were symbolically represented as bodily vulnerabilities as when the orifices of the body were seen to stand for points of entry into or exit from the body politic. Thus, food taboos designed to protect individual bodies from ingesting polluting substances could be understood as a symbolic way of protecting a vulnerable social order from dangerous outside forces. Douglas's work focuses on forms of symbolism that appear to be universal in human cultures, an emphasis that sets her apart from both Turner and Geertz, who both paid far more attention to the particular symbolic practices of specific societies.

Victor Turner (1920–1983) was trained as a structural functionalist in England but became dissatisfied with examining abstract social structure. Rather than emphasizing people's unthinking conformity to the underlying principles that ordered their society, Turner's work emphasized practice and performance. His work came to focus on *social dramas:* people's concrete interactions and conflicts in everyday social life. Turner showed how social dramas not only offered anthropologists insight into the structure of a given society but also revealed how people in that society made sense of their lives. Turner's interest in social dramas led him into studies of ritual (see chapter 4), pilgrimage, and theater. In all of these studies, he was concerned with how the symbols of a particular group of people—those "things that stand for other things"—were used as stores of meaning and as resources for social action. For Turner, what mattered were not the symbols themselves but what they meant to specific people and how they shaped action in specific social situations.

Like Turner, Clifford Geertz (1926–2006) was interested in symbols and their interpretation. For Geertz, culture was a system of symbols and meanings that are publicly displayed in objects and actions. Drawing on literary theory more than on drama theory, Geertz came to see cultures as made up of *texts,* "stories that people tell themselves about themselves." In his view, the anthropologist's job is to learn to read those texts—not the way natives did because it was impossible to get inside the natives' heads, but from within the same cultural context. Geertz proposed the phrase *thick description* for this process of finding the local meanings of cultural texts and in so doing drew attention to the fact that written texts were the typical product of ethnographic fieldwork. Beginning in the early 1970s, many anthropologists increasingly came to see that their task was to *write about* other societies, not merely to collect and analyze data, and that their ethnographies should be understood as texts to be read alongside the natives' own texts. Both Geertz and Turner were influential outside of anthropology in such branches of the humanities as religious studies and literary theory. Indeed, a common complaint about Geertz's work was that by relying so heavily on the interpretive skills of the anthropologist, it made the field appear more like literary criticism than social science.

The mid-twentieth century also saw a revival of evolutionary thinking in North American cultural anthropology. The new evolutionary anthropology rejected biological determinism, together with the racist evolutionary scheme that went with it. At the same time, evolutionary anthropologists accepted current biological understandings of evolution by natural selection and argued that human biological evolution, like the biological evolution of all organisms, involved adaptation to the environment. If varying modes of human adaptation were not the outcome of variations in human biology, some anthropologists reasoned, then perhaps the environments themselves were responsible for human cultural diversity. Anthropologists who ask such questions today usually are described as doing one or another kind of **ecological anthropology** (see chapters 8 and 9).

Ecologists and ecologically inclined anthropologists generally analyze particular human populations as parts of *ecosystems*: that is, they are one group of living organisms that, together with other organisms, make their living within a given environmental setting that exhibits regularities in terms of the variety and size of different populations and the resources they depend on to survive and reproduce.

An important founder of ecological approaches in cultural anthropology was Julian Steward (1902–1972). Steward's analytic framework, which he called **cultural ecology**, focused on the ways in which specific cultures mediated the interactions of human populations with their environments. Steward was an evolutionary thinker: he argued that cultural change over time was conditioned by the specific cultural developments in subsistence technology, and the ways in which members of a society used their culturally specific technology to obtain what they needed to survive from the particular environment in which they lived. As cultural systems changed the way they interacted with their environments, thus changing their adaptations, they evolved to new levels of sociocultural integration. Steward did not accept the universal stages of cultural evolution supported by his contemporary Leslie White (1900–1975). For White, cultural evolution was a general process encompassing all the cultures of humanity. White recast the major stages of cultural evolution proposed by nineteenth-century anthropologists (and by Karl Marx) in terms of how much energy per capita per year was captured by particular cultural systems. For White, cultures evolved as they captured more energy or as their technologies improved, or both. Using these criteria, White identified three major evolutionary turning points: (1) the domestication of plants and animals (the agricultural revolution of antiquity), (2) the beginnings of mechanization (linked to the "fuel revolution" at the beginning of the nineteenth century), and (3) the technological harnessing of atomic energy in the mid-twentieth century. Steward's approach to cultural evolution, by contrast, has been described as **multilineal evolutionism**. Steward focused not on global evolutionary trends but rather on particular sequences of systematic culture change, showing how local, evolutionary trajectories in similar societies could go in different directions, depending on the society's overall culture, its technology, and the particular environment to which each society was adapting. Today, those evolutionary anthropologists who assign symbolic culture a key role in their explanations of human adaptations to their environments (e.g., cultural inheritance theorists) are sometimes said to be continuing the practices of cultural ecology and multilineal evolutionism pioneered by Steward.

Research in ecological anthropology addresses debates about human agency because some ecological anthropologists argue that human adaptations are heavily circumscribed by environmental restrictions. In common with sociobiology, for example, some versions of **behavioral ecology** apply to human societies the same analytic principles that have been used to study the social behavior of animals, especially the social insects (e.g., ants). Indeed, sociobiology inspired behavioral ecological anthropologists to claim that, over the millennia, natural selection operating on individuals in particular environments not only has selected for genes responsible for the physical and behavioral traits of *individuals* but also has operated to increase the frequency in individuals of genes that control our *social* behavior.

Behavioral ecologists thus argue that we have been programmed to respond to others in stereotypical (but individually adaptive) ways that neither cultural conditioning nor individual willpower can modify. Put another way, behavioral ecology stresses that natural selection has produced human beings programmed to automatically find ways of maximizing their own individual self-interest, which in evolutionary terms means getting as many of one's genes into the next generation as possible (see chapter 9). Some versions of behavioral ecology have little or no role for symbolic culture in their accounts of human adaptation because acting in terms of arbitrary symbol systems could potentially mislead individuals into acting in ways that go against their own self-interest, such as taking risks for others with no obvious gain for oneself (or one's genes). If environmental curbs are as extensive as some behavioral ecological anthropologists claim, they would appear to restrict human agency just as much as the kinds of biological programming claimed by the biological determinists. In the twenty-first century, accounts that reduce human behavior to the action of natural selection on genes are giving way to relational accounts that emphasize processes of human development. These relational accounts demonstrate the ways in which growing humans, like other organisms, are shaped over time by a range of ecological, social, cultural, nutritional, and genetic inputs. Such relational accounts of developmental processes illustrate the impossibility of separating "nature" from "culture" in the course of human lives.

By drawing attention to ecological factors that affect cultural adaptations, ecological anthropologists have attempted to show the inadequacies of cultural theories that take no account of the material conditions of human life. Three other theoretical movements in the latter half of the twentieth century, each rather different from the ecological approaches described previously, also tried to argue for theories of culture that take the material world into account.

One such attempt was the **cultural materialism** of Marvin Harris (1927–2001), a theoretical perspective rooted in Harris's idiosyncratic readings of Marx, Engels, White, and Steward. Harris tried to tame what he saw as the extravagant claims of cultural determinists by pointing out the material constraints with which any cultural adaptation must come to terms. He attempted to show that particular customs that shock or disgust us today, such as warfare, cannibalism, or infanticide, were invented to ensure human survival in some past habitat. Although these are cultural inventions, their inventors are no more conscious of why they are doing what they do than are the human beings described by some behavioral ecologists. In both cases, moreover, the same kinds of self-interest calculations are said to govern the selection of particular practices. Indeed, both behavioral ecology and cultural materialism take an essentially *utilitarian* approach to the explanation of the evolution of cultural diversity: that is, in any given case, behaviors are selected because they confer the greatest good (or *utility*) for either a particular individual (behavioral ecology) or the group (cultural materialism).

A second brand of materialism that has been influential in recent cultural anthropology is the **historical materialism** based on the writings of Karl Marx and his followers. The main feature distinguishing Harris's cultural materialism from Marxian historical materialism is the role of the material forces of history. Harris's approach explains cultural adaptation or evolution in terms of local conditions, whereas Marxian approaches explain cultural evolution in world-historical terms. Marx attributed large-scale sociocultural change to the working out of material contradictions within the organization of society (its relations of production). Local ecological constraints are less important than the social constraints and contradictions generated by a particular, culturally constructed mode of production (e.g., between landowners and the people who own no land and so must rent from the owner). Marx's dialectical approach to historical change inspired many anthropologists who were dissatisfied with accounts of culture change that did not take into account social and political conflict, domination, and inequality (discussed in chapters 8, 9, and 10). Marxian ideas were also attractive because, in at least some of his writings, Marx suggested that human beings could exercise agency—could "make history"—albeit not under conditions of their own choosing. The material constraints of history limited the action they could take, limited even the alternatives they could imagine to the present order, but did not necessarily turn them into puppets unable to affect their cultural surroundings. Although the political hopes inspired by historical materialism have dimmed considerably with the end of the Cold War, Marx's crucial insights into the workings of capitalism and the mechanisms of domination continue to stimulate the work of many anthropologists concerned with the ways neoliberal capitalism shapes contemporary patterns of global inequality.

A third attempt to develop a theory of culture that takes the material world into account may be seen in **political ecology**. As we noted in chapter 8, political ecologists draw attention to the ways in which human groups struggle with one another for control of (usually local) material resources. They frequently provide ethnographic accounts that show why a particular local group's economic difficulties are due not to the backwardness of their cultural ecological practices but rather to the fact that political interventions by outsiders have deprived them of the resources they once could count on to help them secure their subsistence. Some political ecologists have pointed out that the material deprivation experienced by some local social groups is occasionally the result of their own decision to live with deprivation rather than succumb to political domination; this choice has been called an *adaptation of resistance*. Some political ecologists have been inspired by Marxian approaches to political and economic issues (see chapter 9). Today, a number of political ecologists describe themselves as "post-Marxists" who reject Marx's deterministic account of the evolution of modes of production. However, even post-Marxist political ecologists in anthropology continue to value the attention that Marx and his followers drew to economic inequality and political oppression, especially in a globalizing world where struggles to control the environment and its resources are multiplying. Many political ecologists believe that anthropologists have much to contribute to help resolve issues of environmental management. Some are active in environmental movements and collaborate with indigenous groups and others in pursuit of environmental justice.

12.5 LATE TWENTIETH-CENTURY DEBATES

At the beginning of the twentieth century, cultural anthropologists wanted to create a science of culture. By the end of the twentieth century, cultural anthropology had split into two camps divided not only over whether a science of culture is possible but also whether science itself, as traditionally conceived, is possible. Since the late 1980s and early 1990s, many anthropologists have concluded that extremist positions are unsatisfactory. The issues are complex, however, because some kinds of progressive politics, such as the condemnation of genocide, seem to rest squarely on the assumption that all human beings everywhere are bearers of universal human rights that *nobody* can be permitted to ignore. It is precisely in the area of human rights that the critics of interpretive, particularistic ethnography have made their most powerful argument. If all action is culturally relative, they argue, and all forms of culture are assumed to be equally valuable, then the grounds for moral outrage at genocide evaporate. Indeed, the leaders of genocide campaigns frequently attempt to silence international critics by defending their actions as culturally appropriate for their societies, and they accuse their critics of ethnocentrism or imperialism. It is for the purpose of exploring these very tensions that research in *moral anthropology* has been proposed (see chapter 1).

One of the reasons why many contemporary anthropologists insist on walking the narrow line between two extremes is that they realize that there is no simple relation between a particular set of knowledge claims and a particular political agenda. Claiming that women are "natural peacemakers," for example, might be a justification for placing women in high political office but has more often been used (at least in the West) as a justification for keeping women outside of politics because of their supposed incapacity to make war. Responsible scholarship (as well as responsible politics) thus requires paying more attention to what Donna Haraway (1944–) calls the *situated knowledges* produced by differently oriented observers engaged in different forms of knowledge production. Taking the orientation of observers into account also makes for better theory. For example, recent work on the history of anthropology has brought to light the significance of intellectual precursors whose work has been overlooked in past histories of the field but whose contributions to the ongoing development of anthropology have been vital. They range from Karl Marx and Max Weber to W. E. B. Du Bois and Zora Neale Hurston.

Attention to the position of a situated observer—to his or her *standpoint*—builds on the insights that emerged when cultural anthropologists began to pay attention to the reflexive dimension of fieldwork. They recognized that making clear the historical, social, cultural, political, and economic contexts within which scholarly research is conducted can actually *increase*, rather than decrease, our ability to recognize where a particular set of knowledge claims are strongest and where they are weakest. For example, ethnographer A's observations about the culture of the X people may be based on fieldwork conducted exclusively among adult males because young people and women refused to talk to ethnographer A. Suppose that ethnographer A then writes an ethnography about the X people based on this research. The knowledge claims ethnographer A makes about the culture of the X people will be stronger if ethnographer A makes it clear from the outset that they are based on situated knowledge: that ethnographer A's information came exclusively from adult males. A different ethnography based on research only among adult females of the X people would be based on differently situated knowledge. The portraits of the X people that are produced by these two ethnographies may be at odds with one another in a number of respects. But readers would not have to decide that only one ethnography was telling the "true story"; surely no single ethnography can capture the "whole truth" about any way of life. If each ethnography clearly identifies the specific kinds of situated knowledge on which it is based, readers might expect them to offer different representations of the way the X people live their lives. People who occupy different standpoints within the same society are unlikely to understand their society in exactly the same way, but distinctly situated points of view can still offer excellent access to *some* of the truths about life in that society. And if these partial truths constructed from different standpoints are not easily reconciled, this may be an accurate reflection of contradictions in the society itself. These days, after all, few anthropologists expect any society to be neatly bounded, internally harmonious, or functioning smoothly (see Sherry Ortner's observation, cited in chapter 6).

This same approach has also led anthropologists to question the assumption that anthropological categories—ritual or kinship, for example—are timeless, universal structures that are not dependent on historical contingencies for the ways in which they are expressed among specific groups of people. The strengths of much recent work in cultural anthropology lie in continuing commitment to ethnographic particularities that frequently resist assimilation into predictable theoretical categories. Much contemporary ethnography relates macroprocesses of globalization to the microlevel of a specific people's everyday life. The enduring anthropological commitment to taking other perspectives seriously keeps cultural anthropology a vibrant, exciting, and compelling discipline with great potential for allowing human beings to come to know and understand themselves better.

12.6 NEW DIRECTIONS IN THE TWENTY-FIRST CENTURY

Cultural anthropologists today have committed themselves to a range of different projects. Probably no form of cultural anthropology being practiced today is carried out in ignorance of or indifference to global interconnections that have been brought into existence since the end of the Cold War. But such interconnections can be studied in many ways.

Some cultural anthropologists root their ethnography among a given local "indigenous" population in a particular location and focus on the way global processes and institutions have come to affect the lives of that local population. For example, work by ethnographers working in sites from the Amazon lowlands to highland Papua New Guinea has documented the arrival of miners, loggers, and other outsiders who turn up and challenge local people for access to their resources. Sometimes the ethnography chronicles the destruction left in the wake of such encounters; often ethnographers use their special relationships with the threatened indigenous groups to become their advocates and defenders in a variety of different settings, from the media to courts of national and international law. This work may include involvement in national and international social movements as ethnographers and those with whom they work join together with like-minded activists and allies on the local, national, or international level to prevent environmental destruction or to protect cultural or human rights. In these kinds of settings, various forms of collaborative research and ethnographic writing are becoming increasingly common.

Some anthropologists prefer to focus their attention on the international political and economic processes that dispossess some populations of their homes and ways of life and push them into new territories as immigrants or refugees. Ethnographers follow the movements of such groups and their resettlement, temporary or permanent, in new locations ranging from refugee camps to neighborhoods in cities in different nation-states or continents. One result has been an increasing number of ethnographies carried out in the United States and Europe among newly arrived groups of all kinds who engage in the complex work of constructing relationships with new neighbors even as they continue to manage relations with those they have left behind. Groups like undocumented migrants and homeless people have also become a focus of ethnographic research motivated by ethnographers' concerns for social justice.

Studies of the international political economy from ethnographic and historical points of view also continue to be produced. Contemporary ethnographers have little patience with ethnographic accounts of contemporary ways of life that ignore history and assume that local affairs have always been the way they were the day the ethnographer first began fieldwork. At a time when numerous global processes are remaking cultural identities and practices before everyone's eyes, many ethnographers find it important to document the way those identities took shape over time and to identify processes that promote current changes. In many parts of the world, this requires paying attention to the history of European colonial conquest and its aftermath, noting carefully the precolonial, colonial, and postcolonial regime changes that have regularly remade the circumstances with which particular populations have had to cope. Such concerns prompt the continuing direction of historical ethnographic attention to European cultural practices in the colonial setting as well as to the cultural responses of colonized peoples (e.g., Comaroff and Comaroff 1991, 1997).

At the beginning of the twenty-first century, for example, cultural anthropology has become well established in many parts of the world; distinct "schools" of Mexican, Brazilian, and Indian anthropology are stronger than ever. Theory and practice have been decentered from institutions in Europe and the United States, and Euro-American cultural practices are fully accepted as viable ethnographic research topics. For example, anthropological studies of science and technology have become increasingly numerous and influential (see chapter 11). Beginning in the late 1970s and early 1980s, scientific laboratories, clinics, and hospitals became increasingly important as settings for ethnographic research. Such work has had an important impact in medical anthropology, especially studies focusing on bioscience and biotechnology. This work is concerned with not only scientific theories and practices, such as stem cell research, but also scientific apparatuses and procedures that may directly intervene in people's lives, such as infertility treatments, new imaging technologies, advances in organ transplantation, and the production of sophisticated artificial implants or prostheses. The unprecedented nature of these developments regularly raises ethical issues about the appropriateness of the research or the procedures as well as how it will be funded, who will benefit from it, and what its negative impacts are likely to be. Developments in biotechnology also blur the boundaries between "nature" and "culture," encouraging ordinary people who have experienced in vitro fertilization or organ transplantation, for example, to refashion the way they understand their own biological and cultural identities. As we saw in Chapter 1, these developments have contributed to anthropological understandings of the Anthropocene. Many anthropologists are concerned with understanding and documenting the potential social, political, and economic consequences of matters of concern like this, which older perspectives struggle to accommodate.

Insights from science studies have been influential among anthropologists whose interests are only tangentially concerned with science and technology themselves. In some cases, this is because certain concepts originally developed in the context of the anthropology of science and technology seem to illuminate the ethnographic materials the anthropologist is studying. For example, some work in science studies has drawn attention to the role of *distributed agency* in the production of scientific knowledge. As we saw in chapter 11, this work argues that successful scientific projects and successful technologies are both *heterogeneous assemblages of components, human and nonhuman, living and nonliving*, all of which exercise some degree of agency, thereby contributing to the final outcome. Despite their often divergent interests, these components have been brought together in a way that allows them to work as one. The loss or breakdown of any component removes its agency, withdraws its contribution, and may destabilize the entire assemblage, whether it be a smoothly functioning piece of technology or the structure of knowledge claims in a particular scientific field.

The notion of a heterogeneous assemblage characterized by distributed agency has been important to some anthropologists who trace the emergence and development of new kinds of social, economic, and political structures in the context of globalization. One illustration is Anna Tsing's analysis of rain-forest destruction and environmental activism in Indonesia, presented in her book *Friction: An Ethnography of Global Connection* (2005). Tsing recounts how, for a short time in the late 1980s and early 1990s, local villagers, "nature-loving" university students, a handful of national bureaucrats concerned with burnishing their "modern" environmentalist credentials, and international environmental movements were able to forge an alliance that successfully kept international loggers out of a particular part of the Indonesian rainforest. This short-lived alliance was surprising, both because it took hold when Indonesia was ruled by a dictatorship and because it held firm even though different allies at different levels had very different understandings of what the alliance was all about. When the dictatorship ended, the alliance fell apart.

A more recent example of what is possible when ethnographers follow the links in heterogeneous assemblages is illustrated in Eduardo Kohn's *How Forests Think* (2013). Kohn traces forms of indexical and iconic signification that allow the Runa people of the Upper Amazon in Ecuador to communicate with their dogs and other living inhabitants of their rainforest world. Kohn draws on work by anthropologist Terrance Deacon, who combines a semiotic framework based on the work of Charles Peirce (introduced in chapter 3), with insights from the biological field of *biosemiotics*, which studies how living organisms communicate with one another. Even if symbolic communication is unique to human beings, Kohn and Deacon make the case that other forms of indexical and iconic communication connect humans to other living organisms in rainforests as well, producing a "thinking" network of various kinds of selves that stretch "beyond the human." Among other things, Kohn's ethnography demonstrates in a fresh and provocative way what is at stake when rainforests and their inhabitants are destroyed. Indeed, contemporary processes such as rainforest destruction, species extinctions, global climate change, ongoing processes of violent conflict, and refugee crises in many parts of the world continue to invite anthropological exploration because ethnographic research situated within an anthropological disciplinary framework continues to provide insights obtainable in no other way. Such research clearly resonates with contemporary anthropological recognition of, and concern about, the Anthropocene and its consequences for all life on earth.

Kohn's effort to undertake anthropology that goes "beyond the human" resonates with the work of anthropologists inspired by science studies who, as we saw in chapter 11, elect to study human beings together with other entities, living and nonliving, material and nonmaterial, with which they are entangled. For example, in *The Mushroom at the End of the World* (2015), Anna Tsing follows the complex connections that link the highly valued matsutake mushroom to the various places where it grows, and the various groups of people who collect, trade, profit and consume it, in a commodity chain that links Japan, China, Canada, Finland, United States, and other places around the globe. Importantly, Tsing observes that some of the places where matsutake grows best are landscapes ruined by capitalist logging practices, such as the overharvested forests of the Pacific Northwest of North America. Indeed, many of those who harvest matsutake mushrooms in this region are immigrants from Southeast Asia whose families arrived in the Western United States following the Vietnam War. The relationships she describes that bring together matsutake mushrooms with different peoples, in different landscapes, making use of different kinds of cultural practices, sketch out possibilities for new ways of life emerging from the ruins left behind by capitalist environmental extraction: "My book . . . offers 'third nature,' that is, what manages to live despite capitalism. To even notice third nature, we must evade assumptions that the future is that singular direction ahead. Like virtual particles in a quantum field, multiple futures pop in and out of possibility. . . . This book sketches open-ended assemblages of entangled ways of life, as these coalesce in coordination across many kinds of temporal rhythms" (2015, viii). (Although she does not describe it this way, it is possible to connect the processes Tsing discusses here to the processes of niche construction, deconstruction, and reconstruction that James Scott highlights in his recent discussion of human subsistence practices, noted in chapter 9). Tsing also situates her ethnography within a complex, expanding network of publications and social media productions reflecting her collaboration with other scholars in different disciplines who make up the Matsutake Worlds Research Group (2015, ix). As we saw in chapter 3, this collaborative effort illustrates how the work of twenty-first century ethnography is proliferating in a variety of new genres and media outlets beyond the traditional, hard-copy scholarly article or ethnographic monograph.

Ethnographic work like that of Kohn, Tsing, and others not only resonates with contemporary anthropological concern about life in the Anthropocene. It also resonates with another influential direction being pursued by those anthropologists who are said to have taken **the ontological turn**. We touched on this emerging theoretical orientation in chapters 1, 2, and 4. Ontology is the branch of philosophy concerned with what exists in the world; what is "really real." Anthropologists who take the ontological turn, as we noted in chapter 1, have chosen to push our discipline's commitment to reflexivity as far as it will go: to the point of being willing to call into question their own previously unquestioned assumptions, rooted in Western Enlightenment thought, about what exists in the world and how the world works. This intense form of reflexivity is considered necessary to open anthropologists more fully to the alternative understandings of the world held by members of the communities with whom they work. The goal is not only to help anthropologists achieve ethnographic insights, but also to convey those insights accurately to others. The challenge is finding appropriate forms of symbolic expression that make room for understandings about the world and its content—alternative ontologies, in other words—that Enlightenment ontology would dismiss or ignore altogether.

In earlier chapters, we saw that ethnographers take the ontological turn in a variety of ways. What they all share, however, is the goal of decentering Western Enlightenment ontology, questioning its overall superiority, and paying adequate attention to alternative ontologies taken for granted by peoples with whom ethnographers work. In chapter 4, we saw the influential scheme proposed by Philippe Descola, who regards the Enlightenment ontology responsible for Western science—which he calls *naturalism*—to be just one of four logically possible ontological orientations that define the relationship between a human being and some other entity (his other three contrasting ontologies are *animism, totemism,* and *analogism*). Other anthropologists concerned with ontological variation do not necessarily subscribe to Descola's scheme. For many, the concern with ontology grows out of particular ethnographic encounters that reveal to them the limits at which their capacities to translate local understandings into anthropological discourse begin to break down. Eduardo Viveiros de Castro, another contributor to the ontological turn, has suggested that such breakdowns cannot be avoided, and that attempts to circumvent them are not innocent but carry a real danger of serious misunderstanding. Viveiros de Castro's solution is for ethnographers to acknowledge this danger openly and to take it into consideration as they translate. He advocates that ethnographers adopt what he calls a method of *controlled equivocation* (2004). To equivocate is to talk around a subject, to use ambiguous language, often to deliberately mislead your audience. Ethnographers ordinarily want to avoid equivocation, to translate accurately. But equivocation may seem inevitable if the reality you are attempting to translate does not match up well with the reality of those for whom you are translating. And so Viveiros de Castro advocates openly acknowledging the inevitable equivocation but attempting to control it by carefully considering options for translation that are more faithful or less faithful to the concept under consideration.

Marisol de la Cadena (2015) adopts Viveiros de Castro's method in her attempt to translate the way Andean *runakuna* understand and deal with the mountain peak of Ausangate, which informed the way she eventually decided to convey this understanding in English. As we saw in chapter 4, her solution was to use the term "earth beings" for these mountain peaks to capture the *runakuna* understanding that the peaks are alive and involved in human activities. Indeed, it is the specific ritual activities of *runakuna* in relation to earth beings like Ausangate that first alerted the ethnographer to the fact that indigenous understandings of these powerful entities cannot be encompassed by traditional categories of religious "belief." However, indigenous understandings of earth beings also overlap in important ways with ideas and practices conventionally understood as "religion" in Western Euro-American thought. The problem of equivocation arises because, although there is overlap, the overlap is not total; and if the translation gives readers the impression that there is no excess in *runakuna* understandings beyond what Western "religion" would accept, then the translation is misleading, false. And so de la Cadena attempts to control her equivocation by drawing attention to the overlaps as well as the lack of fit: "Practices with earth beings . . . can be identified as religious, but they cannot be reduced to such, for the notion of religion may not contain all they are" (2015: 207–208).

New directions in anthropological theorizing that refuse to reduce alternative ontologies to that of Western Euro-American "naturalism" reflect an old and ongoing effort within anthropology to break free of our own cultural assumptions to "see the world as others see it." Together with this intensifying effort to decenter Western views comes another effort to devise theoretical orientations that allow us to find our way past assumptions about the future that foreclose it in advance, either by political limitations, cultural restrictions, or environmental crises that seem too overwhelming to be managed. The work of Tsing and her allies reminds us, however, that unexpected paths can be found even in the blasted remains of forests depleted by commercial logging. Her work echoes the orientation developed by Ingold and Palsson, to which we referred in chapter 1, which invites us to consider ourselves not as static human beings but as dynamic biosocial becomings, caught up in the complex, ongoing, unpredictable living processes of the world. Perhaps fuller consideration of alternative ontologies, and the paths they open for new ways of becoming, may help us find ways of mitigating the worst consequences of life in the Anthropocene. These and other approaches will certainly provide much to occupy anthropologists in the decades to come.

FOR FURTHER READING

Theory   Bernard 2000; Darnell 2001; Geertz 1973; Harrison and Harrison 1999; Kuper 1996; McGee and Warms 2012; Moore and Sanders 2006; Rosaldo 1989.

Reading Ethnography

In chapters 1 and 2, we explored ethnographic research and considered how ethnographic fieldwork is done. In this appendix, we will consider how to read the result of that work. As we saw earlier, an ethnography is a scholarly work about a specific way of life. It is based on the author's lived experience with a specific group of people over a period of time, ideally at least a year. Ordinarily, an ethnography is based on knowledge of the other way of life that is both deep and broad—anthropologists try to learn as much as they can about as much of their hosts' way of life as possible. The anthropologist may then write a general description of the way of life or (as is more common today) explore a particular problem of importance in anthropology from the perspective of the people whom he or she knows. Ethnography is therefore a kind of *writing*; it is not just a straightforward reporting of "the facts." Some of the same techniques that readers have learned for reading in other genres can be applied to reading ethnography. An ethnography is an exercise in representing a set of beliefs and practices, and this raises issues of ethics, politics, and interpretation. In this appendix, we offer you some suggestions for getting as much as possible from your reading of ethnographies.

THE PARTS OF AN ETHNOGRAPHY

How is an ethnography put together? While each ethnography has its own unique characteristics, there are several stylistic features that many ethnographies share. Ethnographies generally begin with a preface in which the author may "set the scene," introduce him or herself, explain how the field research to be reported came about, what the topic of the ethnography will be, and thank a set of people for their help. The preface can be useful to a reader even if he or she doesn't recognize any of the names at the end. It can give the reader an idea about the purpose of the ethnography and why the author wrote it. The reader can learn if the ethnography is a revision of the author's doctoral dissertation or a new work, written after the author received his or her doctorate. It can give the reader an idea of how long ago the author was in the field and perhaps what theoretical directions the author might take.

The preface is usually followed by an introductory chapter that tends to have two major parts: an entrance narrative and the academic context of the work. The entrance narrative dates back to the earliest classic ethnographies in anthropology—both Malinowski's *Argonauts of the Western Pacific* (1922/1984) and Raymond Firth's *We, The Tikopia* (1936/1966), for example, begin with entrance narratives that are well known in anthropology. In the entrance narrative, the author invites the reader to join him or her in experiencing the first impressions of the field—what things looked like at the beginning, sounded like, smelled like; what the local people looked like and how the anthropologist was received at first; and how he or she lived. This narrative is useful in several ways: it gives the reader a sense of the author as a person, acquaints the reader with the author's field situation, and orients the reader to the ethnography. At the same time, it also serves as a way for the author to establish a kind of complicity with the readers, to introduce them to the author's legitimacy as a trustworthy source—to convince readers that they can have confidence in what the author will argue in the rest of the book. At the most basic level, this is the equivalent of saying, "I was there. Trust me." In recent years, when they return from their research, more and more ethnographers are joining writing groups to hone their skills in writing for an audience broader than just other anthropologists. This has led to powerful, even gripping, writing that draws readers into the ethnographic narrative. The contributions of these writing groups are often acknowledged in the preface to an ethnographic monograph.

The other part of the introductory chapter can be difficult for nonspecialists to get through. In a sense, what makes an ethnography an ethnography is that it is part of an ongoing debate within anthropology. Ethnographers do not just write about their experiences—their work is ordinarily intended to address current issues within the discipline of anthropology. Writing an ethnography that is not just for classroom use, then, obliges the author to spell out where his or her work fits in cultural anthropology: Who are the other scholars who have influenced him or her? What are the theoretical issues that the author plans to address? These issues are dealt with early in an ethnography and take the form of a section in which the author reviews (1) the regional and theoretical literature, indicating the strengths and weaknesses of work by other scholars among the same or related people, and (2) the strengths and weaknesses of theorists who have addressed similar issues. This can be challenging for nonspecialists because they usually do not have very much experience with the theoretical issues involved, nor do they recognize any of the names that are being cited by the author (for other anthropologists, this section is very important because it provides hints and clues as to the directions that the author will take in the rest of the ethnography). A further difficulty is that the author may choose to use a highly elaborated theoretical language in this section. You need to ask yourself (or your instructor) how much of this section is required reading. At the very least, you might want to try to apply the theoretical approaches discussed in chapter 12 to put the arguments that the author is making into a theoretical context. It is not necessary to memorize the names of other scholars that are cited in this part of the text, but it is useful to try to follow the argument that the author is making. This section may be one of the points that your instructor will choose to discuss in lecture to help the class make sense of the key issues to be raised in the ethnography.

The style of most ethnographies now changes abruptly as the author shifts to the presentation of data and interpretation of those data. Here is the heart of the ethnography as the author presents a set of descriptions and analyses that will simultaneously represent aspects of a way of life and make an argument about their meaning. Here, the author has carefully and intentionally chosen the order and topics of the chapters. A book is always composed—some material included, other material left out—to make the points that the author wants made. Part of your job as an intelligent reader is to try to figure out why the author has structured the book in *this* particular way.

In some cases, of course, the author tells the readers in the preface or the introduction why the chapters are in the order in which they are found, but sometimes readers have to try to figure out the logic. Sometimes the sequence of chapters is chronological, following a ritual, agricultural, or calendrical cycle, or based on the anthropologist's own acquaintance with the community. More common, perhaps, is a sequence of chapters based on the complexity of the topics to be raised, beginning with the most straightforward and ending with the most complex, or where the topics of later chapters require information that can only be presented in earlier chapters.

Another common format is to begin with the environmental setting or history of the community or people who are the subjects of the ethnography; and then once the historical and ecological background is established, the author turns to the social and cultural worlds of the community. In other cases, authors may choose to arrange their chapters by the emotional difficulty or cultural unfamiliarity of the topics presented. Authors may feel that all the details of their arguments must be presented first before getting to material that their readers might find difficult to accept without the necessary background. Alternatively, they may have concluded that their readers need to know and sympathize with their informants before readers are introduced to aspects of informants' lives that might be difficult for readers to understand or accept.

There are many other ways to structure an ethnography, but in all cases that structure is something to which the author has given considerable thought. This doesn't mean that the author is always successful, by the way. Once they have figured out the logic, readers may decide that the author has not presented the material in a way that convinces them, satisfies them ("I wish she had written in greater detail about . . . "), or explains to them what the author wanted them to know ("I still don't understand why the people in the ethnography do . . . "). Sometimes authors may have omitted material that readers consider important. Sometimes there may be too much material that readers find tangential or that becomes overly repetitive. In other cases, readers may have had experiences that differ so much from the ethnographer's interpretation that they cannot accept either the accuracy of the ethnography or the universality of the claims ("I was in high school at the same time the author was doing his research in a high school. We did things very differently. Maybe what the author found was true in that school because it was not like other high schools.").

Following the body of the ethnography is the conclusion. Here, the style often changes again, as the author attempts to tie up the loose ends, summarize, and connect the body of the work with the theoretical issues, which are set out in the introduction, that motivated him or her. This is also a place where authors may return to a style that resembles the style of the first chapter because they wish to situate their work in the context of other work on similar topics: There may be more discussions of theory, more citations of work by other scholars, and an attempt to make a statement that is more general and abstract than anything in the preceding chapters. Here, your job is to try to figure out where the concluding remarks come from. Do they seem justified, based on what has been presented before, or does the author go too far or not far enough? Does the author connect the ethnographic chapters to the conclusion in a way that makes sense to you? Having finished the book, do you feel that you know something about the world that you had not known before, that you have gotten a sense of "being there"?

THE USE OF INDIGENOUS AND LOCAL TERMS

One of the most distinctive stylistic features of ethnographic writing is the use of indigenous or local terms. Readers of ethnography may have been taken aback and perhaps puzzled by this ethnographic usage; they may even find it makes reading the ethnography more difficult. There are several reasons why ethnographers may use many indigenous or local terms. At one level, it is further proof to the readers that authors know what they are talking about—they have learned the language that the local people use and they can demonstrate this in their writing. Also, there may be other people who speak that language who read the book. Whether the language in question is the Kiriwinian that Malinowski learned in the Trobriand Islands in 1915–1918 or the German that Daphne Berdahl used in the small town of Kella in the 1990s, scholarly professionalism requires that ethnographers record information about the languages of research as accurately as possible so that other fluent speakers will be able to recognize how the ethnographer has made sense of the language. Such linguistic accuracy is further proof that the authors can be trusted.

In a way, this is the equivalent of "showing your work" in a math class. But more important, it is a reflection of one of the fundamental assumptions in anthropology—that other people create through their languages coherent and meaningful ways to look at the world and that the language used to live in those worlds *does not map perfectly onto English.* Using indigenous or local terms becomes a way of signaling dimensions of a way of life that are different from that of the ethnographer. Part of the ethnographer's job, as Bruce Knauft (2013, 18) puts it, is "learning and conveying concepts that are important to other people even when they exceed our initial understanding." For all of these reasons, then, the use of indigenous or local terms can be seen as a characteristic of the style of writing we call *ethnographic*. So, in reading ethnography, readers should not panic over the many indigenous or local terms that appear—it's unlikely that your instructor expects you to memorize all of them!—but you should use the terms as indicators of important points of entry into understanding a way of life that is different from their own.

THE PHOTOGRAPHS

Many ethnographies are illustrated, usually with photographs. This is also an area that should draw the reader's attention. Photographs have been part of ethnographic writing since the first ethnographies—Malinowski's *Argonauts of the Western Pacific* (1922/1984) contains 66 photographs, and he was following a guide to field photography first published in 1899. It is likely the case that the use of the camera in early ethnography was based on the idea that the camera was a tool of "scientific" recording, and it is certainly the case that Malinowski was very thorough in his use of cameras in the Trobriand Islands (see Young 1998). But it is well worth the reader's time to examine the photographs in any ethnography that he or she is reading and think about why they are there and what they contribute to the ethnography. After all, it adds to the expense of publishing a book to include photographs, and so they are not there just because the author thought it would be nice to include a few. First, the photographs are yet another way for the ethnographer to establish credentials—the photographs, especially when taken by ethnographers or their companions, are a testimony to the fact that the ethnographer was there; often they signify that the author was well accepted by local people (many ethnographies have at least one image of the author interacting with local people). In both cases, the message is "I was there. You can trust what I am telling you."

Second, the photographs can set the scene, moving the reader from imagining the scene to having a picture of the scene. Sometimes even the most vivid writing cannot express the distinctive reality that the ethnographer wishes to convey. The photographs can help by giving the readers a visual reference for the ethnographer's descriptions and analyses. The photographs can also communicate details of the social and physical environment that the ethnographer may have neglected or found excessively complex to describe. Indeed, the photographs can allow readers a kind of complicity with the author by allowing them to check their interpretation of a scene against the author's. Third, the photographs can humanize the people with whom the ethnographer lived. For example, a tightly composed portrait that fills the photographic frame with a face is not a very useful photograph for seeing the social and physical world in which people live, but it is very effective at establishing the common humanity of subject, photographer, and viewer. Finally, from the use of captions and references in the text to the photographs, the ethnographer can create a dialogue between the text and the photographs that will allow the reader to understand better the world that the ethnographer is trying to evoke.

It must be said, however, that photographs have sometimes been used to exoticize the people in them. Some ways of drawing attention to costume, facial or body painting, body mutilations, ritual postures, activities, housing, or material objects can portray people as so alien that readers viewing the photos may see them as being socially or culturally abnormal or inferior or may see only differences, losing sight of the commonalities that they may share. For example, a text that includes photographs of people only in "traditional" costume can leave the impression of quaintness or exoticism: that this is how people dress on a daily basis, even when the traditional costume is only worn once a year or just for photographs. In recent years, anthropologists have critically examined the use of photographs in ethnography and consider very carefully the photographs they include with their own work. It is important to remember that photographs do not speak for themselves. Photographs are ambiguous, which is why they are given captions or discussed in the text of the ethnography itself.

As you read an ethnography with photographs, you might ask yourself some questions about the way that these images are treated. Are there extensive captions? Do the captions refer to the text, and does the text refer to the photographs? Are the photographs of people? Places? Activities? All three? How much of the scene is included in the photographs (i.e., are most of the photographs close-ups of people, or are the people always surrounded by their environment)? Do the photographs draw you into the society or do they distance you? Are there things in the text that you wish were illustrated with a photograph? Can you figure out why the author chose the photographs that appear in the book? Do the photographs make you want to go where the ethnographer has been? Do you feel that you know the society better having seen the photographs?

WHY ARE YOU READING THIS ETHNOGRAPHY (AND HOW SHOULD YOU READ IT)?

Even before you open an ethnography, you should ask yourself (and perhaps your instructor, too) why you are reading it because why you are reading it will affect *how* you read it. The goal of reading an ethnography is not to memorize the multitude of details that are found within it. Frequently, the goal of reading an ethnography is to get a sense of a way of life very different from your own as well as to learn how the people described in the ethnography make sense out of their lives. The explicit focus of the ethnography might be economic activities or kinship reckoning, but your first goal ought to be to look for overall patterns rather than to remember details like the term for "Father's-Sister's-Daughter marriage" or the exact sequence of events in spirit possession.

You might be asked to read more than one ethnography to compare the ways of life of peoples on different continents or with different ways of making a living, or to find out what has happened to people whose ancestors used to farm but who now work in a factory in Malaysia or Mexico. You might also be reading an ethnography set in your own world, and the instructor's goal may be to get you to think about the ways in which your way of life, like that of other people elsewhere, is also a social and cultural construction. Even if your instructor has not told you why you are being asked to read this ethnography or specifically what to look for, you can often figure this out if you think about what the instructor has been discussing in class or where this ethnography is placed on the course syllabus.

In all cases, you should read actively and with paper and pencil handy. As noted earlier, all writing in anthropology is part of an ongoing dialogue within the field, and you should make yourself part of that dialogue: Reading is active, not passive. If you don't understand what the author is saying, make a note on your computer, on paper, or in the margin of the book (only if it's yours, of course!). If you don't agree with something that the author has written, make a note. If you are really impressed with something that the author has written, make a note. If you want to know more about something the author has written, make a note. You and the author are in this together, and what you write in (and about) the book becomes part of the text.

Although it is difficult to do, especially when you are just starting out, think about what the author may have omitted or not discussed. Does the author not write about men? Or women? Does the author talk about globalization or the effects that nation-building efforts may have had on the people about whom you are reading? Does the author ignore or pay attention to conflicts within the group the ethnography is about? Are there topics that you would like to know more about? Is there anything that would make this book speak more directly to you?

One final set of questions to ask has to do with the ethnographer him or herself. How does the ethnographer appear in the book? What role does the ethnographer take? Does the ethnographer give the impression of being a detached, outside observer, or does the ethnographer take a political position? Was the ethnographer an advocate for the people or working in an applied way with or for a group of people? Does the ethnographer take a position about any of the issues that are raised? What does the ethnographer reveal about him or herself? About the purposes of the research? About how it came about? About who paid for it? About the nature of his or her interactions with the people in the study? In some cases, particularly in older ethnographies, the author appears as a character in the entrance narrative and then never makes another entrance. In other cases, the ethnographer is one of the characters in the book, sometimes as an observer, sometimes a narrator, sometimes as someone whose experiences become part of the data being collected. More recently, ethnographers and the people they work with have begun to cowrite ethnographic texts based on the fieldwork that they did together. It will be valuable to you to think about the effect these strategies have on your reading and on the ethnography more generally.

It has been a long time since ethnographies were taken at face value. Contemporary ethnographers are aware as never before that their texts are not innocent documents—they are not simply objective reports of the heaps of data that the ethnographer collected like ripe fruit on the trees of knowledge. They are part of an ongoing debate within the discipline of anthropology; they are based on an unequal, carefully negotiated relationship between the ethnographer and the set of people with whom he or she worked; they are necessarily partial (there were subjects left unstudied and events that the ethnographer did not or was not allowed to see); and they have political implications. They can be used by governments, by political groups within the society, and by scholars in other fields for purposes not intended by the ethnographer. As a result, ethnographers have become increasingly diligent about positioning themselves and their research in explicit contexts. They make clear who they are, how they were received both personally and politically, who they were able to spend time with, who paid for their research, how it was managed and carried out, and what parts of it may have been used by or objected to by local people of various kinds. They do this so that the significance of their data will be neither under- nor overestimated. Knowing who collected the data, how they were collected, from whom, and how they were interpreted makes the significance of ethnography stronger and more precise.

That said, it is important not to lose sight of the fact that a key factor motivating ethnography itself is an undeniable fascination with the varied ways of life people continue to make for themselves in different geographic, historical, political, and cultural settings. Ethnographies reveal the sometimes, surprising inventiveness and resilience of people facing challenges of many kinds. Reading ethnography is an excellent pathway into the richness of the human experience. Enjoy!

Bibliography

Abu-Lughod, Janet. *Before European Hegemony: The World System A.D. 1250–1350*. New York: Oxford University Press, 1989.

Agar, Michael. *Language Shock: Understanding the Culture of Conversation*. New York: Morrow, 1994.

Agar, Michael. *The Professional Stranger*. 2nd ed. San Diego: Academic Press, 1996.

Agrawal, Arun. *Environmentality: Technologies of Government and the Making of Subjects*. Durham, NC: Duke University Press, 2005.

Akmajian, Adrian et al. *Linguistics: An Introduction to Language and Communication*. 7th ed. Cambridge, MA: MIT Press, 2017.

Alim, H. Samy. "Introducing Raciolinguistics: Racing Language and Languaging Race in Hyperracial Times." In *Raciolinguistics: How Language Shapes Our Ideas About Race*, edited by H. Samy Alim, John R. Rickford, and Arnetha Ball, 1–30. New York: Oxford University Press. 2016a.

Alim, H. Samy. "Who's Afraid of the Transracial Subject?" In *Raciolinguistics: How Language Shapes Our Ideas About Race*, edited by H. Samy Alim, John R. Rickford, and Arnetha Ball, 33–50. New York: Oxford University Press. 2016b.

Alim, H. Samy, John R. Rickford, and Arnetha F. Ball, eds. *Raciolinguistics: How Language Shapes Our Ideas about Race*. New York: Oxford University Press, 2016.

Alim, H. Samy, and Geneva Smitherman. *Articulate While Black: Barack Obama, Language, and Race in the U.S.* Oxford, England: Oxford University Press, 2012.

Alland, Alexander. *The Artistic Animal*. New York: Doubleday Anchor, 1977.

Amrute, Sareeta Bipin. *Encoding Race, Encoding Class: Indian it Workers in Berlin*. Durham, NC. Duke University Press, 2016.

Anand, Nikhil. *Hydraulic City: Water and the Infrastructures of Citizenship in Mumbai*. Durham; London: Duke University Press, 2017.

Anderson, Benedict. *Imagined Communities*. London: Verso, 1983.

Andersen, Margaret and Patricia Hill Collins, eds. *Race, Class, and Gender: An Anthology*. 8th ed. Independence, KY: Cengage Learning, 2012.

Anderson, Richard L. *Calliope's Sisters: A Comparative Study of Philosophies of Art*. 2nd ed. Upper Saddle River, NJ: Pearson Prentice Hall, 2004.

Appadurai, Arjun. *Modernity at Large: Cultural Dimensions of Globalization*. Minneapolis: University of Minnesota Press, 1996.

Arens, W., and Ivan Karp. *Creativity of Power: Cosmology and Action in African Societies.* Washington, DC: Smithsonian Institution Press, 1989.

Asad, Talal. *Formations of the Secular: Christianity, Islam, Modernity.* Palo Alto, CA: Stanford University Press, 2003.

Ashmore, Wendy, and Robert J. Sharer. *Discovering Our Past: A Brief Introduction to Archaeology.* 5th ed. New York: McGraw-Hill, 2009.

Askew, Kelly, and Richard R. Wilk, eds. *The Anthropology of Media: A Reader.* Malden, MA: Wiley-Blackwell, 2002.

Baer, Hans, Merrill Singer, and Ida Susser, eds. *Medical Anthropology and the World System.* 2nd ed. Westport, CT: Praeger, 2003.

Baker, Lee D. *From Savage to Negro: Anthropology and the Construction of Race, 1896–1954.* Berkeley: University of California Press, 1998.

Bakke, Gretchen, and Marina Peterson, eds. *Anthropology of the Arts: A Reader.* London: Bloomsbury Academic, 2016.

Becker, Gaylene. *The Elusive Embryo: How Women and Men Approach New Reproductive Technologies.* Berkeley: University of California Press, 2000.

Behar, Ruth, and Deborah Gordon, eds. *Women Writing Culture.* Berkeley: University of California Press, 1996.

Bell, Sandra, and Simon Coleman. "The Anthropology of Friendship: Enduring Themes and Future Possibilities." In *The Anthropology of Friendship*, edited by Sandra Bell and Simon Coleman, 1–19. Oxford, England: Berg, 1999.

Bernard, Alan. *History and Theory in Anthropology.* New York: Cambridge University Press, 2000.

Bernard, H. Russell. *Research Methods in Anthropology: Qualitative and Quantitative Approaches.* 6th ed. Lanham, MD: Roman & Littlefield, 2017.

Biehl, João. *Will to Live: AIDS Therapies and the Politics of Survival.* Princeton, NJ: Princeton University Press, 2007.

Biehl, João, and Adriana Petryna. *When People Come First: Critical Studies in Global Health.* Princeton, NJ: Princeton University Press, 2013.

Biersack, Aletta, and James B. Greenberg. *Reimagining Political Ecology.* Durham, NC: Duke University Press, 2006.

Blackwood, Evelyn, and Saskia E. Wieringa, eds. *Female Desires: Same Sex Relations and Transgender Practices across Cultures.* New York: Columbia University Press, 1999.

Blount, Ben G., ed. *Language, Culture, and Society: A Book of Readings.* 2nd ed. Prospect Heights, IL: Waveland Press, 1995.

Blum, Susan. *Making Sense of Language: Readings in Culture and Communication* 3rd ed. New York: Oxford University Press, 2016.

Boellstorff, Tom. *Coming of Age in* Second Life: *An Anthropologist Explores the Virtually Human.* Princeton, NJ: Princeton University Press, 2008.

Bohannan, Paul. *How Culture Works.* New York: Free Press, 1995.

Bonvillain, Nancy. *Language, Culture, and Communication: The Meaning of Messages.* 5th ed. Upper Saddle River, NJ: Pearson Prentice Hall, 2008.

Bonvillain, Nancy. *Women and Men: Cultural Constructs of Gender.* 4th ed. Upper Saddle River, NJ: Pearson Prentice Hall, 2006.

Bowen, John. *Religions in Practice: An Approach to the Anthropology of Religion.* 7th ed. Needham Heights, MA: Allyn & Bacon, 2017.

Bowie, Fiona. *The Anthropology of Religion: An Introduction.* 2nd ed. Malden, MA: Wiley-Blackwell, 2006.

Boyd, Robert, and Peter J. Richerson. *Culture and the Evolutionary Process*. Chicago: University of Chicago Press, 1985.

Bradburd, Daniel. *Being There: The Necessity of Fieldwork*. Washington, DC: Smithsonian Institution Press, 1998.

Breckenridge, Carol, Sheldon Pollock, Homi Bhabha, and Dipeesh Chakrabarty, eds. *Cosmopolitanism*. Durham, NC: Duke University Press, 2002.

Brenneis, Donald, and Ronald Macaulay, eds. *The Matrix of Language: Contemporary Linguistic Anthropology*. Boulder, CO: Westview Press, 1996.

Brettell, Caroline B., and Carolyn F. Sargent, eds. *Gender in Cross Cultural Perspective*. 6th ed. Upper Saddle River, NJ: Pearson Prentice Hall, 2013.

Brosius, J. Peter et al. *Communities and Conservation: Histories and Politics of Community-Based Natural Resource Management*. Walnut Creek, CA: AltaMira Press, 2005.

Bunten, Alexis. "Commodities of Authenticity: When Native People Consume Their Own 'Tourist Art.'" In *Exploring World Art*, edited by Eric Venbrux et al., 317–336. Long Grove, IL: Waveland Press, 2006.

Burling, Robbins. *The Talking Ape: How Language Evolved*. New York: Oxford University Press, 2005.

Burt, Ben. *World Art: An Introduction to the Art in Artefacts*. London: Bloomsbury, 2013.

Butler, Judith. *Gender Trouble: Feminism and the Subversion of Identity (Routledge Classics, 36)*. New York: Routledge, 2006..

Caldwell, Melissa L. "Domesticating the French Fry: McDonald's and Consumerism in Moscow." In *The Cultural Politics of Food and Eating: A Reader*, edited by James Watson and Melissa L. Caldwell, 180–196. Malden, MA: Blackwell, 2005.

Campbell, Christina J. et al., eds. *Primates in Perspective*. 2nd ed. New York: Oxford University Press, 2011.

Carrier, James G., ed. *A Handbook of Economic Anthropology*. Northampton, MA: Edward Elgar 2006.

Carsten, Janet. *After Kinship*. Cambridge, England: Cambridge University Press, 2003.

Carsten, Janet, ed. *Cultures of Relatedness: New Approaches to the Study of Kinship*. Cambridge, England: Cambridge University Press, 2000.

Carsten, Janet. *Ghosts of Memory: Essays on Remembrance and Relatedness*. Malden, MA: Wiley-Blackwell, 2007.

Chambers, Erve. *Native Tours: The Anthropology of Travel and Tourism*. 2nd ed. Long Grove, IL: Waveland Press, 2010.

Clifford, James. *The Predicament of Culture*. Cambridge, MA: Harvard University Press, 1988.

Coe, Sophie, and Michael Coe. *The True History of Chocolate*. London: Thames & Hudson, 1996.

Collier, Jane Fishburne, and Sylvia Junko Yanigasako, eds. *Gender and Kinship*. Stanford, CA: Stanford University Press, 1987.

Collins, Patricia Hill. *Black Feminist Thought*. New York, Routledge, 2008.

Colloredo-Mansfeld, Rudi. *The Native Leisure Class: Consumption and Cultural Creativity in the Andes*. Chicago: University of Chicago Press, 1999.

Comaroff, John, and Jean Comaroff. *Of Revelation and Revolution, Volume 1: Christianity, Colonialism and Consciousness in South Africa*. Chicago: University of Chicago Press, 1991.

Comaroff, John, and Jean Comaroff. *Of Revelation and Revolution, Volume 2: The Dialectics of Modernity on a South African Frontier*. Chicago: University of Chicago Press, 1997.

Counihan, Carole M. *Around the Tuscan Table: Food, Family, and Gender in Twentieth Century Florence*. New York: Routledge, 2004.

Counihan, Carole, and Penny Van Esterik. *Food and Culture: A Reader*. 2nd ed. New York: Routledge, 2008.

Dalsgaard, Steffen. "Facework on Facebook: The Presentation of Self in Virtual Life and Its Role in the US Elections." *Anthropology Today* 24, no. 6 (2008): 8–12.

Daniel, E. Valentine, and John Knudsen, eds. *Mistrusting Refugees*. Berkeley: University of California Press, 1995.

Darnell, Regna. *Invisible Genealogies: A History of Americanist Anthropology*. Lincoln: University of Nebraska Press, 2001.

Das, Veena, Arthur Kleinman, Margaret Lock, and Mamphela Ramphele. *Remaking a World: Violence, Social Suffering, and Recovery*. Berkeley: University of California Press, 2001.

De Genova, Nicholas. *The Borders of "Europe": Autonomy of Migration, Tactics of Bordering*. Durham, NC: Duke University Press, 2017a.

De Genova, Nicholas. "Introduction: The Borders of "Europe" and the European Question." In *The Borders of "Europe" Autonomy of Migration, Tactics of Bordering*, Nicholas De Genova (ed), 1–36. 2017b.

de la Cadena, Marisol. *Earth Beings: Ecologies of Practice Across Andean Worlds*. Durham, NC: Duke University Press, 2015.

De Léon, Jason. *The Land of Open Graves: Living and Dying on the Migrant Trail*. Berkeley: University of California Press, 2015.

Descola, Philippe. *Beyond Nature and Culture*. Translated by Janet Lloyd. Chicago: The University of Chicago Press, 2013.

Descola, Philippe. "Modes of Being and Forms of Predication." *Hau: Journal of Ethnographic Theory* 4, no. 1 (2014): 271–280.

DeWalt, Kathleen M., and Billie R. DeWalt. *Participant Observation: A Guide for Fieldworkers*. 2nd ed. Lanham, MD: AltaMira Press, 2010.

Di Leonardo, Micaela, ed. *Gender at the Crossroads of Knowledge: Feminist Anthropology in the Postmodern Era*. Berkeley: University of California Press, 1991.

Dirks, Nicholas B. *The Scandal of Empire: India and the Creation of Imperial Britain*. Cambridge, MA: Harvard University Press, 2006.

Douglas, Mary. *Natural Symbols: Explorations in Cosmology*. London: Routledge, 1970.

Douglas, Mary. *Purity and Danger*. London: Routledge and Kegan Paul, 1966.

Douglas, Mary. "Introduction." In *Witchcraft Confessions and Accusations*, edited by Mary Douglas, xi–xxxviii. London: Tavistock, 1970.

Duranti, Alessandro, ed. *A Companion to Linguistic Anthropology*. Malden, MA: Wiley-Blackwell, 2006.

Duranti, Alessandro. *Linguistic Anthropology*. Cambridge, England: Cambridge University Press, 1997.

Duranti, Alessandro, ed. *Linguistic Anthropology: A Reader*. Malden, MA: Blackwell 2001.

Durham, William H. *Coevolution: Genes, Culture, and Human Diversity*. Stanford, CA: Stanford University Press, 1991.

Edelman, Marc, and Angelique Haugerud, eds. *The Anthropology of Development and Globalization: From Classical Political Economy to Contemporary Neoliberalism*. Malden, MA: Wiley-Blackwell, 2005.

Eller, Jack David. *Introducing Anthropology of Religion: Culture to the Ultimate*. 2nd ed. New York; London: Routledge, 2015.

Erazo, Juliet S. *Governing Indigenous Territories: Enacting Sovereignty in the Ecuadorian Amazon*. Durham, NC: Duke University Press, 2013.

Eriksen, Thomas Hylland. *Ethnicity and Nationalism: Anthropological Perspectives*. London: Pluto Press, 2010.

Errington, Shelly. *The Death of Authentic Primitive Art and Other Tales of Progress*. Berkeley: University of California Press, 1998.

Ervin, Alexander M. *Applied Anthropology: Tools and Perspectives for Contemporary Practice*. 2nd ed. Upper Saddle River, NJ: Pearson Allyn & Bacon, 2004.

Evans-Pritchard, E. E. *Witchcraft, Oracles, and Magic Among the Azande*. Oxford: Oxford University Press, 1976.

Farmer, Paul. *Pathologies of Power: Health, Human Rights, and the New War on the Poor*. Berkeley: University of California Press, 2003.

Fassin, Didier. *Humanitarian Reason*. Berkeley: University of California Press, 2012.

Fassin, Didier, and Mariella Pandolfi. *Contemporary States of Emergency: The Politics of Military and Humanitarian Interventions*. New York: Zone Books, 2010.

Fausto-Sterling, Anne. "Nature." In *Critical Terms for the Study of Gender*, edited by Catharine R. Stimpson and Gilbert Herdt, 294–319. Chicago: University of Chicago Press, 2014.

Fausto-Sterling, Anne. *Sex/Gender: Biology in a Social World*. New York: Routledge, 2012.

Featherstone, Mike, ed. *Global Culture: Nationalism, Globalization, and Modernity*. London: Sage, 1990.

Feder, Kenneth. *The Past in Perspective: An Introduction to Human Prehistory*, 7th ed. New York: Oxford University Press, 2016.

Ferguson, R. Brian. "Pinker's List: Exaggerating Prehistoric War Mortality." In *War, Peace and Human Nature*, edited by Douglas P. Fry, 112–131. New York: Oxford University Press, 2013.

Fiddis, Nick. *Meat: A Natural Symbol*. London: Routledge, 1991.

Firth, Raymond. *We, The Tikopia*. Boston: Beacon Press, 1966 [1936].

Fischer, Edward, and Peter Benson. *Broccoli and Desire*. Stanford, CA: Stanford University Press, 2006.

Fortes, Meyer, and E. E. Evans-Pritchard. *African Political Systems*. London: Pub. for the International institute of African languages & cultures by the Oxford university press, H. Milford, 1940.

Foucault, Michel. *Discipline and Punish*. New York: Vintage, 1995.

Foucault, Michel. *The History of Sexuality, Volume 1. An Introduction*. New York: Vintage, 1980.

Foucault, Michel. *The History of Sexuality, Volume 2. The Use of Pleasure*. New York: Vintage, 1990.

Foucault, Michel. *The History of Sexuality, Volume 3. The Care of the Self*. New York: Vintage, 1988.

Fox, Richard G., and Barbara J. King, eds. *Anthropology Beyond Culture*. Oxford, UK: Berg, 2002.

Fried, M. H. *The Evolution of Political Society*. New York: Random House, 1967.

Galison, Peter. *How Experiments End*. Chicago: University of Chicago Press, 1987.

Galison, Peter. *Image and Logic: A Material Culture of Microphysics*. Chicago: University of Chicago Press, 1997.

Gamst, F. C., and E. Norbeck, eds. *Ideas of Culture*. New York: Holt, Rinehart & Winston, 1976.

Gardner, Katy, and David Lewis. *Anthropology, Development and the Post-Modern Challenge*. London: Pluto Press, 1996.

Geertz, Clifford. *The Interpretation of Cultures*. New York: Basic Books, 1973.

Geismar, Haidy. "Anthropology and Heritage Regimes." *Annual Review of Anthropology* 44 (2015): 71–85.

Gentner, Dedre, and Susan Goldin-Meadow. "Language in Mind: Advances in the Study of Language and Thought." In *Whither Whorf?*, edited by Dedre Gentner, and Susan Goldin-Meadow, 3–14. Cambridge, MA: MIT Press. 2003.

Gershon, Ilana. "Email My Heart: Remediation and Romantic Break-Ups." *Anthropology Today* 24 (2008): 13–15.

Gershon, Ilana. "Language and the Newness of Media." *Annual Review of Anthropology* 46 (2017): 15–31.

Ginsburg, Faye, and Rayna Rapp. *Conceiving the New World Order: The Global Politics of Reproduction.* Berkeley: University of California Press, 1995.

Ginsburg, Faye D., Lila Abu-Lughod, and Brian Larkin, eds. *Media Worlds: Anthropology on New Terrain.* Berkeley: University of California Press, 2002.

Gmelch, Sharon. *Tourists and Tourism: A Reader.* 2nd ed. Long Grove, IL: Waveland Press, 2010.

Good, Byron et al. *A Reader in Medical Anthropology: Theoretical Trajectories, Emergent Realities.* Malden, MA: Wiley-Blackwell, 2010.

Goodale, Mark. *Human Rights: An Anthropological Reader.* Malden, MA: Wiley-Blackwell, 2009.

Goodman, Alan H., and Thomas Leland Leatherman, eds. *Building a New Biocultural Synthesis: Political-Economic Perspectives on Human Biology.* Ann Arbor: University of Michigan Press, 1999.

Goody, Jack, and Stanley Tambiah. *Bridewealth and Dowry.* Cambridge, England: Cambridge University Press, 1973.

Graburn, Nelson, ed. *Readings in Kinship and Social Structure.* New York: Harper & Row, 1971.

Gregory, Melissa, and Gregory J. Seigworth, eds. *The Affect Theory Reader.* Durham, NC: Duke University Press, 2010.

Grosz, Elizabeth. *Volatile Bodies: Toward a Corporeal Feminism.* Bloomington: Indiana University Press, 1994.

Gudeman, Stephen. *The Anthropology of Economy.* Cambridge: Cambridge University Press, 2016.

Gutmann, Matthew. "Trafficking in Men: The Anthropology of Masculinity." *Annual Review of Anthropology* 26 (1997): 385–409.

Gwynne, Margaret A. *Applied Anthropology: A Career-Oriented Approach.* Upper Saddle River, NJ: Pearson Allyn & Bacon, 2003.

Hackett, Edward J. et al. *The Handbook of Science and Technology Studies.* 3rd ed. Cambridge, MA: MIT Press, 2008.

Halperin, David. "Sex, Sexuality, and Sexual Classification." In *Critical Terms for the Study of Gender*, edited by Catharine R. Stimpson and Gilbert Herdt, 449–486. Chicago: University of Chicago Press, 2014.

Halperin, Rhoda H. *Cultural Economies: Past and Present.* Austin: University of Texas Press, 1994.

Hann, C. M., and Keith. Hart. *Economic Anthropology: History, Ethnography, Critique.* Cambridge, UK; Malden, MA: Polity Press, 2011.

Hannerz, Ulf. *Transnational Connections: Culture, People, Places.* London: Routledge, 1996.

Haraway, Donna. *Modest-Witness@Second-Smillennium.Femaleman-Meets-Oncomouse: Feminism and Technoscience.* New York: Routledge, 1997.

Haraway, Donna. *Simians, Cyborgs and Women: The Reinvention of Nature.* New York: Routledge, 1991.

Hardon, Anita, and Emilia Sanabria. "Fluid drugs: Revisiting the Anthropology of Pharmaceuticals." *Annual Review of Anthropology* 46 (2017): 117–132.

Harris, Olivia, ed. *Inside and Outside the Law: Anthropological Studies of Authority and Ambiguity.* New York: Routledge, 1997.

Harrison, Faye, ed. "Contemporary Issues Forum: Race and Racism." *American Anthropologist* 100, no. 3 (1998): 605–715.

Harrison, Faye. "Introduction: Expanding the Discourse on 'Race.'" *American Anthropologist* 100, no. 3 (1998): 609–631.

Harrison, Ira, and Faye Harrison, eds. *African-American Pioneers in Anthropology.* Champaign: University of Illinois Press, 1999.

Hartigan, John. *Race in the 21st Century: Ethnographic Approaches.* 2nd ed. New York: Oxford University Press, 2015.

Hartigan, John, ed. *Anthropology of Race: Genes, Biology, and Culture.* Santa Fe: School for Advanced Research Press, 2013.

Herdt, Gilbert, ed. *Third Sex, Third Gender: Beyond Sexual Dimorphism in Culture and History.* New York: Zone Books, 1994.

Hicks, David, ed. *Religion and Belief: Readings in the Anthropology of Religion.* 3rd ed. Lanham, MD: AltaMira Press, 2010.

Hinkson, Melinda. "Precarious Placemaking." *Annual Review of Anthropology* 46, 2017: 49–64.

Hill, Jane, and Judith Irvine, eds. *Responsibility and Evidence in Oral Discourse.* Cambridge, England: Cambridge University Press, 1992.

Hinton, Alexander Laban. *Annihilating Difference: The Anthropology of Genocide.* Berkeley: University of California Press, 2002.

Hirsch, Jennifer S., and Holly Wardlow. *Modern Loves: The Anthropology of Romantic Courtship & Companionate Marriage.* Ann Arbor: University of Michigan Press, 2006.

Hobsbawm, Eric, and Terence Ranger. *The Invention of Tradition.* Cambridge, England: Cambridge University Press, 1992.

Hodgson, Dorothy L. *Once Intrepid Warriors: Gender, Ethnicity, and the Cultural Politics of Maasai Development.* Bloomington: Indiana University Press, 2004.

Holbraad, Martin, and Morten Axel Pedersen. *The Ontological Turn: An Anthropological Exposition.* Cambridge, England: Cambridge University Press, 2017.

Howe, Cymene. *Intimate Activism: The Struggle for Sexual Rights in Postrevolutionary Nicaragua.* Durham, NC: Duke University Press, 2013.

Hughey, Michael. *New Tribalisms: The Resurgence of Race and Ethnicity.* New York: New York University Press, 1998.

Inda, Jonathan Xavier, and Renato Rosaldo, eds. *The Anthropology of Globalization: A Reader.* 2nd ed. Malden, MA: Wiley-Blackwell, 2007.

Ingold, Tim, and Gisli Palsson. *Biosocial Becomings: Integrating Social and Biological Anthropology.* New York: Cambridge University Press, 2013.

Kahn, Susan Martha. *Reproducing Jews: A Cultural Account of Assisted Conception in Israel.* Durham, NC: Duke University Press, 2000.

Karkazis, Katrina. *Fixing Sex: Intersex, Medical Authority, and Lived Experience.* Durham, NC: Duke University Press, 2008.

Kaur, Raminder, and Parul Dave Mukherji, eds. *Arts and Aesthetics in a Globalizing World.* New York: Bloomsbury Academic, 2014.

Kawa, Nicholas. *Amazonia in the Anthropocene.* Austin: University of Texas Press, 2016.

Keane, Webb. "Signs Are Not the Garb of Meaning: On the Social Analysis of Material Things." In *Materiality*, edited by Daniel Miller, 182–205. Durham, NC: Duke University Press, 2005.

Keane, Webb. "Semiotics and the Social Analysis of Material Things." *Language and Communication* 23 no. 3-4 (2003): 409–435.

Kearney, Michael. "The Local and the Global: The Anthropology of Globalization and Transnationalism." *Annual Review of Anthropology* 24 (1995): 547–565.

Kearney, Michael. *Reconceptualizing the Peasantry: Anthropology in Global Perspective.* Boulder, CO: Westview Press, 1996.

Kedia, Satish, and John van Willigen, eds. *Applied Anthropology: Domains of Application.* Westport, CT: Praeger, 2006.

Kelty, Christopher M. *Two Bits: The Cultural Significance of Free Software.* Durham, NC: Duke University Press, 2008.

Kiddey, R. *Homeless Heritage: Collaborative Social Archaeology as Therapeutic Practice.* PhD Diss., University of York, York, UK, 2014a.

Kiddey, R. "Punks and Drunks: Counter Mapping Homelessness in Bristol and York." In *Who Needs Experts? Counter-Mapping Cultural Heritage,* edited by J. Schofield, 165–179. Farhham, UK: Ashgate, 2014b.

Kiefer, Christie W. *Doing Health Anthropology: Research Methods for Community Assessment and Change.* New York: Springer, 2007.

Killick, Evan, and Amit Desai. "Introduction: Valuing Friendship." In *The Ways of Friendship: Anthropological Perspectives,* edited by Amit Desai and Evan Killick, Oxford: Berghahn Books, 2010.

Kirksey, Eben. *Emergent Ecologies.* Durham, NC: Duke University Press, 2015.

Kirsch, Stuart. *Engaged Anthropology: Politics Beyond the Text.* Berkeley: University of California Press, 2018.

Kleinman, Arthur, Veena Das, and Margaret Lock, eds. *Social Suffering.* Berkeley: University of California Press, 1997.

Knauft, Bruce. *The Gebusi.* 3rd ed. New York: McGraw-Hill, 2013.

Knauft, Bruce. *Genealogies for the Present in Cultural Anthropology.* New York: Routledge, 1996.

Koenig, Barbara A., Sandra Soo-Jin Lee, and Sarah S. Richardson. *Revisiting Race in a Genomic Age.* New Brunswick, N.J.: Rutgers University Press, 2008.

Kohn, Eduardo. *How Forests Think: Toward an Anthropology Beyond the Human.* Berkeley: University of California Press, 2013.

Kotef, Hagar. *Movement and the Ordering of Freedom: On Liberal Governances of Mobility.* Durham, NC: Duke University Press, 2015.

Kuhn, Thomas S. *The Structure of Scientific Revolutions.* 3rd ed. Chicago: University of Chicago Press, 1996.

Kuper, Adam. *Anthropology and Anthropologists: The Modern British School.* 3rd ed. London: Routledge, 1996.

Kuper, Adam. *Culture: The Anthropologists Account.* Cambridge, MA: Harvard University Press, 1999.

Labinger, Jay A., and H. M. Collins. *The One Culture? A Conversation About Science.* Chicago: University of Chicago Press, 2001.

Lambek, Michael, ed. *A Reader in the Anthropology of Religion.* 2nd ed. Malden, MA: Wiley-Blackwell, 2008.

Lancaster, Roger N. *Life Is Hard.* Berkeley: University of California Press, 1992.

Lancaster, Roger N., and Micaela Di Leonardo, eds. *The Gender/Sexuality Reader: Culture, History, Political Economy.* London: Routledge, 1997.

Latour, Bruno. *Science in Action: How to Follow Scientists and Engineers Through Society.* Cambridge, MA: Harvard University Press, 1987.

Latour, Bruno. *We Have Never Been Modern*. Cambridge, MA: Harvard University Press, 2007.

Latour, Bruno, and Steve Woolgar. *Laboratory Life: The Construction of Scientific Facts*. Princeton, NJ: Princeton University Press, 1986.

Leacock, Eleanor. *Myths of Male Dominance: Collected Articles on Women Cross-Culturally*. New York: Monthly Review Press, 1981.

Lee, Richard B. *The Dobe Ju/'hoansi*. 4th ed. Belmont, CA: Wadsworth, 2013.

Leslie, Charles M. *Asian Medical Systems: A Comparative Study*. Berkeley: University of California Press, 1976.

Levine, Nancy. *The Dynamics of Polyandry: Kinship, Domesticity, and Population on the Tibetan Border*. Chicago: University of Chicago Press, 1988.

Lewellen, Ted C. *The Anthropology of Globalization: Cultural Anthropology Enters the 21st Century*. Westport, CT: Bergin & Garvey Paperback, 2002.

Lewellen, Ted C. *Dependency and Development*. Westport, CT: Bergin & Garvey, 1995.

Lewellen, Ted C. *Political Anthropology: An Introduction*. 3rd ed. Westport, CT: Praeger, 2003.

Lewin, Ellen. *Feminist Anthropology: A Reader*. Malden, MA: Wiley-Blackwell, 2006.

Li, Tania. *The Will to Improve: Governmentality, Development, and the Practice of Politics*. Durham, NC: Duke University Press, 2007.

Littlefield, Alice, and Hill Gates, eds. *Marxist Approaches in Economic Anthropology*. Lanham, MD: University Press of America and Society for Economic Anthropology, 1991.

Lock, Margaret M., and Vinh-Kim Nguyen. *An Anthropology of Biomedicine*. Malden, MA: Wiley-Blackwell, 2010.

Lykke, Nina. *Feminist Studies: A Guide to Intersectional Theory, Methodology and Writing*. New York: Routledge, 2012.

Malinowski, Bronislaw. *Argonauts of the Western Pacific*. Long Grove, IL: Waveland Press, 1984 [1922].

Malkki, Liisa H. "Refugees and Exile: From 'Refugee Status' to the National Order of Things." *Annual Review of Anthropology* 24 (1995): 495–523.

Mankekar, Purnima. *Screening Culture, Viewing Politics: An Ethnography of Television, Womanhood, and Nation in Postcolonial India*. Durham, NC: Duke University Press, 1999.

Marcus, George. "Ethnography in/of the World System: The Emergence of Multi-Sited Ethnography." *Annual Review of Anthropology* 24 (1995): 95–117.

Marcus, George, and Michael Fischer. *Anthropology as Cultural Critique: An Experimental Moment in the Human Sciences*. Chicago: University of Chicago Press, 1986.

Marks, Jonathan. *The Alternative Introduction to Biological Anthropology*. New York: Oxford University Press, 2011.

Martin, Emily. *The Woman in the Body*. Boston: Beacon Press, 2001.

McDonald, James H. *The Applied Anthropology Reader*. Upper Saddle River, NJ: Pearson Allyn & Bacon, 2001.

McElroy, Ann, and Patricia K. Townsend. *Medical Anthropology in Ecological Perspective*. 5th ed. Boulder, CO: Westview Press, 2008.

McGee, R. Jon, and Richard Warms. *Anthropological Theory: An Introductory History*. 5th ed. New York: McGraw-Hill, 2012.

Meintjes, Louise. *Dust of the Zulu: Ngoma Aesthetics After Apartheid*. Durham, NC: Duke University Press, 2017.

Merry, Sally Engle. *Human Rights and Gender Violence: Translating International Law into Local Justice*. Chicago: University of Chicago Press, 2006.

Merry, Sally Engle. "Legal Transplants and Cultural Translation: Making Human Rights in the Vernacular." In *Human Rights: An Anthropological Reader*, edited by Mark Goodale, 265–302. 2009.

Messer, Ellen. "Anthropology and Human Rights." *Annual Review of Anthropology* 22 (1993): 221–249.

Miller, Barbara Diane, ed. *Sex and Gender Hierarchies*. Cambridge, England: Cambridge University Press, 1993.

Miller, Claire Cain. "Searching for a Best Estimate of the Transgender Population." *New York Times*, June 9, 2015, A3.

Miller, Daniel. "Coca-Cola: A Black Sweet Drink from Trinidad." In *Material Cultures: Why Some Things Matter*, edited by Daniel Miller, 169–188. Chicago: University of Chicago Press, 1998.

Miller, Daniel. "Consumption and Commodities." *Annual Review of Anthropology* 24 (1995): 141–161.

Miller, Daniel, and Don Slater. *The Internet: An Ethnographic Approach*. Oxford: Berg, 2000.

Mintz, Sidney W. *Sweetness and Power: The Place of Sugar in Modern History*. New York: Penguin Books, 1985.

Mintz, Sidney W. *Tasting Food, Tasting Freedom: Excursions into Eating, Culture, and the Past*. Boston: Beacon Press, 1996.

Moore, Henrietta L., and Todd Sanders, eds. *Anthropology in Theory: Issues in Epistemology, 2md edition*. Malden, MA: Wiley Blackwell, 2014.

Moore, Jerry D. *Visions of Culture: An Introduction to Anthropological Theories and Theorists*. Walnut Creek, CA: AltaMira Press, 1997.

Morgan, Marcyliena H. *Language, Discourse, and Power in African American Culture*. Cambridge, England: Cambridge University Press, 2002.

Morgan, Marcyliena H. *The Real Hiphop: Battling for Knowledge, Power, and Respect in the LA Underground*. Durham, NC: Duke University Press, 2009.

Morgan, Marcyliena H. *Speech Communities*. Cambridge, England: Cambridge University Press, 2014.

Moro, Pamela, and James Myers. *Magic, Witchcraft, and Religion*. 9th ed. New York: McGraw-Hill, 2012.

Murthy, Dhiraj. "Muslim Punks Online: A Diasporic Pakistani Music Subculture on the Internet." *South Asian Popular Culture* 8 (2010): 181–194.

Myers, Fred. *Painting Culture: The Making of an Aboriginal High Art*. Durham, NC: Duke University Press, 2003.

Nader, Laura. *Law in Culture and Society*. Berkeley: University of California Press, 1997.

Nagata, Judith. "Beyond Theology: Toward an Anthropology of 'Fundamentalism.'" *American Anthropologist* 103, no. 2 (2001): 481–498.

Nagengast, Carole. "Violence, Terror, and the Crisis of the State." *Annual Review of Anthropology* 23 (1994): 109–136.

Nardi, Bonnie A. *My Life as a Night Elf Priest: An Anthropological Account of* World of Warcraft. Ann Arbor: University of Michigan Press, 2010.

Netting, Robert. *Smallholders, Householders: Farm families and the Ecology of Intensive, Sustainable Agriculture*. Stanford, CA: Stanford University Press, 1993.

Netting, Robert, Richard Wilk, and E. J. Arnould, eds. *Households: Comparative and Historical Studies of the Domestic Group*. Berkeley: University of California Press, 1984.

Niezen, Ronald, and Maria Sapignoli. "Introduction." In *Palaces of Hope: The Anthropology of Global Organizations*, edited by Ronald Niezen, and Maria Sapignoli. New York: Cambridge University Press. 2017.

Ong, Aihwa. *Flexible Citizenship: The Cultural Logics of Transnationality*. Durham, NC: Duke University Press, 1999.

Ong, Aihwa, and Stephen J. Collier. *Global Assemblages: Technology, Politics, and Ethics as Anthropological Problems*. Malden, MA: Blackwell, 2005.

Ortner, Sherry. *Anthropology and Social Theory: Culture, Power, and the Acting Subject*. Durham, NC: Duke University Press, 2006.

Ortner, Sherry. "Is Female to Male as Nature is to Culture?" In *Women, Culture and Society*, edited by Michelle Rosaldo and Louise Lamphere, 67–88. Stanford, CA: Stanford University Press, 1974.

Ottenheimer, Harriet Joseph. *The Anthropology of Language: An Introduction to Linguistic Anthropology*. 2nd ed. Belmont, CA: Wadsworth, 2009.

Ottenheimer, Martin. *Kinship: An Introduction to the Anthropological Study of Family and Marriage*. Belmont, CA: Wadsworth, 2006.

Padilla, Mark et al. *Love and Globalization: Transformations of Intimacy in the Contemporary World*. Nashville, TN: Vanderbilt University Press, 2007.

Park, Michael Alan. *Biological Anthropology*. 6th ed. New York: McGraw-Hill, 2009.

Parkin, Robert. *Kinship: An Introduction to Basic Concepts*. Oxford: Blackwell, 1997.

Parkin, Robert, and Linda Stone, eds. *Kinship and Family: An Anthropological Reader*. Oxford, UK: Wiley-Blackwell, 2004.

Pavlenko, Aneta. *The Bilingual Mind: And What It Tells US About Language and Thought*. Cambridge, England: Cambridge University Press, 2014.

Peletz, Michael. "Kinship Studies in Late Twentieth-Century Anthropology." *Annual Review of Anthropology* 24 (1995): 343–372.

Pels, Peter. "The Anthropology of Colonialism: Culture, History, and the Emergence of Western Governmentality." *Annual Review of Anthropology* 26 (1997): 163–183.

Pels, Peter, and Oscar Salemink. *Colonial Subjects: Essays on the Practical History of Anthropology*. Ann Arbor: University of Michigan Press, 1999.

Petryna, Adriana. *When Experiments Travel: Clinical Trials and the Global Search for Human Subjects*. Princeton, NJ: Princeton University Press, 2009.

Pickering, Andrew. *The Mangle of Practice: Time, Agency and Science*. Chicago: University of Chicago Press, 1995.

Plattner, Stuart, ed. *Economic Anthropology*. Stanford, CA: Stanford University Press, 1989.

Pospisil, Leonard *Anthropology of Law: A Comparative Theory*. New York: Harper & Row, 1971.

Preucel, Robert W. *Archaeological Semiotics*. Malden, MA: Wiley-Blackwell, 2010.

Rabinow, Paul. *Reflections on Fieldwork in Morocco*. Berkeley: University of California Press, 1977.

Raffles, Hugh. *In Amazonia: A Natural History*. Princeton, NJ: Princeton University Press, 2002.

Reardon, Jenny. *Race to the Finish: Identity and Governance in an Age of Genomics*. Princeton: Princeton University Press, 2005.

Relethford, John. *The Human Species: An Introduction to Biological Anthropology*. 8th ed. New York: McGraw-Hill, 2009.

Robbins, Richard H. *Global Problems and the Culture of Capitalism*. 3rd ed. Upper Saddle River, NJ: Pearson Allyn & Bacon, 2004.

Robertson, Jennifer. *Robo Sapiens Japanicus: Robots, Gender, Family, and the Japanese Nation*. Berkeley: University of California Press, 2018.

Rosaldo, Renato. *Culture and Truth: The Remaking of Social Analysis*. Boston: Beacon Press, 1989.

Rubin, Gayle. "The Traffic in Women: On the 'Political Economy' of Sex." In *Toward an Anthropology of Women*, edited by Rayna R. Reiter, 157–210. New York: Monthly Review Press, 1975.

Sacks, Karen. *Sisters and Wives*. Westport, CT: Greenwood Press, 1979.

Sahlins, Marshall. *Culture and Practical Reason*. Chicago: University of Chicago Press, 1976.

Sahlins, Marshall. *Stone Age Economics*. Chicago: Aldine, 1972.

Salzmann, Zdenek. *Language, Culture, and Society: An Introduction to Linguistic Anthropology*. 4th ed. Boulder, CO: Westview Press, 2006.

Savage-Rumbaugh, Sue et al. "Spontaneous Symbol Acquisition and Communicative Use by Pygmy Chimpanzees (Pan Paniscus)." *Journal of Experimental Psychology: General* 115 (1986): 211–235.

Sawyer, Suzana. *Crude Chronicles: Indigenous Politics, Multinational Oil, and Neoliberalism in Ecuador*. Durham, NC: Duke University Press, 2004.

Scheper-Hughes, Nancy. *Death without Weeping: The Violence of Everyday Life in Brazil*. Berkeley: University of California Press, 1992.

Scheper-Hughes, Nancy, and Loïc Wacquant. *Commodified Bodies*. Thousand Oaks, CA: Sage Publications, 2003.

Schieffelin, Bambi, Kathryn Woolard, and Paul V. Kroskrity, eds. *Language Ideologies: Practice and Theory*. New York: Oxford University Press, 1998.

Schiller, Nina Glick, and Georges Fouron. "Long-Distance Nationalism Defined." In *The Anthropology of Politics*, edited by Joan Vincent, 356–365. Malden, MA: Blackwell, 2002.

Schneider, David. *American Kinship*. Englewood Cliffs, NJ: Prentice Hall, 1968.

Schneider, David. *A Critique of the Study of Kinship*. Ann Arbor: University of Michigan Press, 1984.

Schuler, Sindey Ruth. *The Other Side of Polyandry*. Boulder, CO: Westview Press, 1987.

Schultz, Emily. *Dialogue at the Margins: Whorf, Bakhtin, and Linguistic Relativity*. Madison: University of Wisconsin, 1990.

Scott, James C. *Against the Grain: A Deep History of the Earliest States*. New Haven: Yale University Press, 2017.

Scott, James C. *The Art of Not Being Governed: An Anarchist History of Upland Southeast Asia*. New Haven: Yale University Press, 2009.

Scott, James C. *Domination and the Arts of Resistance*. New Haven, CT: Yale University Press, 1992.

Scott, James C. *Seeing Like a State: How Certain Schemes to Improve the Human Condition Have Failed*. New Haven, CT: Yale University Press, 1998.

Scott, James C. *Weapons of the Weak*. New Haven, CT: Yale University Press, 1987.

Service, Elman. *Origins of the State and Civilization*. New York: Norton, 1975.

Service, Elman. *Primitive Social Organization*. New York: Random House, 1962.

Shapin, Steven. *Never Pure: Historical Studies of Science as if It Was Produced by People with Bodies, Situated in Time, Space, Culture, and Society, and Struggling for Credibility and Authority*. Baltimore, MD: Johns Hopkins University Press, 2010.

Shapin, Steven. *The Scientific Revolution*. Chicago: University of Chicago Press, 1996.

Shapin, Steven, and Simon Schaffer. *Leviathan and the Air-Pump: Hobbes, Boyle, and the Experimental Life*. Princeton, NJ: Princeton University Press, 1985.

Sharma, Aradhana, and Akhil Gupta. *The Anthropology of the State: A Reader*. Malden, MA: Wiley-Blackwell, 2006.

Sharp, Lesley. *Strange Harvest: Organ Transplants, Denatured Bodies, and the Transformed Self*. Berkeley: University of California Press, 2006.

Sherwood, Chet, and Aída Gómez-Robles. "Brain Plasticity and Human Evolution." *Annual Review of Anthropology* 46 (2017): 399–419.

Shoshan, Nitzan. *The Management of Hate: Nation, Affect, and the Governance of Right-Wing Extremism in Germany*. Princeton, New Jersey: Princeton University Press, 2016.

Silverstein, Michael. "Metapragmatic Discourse and Metapragmatics Function." In *Reflexive Language: Reported Speech and Metapragmatics*, edited by John Lucy, 33–58. New York: Cambridge University Press. 1993.

Silverstein, Michael. "Language and the Culture of Gender: At the Intersection of Structure, Usage, and Ideology." In *Semiotic Mediation: Sociocultural and Psychological Perspectives*, edited by Elizabeth. Mertz, and Richard J. Parmentier, 210–60. Orlando: Academic Press. 1985.

Silverstein, Michael. "Shifters, Linguistic Categories, and Cultural Description." In *Meaning in Anthropology*, edited by Keith Basso, and Henry A. Selby, 11–55. Albuquerque, NM: University of New Mexico Press, 1976.

Singer, Merrill, and Hans Baer. *Introducing Medical Anthropology: A Discipline in Action*. Lanham, MD: AltaMira Press, 2007.

Slobin, Dan. "Thinking for Speaking." *Proceedings of the Berkeley Linguistics Society* 13, 1987: 435–44.

Smedley, Audrey. *Race in North America*. 2nd ed. Boulder, CO: Westview, 1999.

Smith, Valene L. *Hosts and Guests: The Anthropology of Tourism*. 2nd ed. Philadelphia: University of Pennsylvania Press, 1989.

Spady, James G., Samir Meghelli, and H. Samy Alim. *Tha Global Cipha: Hip Hop Culture and Consciousness*. Philadelphia, PA: Black History Museum Press, 2006.

Sopranzetti, Claudio. *Owners of the Map: Motorcycle Taxi Drivers, Mobility, and Politics in Bangkok*. Oakland, California: University of California Press, 2017.

Stanlaw, James, Nobuko Adachi, and Zdenek Salzmann. *Language, Culture, and Society: An Introduction to Linguistic Anthropology*. 7th ed. New York: Routledge, 2017.

Stein, Rebecca, and Philip L. Stein. *Anthropology of Religion, Magic, and Witchcraft*. 4th ed. New York: Routledge, 2017.

Stimpson, Catharine R., and Gilbert H. Herdt. *Critical Terms for the Study of Gender*. Chicago; London: The University of Chicago Press, 2014.

Stoler, Ann Laura. *Carnal Knowledge and Imperial Power: Race and the Intimate in Colonial Rule*. Berkeley: University of California Press, 2002.

Stone, Linda. *Kinship and Gender: An Introduction*. 5th ed. Boulder, CO: Westview Press, 2014.

Stone, Linda, ed. *New Directions in Anthropological Kinship*. Lanham, MD: Rowman & Little field, 2001.

Strathern, Marilyn. "Cutting the Network." *Journal of the Royal Anthropological Institute* 2, no. 3 (1996): 517–535.

Strathern, Marilyn. *Reproducing the Future: Anthropology, Kinship, and the New Reproductive Technologies*. New York: Routledge, 1992.

Suggs, David, and Andrew Miracle. *Culture and Human Sexuality*. Pacific Grove, CA: Brooks/Cole, 1993.

Tambiah, Stanley. *Leveling Crowds: Nationalist Conflict and Collective Violence in South Asia*. Berkeley: University of California Press, 1997.

Traweek, Sharon. *Beamtimes and Lifetimes*. Cambridge, MA: Harvard University Press, 1992.

Tsing, Anna. *Friction: An Ethnography of Global Connection*. Princeton, NJ: Princeton University Press, 2005.

Tsing, Anna. *The Mushroom At the End of the World*. Princeton, NJ: Princeton University Press, 2015.

van Willigen, John. *Applied Anthropology*. 3rd ed. Westport, CT: Bergin & Garvey, 2002.

Venbrux, Eric, Pamela Sheffield Rosi, and Robert L Welsch. *Exploring World Art*. Long Grove, IL: Waveland Press, 2006.

Vincent, Joan. *The Anthropology of Politics: A Reader in Ethnography, Theory, and Critique*. Malden, MA: Wiley-Blackwell, 2002.

Viveiros de Castro, Eduardo. "Perspectival Anthropology and the Method of Controlled Equivocation." *Tipiti: Journal of the Society for the Anthropology of Lowland South America* 2, no. 1, 2004: 3–22.

Vogel, Susan M. *Baule: African Art Western Eyes*. New Haven, CT: Yale University Press, 1997.

Von Schnitzler, Antina. *Democracy's Infrastructure: Techno-Politics and Citizenship After Apartheid*. Princeton: Princeton University Press, 2016.

Wade, Peter. *Degrees of Mixture, Degrees of Freedom: Genomics, Multiculturalism, and Race in Latin America*. Durham, NC: Duke University Press, 2017.

Wade, Peter. *Race and Ethnicity in Latin America*. New York: Pluto Press; distributed in the United States of America exclusively by Palgrave Macmillan, 2010.

Wade, Peter, Carlos López Beltrán, Eduardo Restrepo, and Ricardo Ventura Santos. "Introduction: Genomics, Race Mixture, and Nation in Latin America." In *Mestizo Genomics: Race Mixture, Nation, and Science in Latin America*, edited by Peter Wade, Carlos López Beltrán, Eduardo Restrepo, and Ricardo Ventura Santos, 1–30. Durham, NC: Duke University Press, 2014a.

Wade, Peter, Carlos López Beltrán, Eduardo Restrepo, and Ricardo Ventura Santos, eds. *Mestizo Genomics: Race Mixture, Nation, and Science in Latin America*. Durham, NC: Duke University Press, 2014b.

Wallace, Anthony F. C. *Religion: An Anthropological View*. New York: Random House, 1966.

Warms, Richard L., James. Garber, and R. Jon McGee, eds. *Sacred Realm: Readings in the Anthropology of Religion*, 2nd edition. New York: Oxford University Press, 2009.

Watson, James L. *Golden Arches East: McDonald's in East Asia*. 2nd ed. Stanford, CA: Stanford University Press, 2006.

Watson, James L., and Melissa L. Caldwell. *The Cultural Politics of Food and Eating: A Reader*. Malden, MA: Blackwell, 2005.

Weatherford, Jack. *The History of Money*. New York: Crown, 1997.

Weismantel, Mary. *Food, Gender, and Poverty in the Ecuadorian Andes*. Prospect Heights, IL: Waveland Press, 1998.

Weismantel, Mary. "Making Kin: Kinship Theory and Zumbagua Adoptions." *American Ethnologist* 22, no. 4 (1995): 685–709.

Welsch, Robert L. "The Authenticity of Contemporary World Art: Afterword." In *Exploring World Art*, edited by Eric Venbrux et al., 389–398. Long Grove, IL: Waveland Press, 2006.

West, Paige. *Conservation is Our Government Now: The Politics of Ecology in Papua New Guinea*. Durham, NC: Duke University Press, 2006.

Weston, Kath. *Families We Choose: Lesbians, Gays, Kinship*. New York: Columbia University Press, 1991.

Weston, Kath. "Lesbian/Gay Studies in the House of Anthropology." *Annual Review of Anthropology* 22 (1993): 339–367.

Wiley, Andrea S., and John S. Allen. *Medical Anthropology: A Biocultural Approach*. New York: Oxford University Press, 2009.

Wilk, Richard R., and Lisa Cliggett. *Economies and Cultures: Foundations of Economic Anthropology*. 2nd ed. Boulder, CO: Westview Press, 2007.

Williams, Brackette. "A Class Act: Anthropology and the Race to Nation across Ethnic Terrain." *Annual Review of Anthropology* 18 (1989): 401–444.

Williams-Forson, Psyche A., and Carole Counihan. *Taking Food Public: Redefining Foodways in a Changing World*. New York: Routledge, 2011.

Winzeler, Robert L. *Anthropology and Religion: What We Know, Think, and Question*. 2nd. ed. Lanham, MD: AltaMira Press, 2013.

Wolcott, Harry F. *The Art of Fieldwork*. 2nd ed. Lanham, MD: AltaMira Press, 2004.

Wolcott, Harry F. *Ethnography: A Way of Seeing*. 2nd ed. Lanham, MD: AltaMira Press, 2008.

Wolf, Eric. *Envisioning Power: Ideologies of Dominance and Resistance*. Berkeley: University of California Press, 1999.

Wolf, Eric. *Europe and the People without History*. Berkeley: University of California Press, 1982.

Wolf, Eric. *Peasants*. Englewood Cliffs, NJ: Prentice Hall, 1962.

Yan, Yunxiang. "Of Hamburger and Social Space: Consuming McDonald's in Beijing." In *The Cultural Politics of Food and Eating*, edited by James Watson and Melissa L. Caldwell, 80–103. Malden, MA: Blackwell, 2005.

Young, Michael W. *Malinowski's Kiriwina: Fieldwork Photography 1915–1918*. Chicago: University of Chicago Press, 1998.

Zentella, Ana Celia. *Growing Up Bilingual: Puerto Rican Children in New York*. Malden, MA: Wiley-Blackwell, 1997.

Index

Key terms are defined on boldfaced page numbers.